ENOCH

STUDIES ON PERSONALITIES
OF THE OLD TESTAMENT
James L. Crenshaw, *General Editor*

E N O C H
A MAN FOR ALL GENERATIONS

JAMES C. VANDERKAM

UNIVERSITY OF SOUTH CAROLINA PRESS

Published in·Columbia, South Carolina, by the
University of South Carolina Press

Manufactured in the United States of America

VanderKam, James C.
    Enoch, a man for all generations / James C. VanderKam.
    p. cm. — (Studies on personalities of the Old Testament)
    Includes bibliographical references and index.
    ISBN 1–57003–060–X
    1. Enoch.   2. Apocryphal literature (Old Testament) — Criticism,
interpretation, etc.   3. Apocalyptic literature — History and
criticism.   4. Christian literature, Early — History and criticism.
I. Title.   II. Series.
BS580.E6V357   1996
229'.913 — dc20   95–4384

CONTENTS

PREFACE

The Dead Sea Scrolls have made many contributions to our knowledge about the Jewish world in the last centuries B.C.E and the first century C.E. Among those contributions is a new appreciation for the literature about Enoch, the seventh patriarch from Adam, and the status that he and his writings had attained within some Jewish groups. The traditions associated with Enoch preserve for us a glimpse at a different option within ancient Judaism—that is, a perspective that put almost no emphasis on the Mosaic law. It focused its attention, rather, on special revelations granted to Enoch before the flood. These revelations dealt not only with the past but also with the future and its meaning for the present. It was a tradition that was hardly to survive but which for a time exercised a noticeable influence among some Jewish people and certainly among some early Christians.

The purpose of this study is to provide a survey of the ancient Jewish and Christian references to Enoch and Enochic themes, from the beginning to about 300 C.E. It is not meant to be an exhaustive account in the sense that all textual and historical problems are treated or that all relevant secondary literature is recorded or discussed. Rather, it is intended to provide for readers who may not be familiar with the mostly extrabiblical traditions about Enoch an opportunity to appreciate the range and character of ancient testimonies to this man, his teachings, and his work. As a consequence, a large number of texts are covered fairly rapidly. In the course of the survey an effort is made to point out lines of continuity, possible influences, and areas of change, with only a modest number of bibliographical references in footnotes. The reader is at times referred to other sources for more in-depth coverage of a particular text or passage.

Work on this book has given me opportunity to draw together the results of other investigations that I have made into the various parts of the Enochic traditions and also to move into areas on which I have not written before. In *Enoch and the Growth of an Apocalyptic Tradition* I covered in more detail and depth many of the texts presented here in chapters 1–4—that is, from the beginning of the tradition through the *Book of Jubilees* (ca. 150 B.C.E.). The data in that work are used here, although they are at times modified—often abbreviated and occasionally expanded. I have also been able to draw upon a series of other studies that I have written on smaller segments of the Enochic texts; references are made to these in the notes when appropriate. Unless otherwise indicated, translations of *1 Enoch* are from M. Knibb, *The Ethiopic Book of Enoch*; scriptural citations are from the NRSV.

Readers who know the Enoch material well will notice that I have not included *3 Enoch* in the book. One reason for doing this is that *3 Enoch* was written at a much later time than almost all of the other texts cited. It seemed best, in a book that is appearing in a series called "Studies on Personalities of the Old Testament," to cut the survey off at some point not too long after the biblical period. The end of the third century was chosen as a reasonable point. There are some violations of this rule, particularly in the section on later Jewish interpretations, in which passages from the targums and *Genesis Rabbah* are included. These texts, however, clearly reflect older interpretations and are adduced because they illustrate Jewish attitudes toward Enoch at a time when some Christians were attributing high status to his writings.

I wish to thank Professor James Crenshaw, the editor of the series, for inviting me to write this volume and for his encouragement and patience as it was being prepared and for his helpful and prompt suggestions when it was submitted. I am also grateful to Monica Walsh and Tobin Rachford, both of whom are talented doctoral students at Notre Dame, for their assistance in compiling the indexes.

ABBREVIATIONS

AB	Astronomical Book
ABD	*Anchor Bible Dictionary*, ed. D. N. Freedman
ANF	The Ante-Nicene Fathers, ed. Alexander Roberts and James Donaldson
Ant.	*Antiquities of the Jews* (Josephus)
BD	Book of Dreams
BibOr	Biblica et orientalia
BJS	Brown Judaic Studies
BW	Book of the Watchers
CBQ	*Catholic Biblical Quarterly*
CBQMS	Catholic Biblical Quarterly – Monograph Series
CRINT	Compendia rerum iudaicarum ad novum testamentum
CSCO	Corpus scriptorum christianorum orientalium
DJD	Discoveries in the Judaean Desert
EE	Epistle of Enoch
Gen. Apoc.	*Genesis Apocryphon*
Gen. Rab.	*Genesis Rabbah*
JBL	*Journal of Biblical Literature*
JCS	*Journal of Cuneiform Studies*
JSOT	*Journal of the Study of the Old Testament*
JSP	*Journal for the Study of the Pseudepigrapha*
Jub.	*Book of Jubilees*
LCL	Loeb Classical Library
LXX	Septuagint
NRSV	New Revised Standard Version
OTP	*The Old Testament Pseudepigrapha*, ed. J. H. Charlesworth
RSR	*Recherches de sciences religieuses*
SBLEJL	Society of Biblical Literature Early Judaism and Its Literature
SBLSP	Society of Biblical Literature Seminar Papers
SBLTT	Society of Biblical Literature Texts and Translations
SVTP	Studia in Veteris Testamenti pseudepigrapha
TDOT	*Theological Dictionary of the Old Testament*, ed. G. J. Botterweck and H. Ringgren
WB	Weld-Blundell
WBC	Word Biblical Commentary
WMANT	Wissenschaftliche Monographien zum Alten und Neuen Testament

ENOCH

CHAPTER 1

THE BEGINNING
OF A CAREER

A character named Enoch appears in two biblical genealogies: Gen.
5:21–24 and 1 Chron. 1:3. The verses in Genesis proved to be such
fertile exegetical ground that luxurious and complex traditions were later
to grow from it. Paying careful attention to the primary reference to
Enoch should show something of its cryptic character and potential for
imaginative, learned elaboration.

A. ENOCH IN GEN. 5

The first place in which one meets this Enoch is in Gen. 5, a chapter
that gives the second biblical genealogy. The first genealogy names the
descendants of Cain, the oldest son of Adam and Eve (see Gen. 4:1–2),
for five generations (Gen. 4:17–22). They are worth mentioning here
because there is something strongly similar between this family tree and
the one that includes Enoch in Gen. 5. Actually, the list in Gen. 4 stems
from a different literary source than that of chapter 5. Gen. 2:4b–4:26 is
normally identified as coming from the J (Yahwist) source, while Gen. 5
is traced to the P (Priestly) source. The J story in Gen. 2–4 speaks of
Adam and Eve and their two sons, Cain and Abel. After Cain murdered
his brother, he was banished, but Abel's place was taken by another son
born to the original parents, Seth, who in turn became the father of
Enosh (4:25–26).

With this information in mind, one can reproduce the genealogy that
emerges from the J sections in this way:

Adam
Cain   Seth
Enoch   Enosh
Irad
Mehujael
Methushael
Lamech

1

So, the J source names these seven generations in the Adam-Cain line and places alongside them a three-generation sequence in the Adam-Seth branch.

The editor next calls on the P source to supply a list, traced this time not through Cain but, rather, through his brother Seth (there is, of course, no genealogy for Abel, who, one should assume, died before fathering any children). The priestly list not only supplies the names of the ancient heads of humanity but also specifies their ages when they became fathers for the first time, the number of years they lived after that event, and the sum of the years in their lives.

Adam	130 + 800	= 930
Seth	105 + 807	= 912
Enosh	90 + 815	= 905
Kenan	70 + 840	= 910
Mahalalel	65 + 830	= 895
Jared	162 + 800	= 962
Enoch	65 + 300	= 365
Methuselah	187 + 782	= 969
Lamech	182 + 595	= 777
Noah	500 + 450	= 950 (Gen. 9:28)[1]

The first point to notice from the Gen. 5 genealogy is that Enoch occupies the telling seventh position, a fact noted in, among other places, the New Testament book of Jude (v. 14). Not only does he fill that slot; it also seems that the genealogist purposely moved him to it from a less conspicuous place in the J arrangement in which there is a total of seven members (counting Adam). This inference follows from a comparison of the two genealogies in Gen. 4 and 5. If they are set side by side, it soon becomes evident that they share a number of names.

Gen. 4	Gen. 5
1. Adam	1. Adam
2. Cain	2. Seth

---

1. Gen. 5:32 gives Noah's age at the time when triplets were born to him as 500 years. To this total one has to add another 100 years to reach the time of the flood (7:6) and then 350 more for the time that he lived after the flood (9:28). The numbers reproduced here are those of the Hebrew text of Genesis. The Greek translation differs for some (usually by 100 years), and other systems are also attested.

3. Enoch	3. Enosh
4. Irad	4. Kenan
5. Mehujael	5. Mahalalel
6. Methushael	6. Jared
7. Lamech	7. Enoch
8.	8. Methuselah
9.	9. Lamech
10.	10. Noah

Obviously, some of the names are the same (Adam, Enoch, Lamech) and others are similar (e.g., Methushael and Methuselah), but, if one sets the names in the first and shorter list next to those with which they are most closely parallel in the second genealogy, interesting results emerge.

Gen. 4	Gen. 5
3. Enoch	5. Mahalalel
4. Irad	6. Jared
5. Mehujael	7. Enoch
6. Methushael	8. Methuselah
7. Lamech	9. Lamech

It is very likely that the priestly genealogist had before him a list much like, or even identical with,[2] the one in Gen. 4 along with the names from Gen. 4:25–26 (Adam, Seth, Enosh) and that he simply switched the positions of number 3 Enoch and number 5 Mehujael (the name that most closely resembles Mahalalel in Gen. 5), perhaps added one name (no. 4),[3] and thus was able to make Enoch the seventh. Otherwise he retained the names (with slight changes) and order of the J genealogy.[4] That is, it was so important for the writer of the Gen. 5 genealogy to give Enoch an especially prominent position that he altered the givens of his source.

2. H. S. Kvanvig, *Roots of Apocalyptic: The Mesopotamian Background of the Enoch Figure and of the Son of Man*, WMANT 61 (Neukirchen-Vluyn: Neukirchener Verlag, 1988), 44.
3. It has been suggested that the name Kenan is a variant of Cain; the Hebrew spelling of the two differs by one letter. See C. Westermann, *Genesis 1–11: A Commentary* (Minneapolis: Augsburg, 1984), 357.
4. This explanation presupposes, as scholars have usually maintained, that the J source was written at an earlier time than the priestly document. Several experts have argued recently that the order of the sources should be reversed,

3

A second point is that Enoch serves as a highly unusual link in the chain. His age at the birth of his first son is 65 years, a number that ties him with Mahalalel, the fifth member, for the lowest in the list. While Mahalalel goes on to live an additional 830 years, only 300 years separate the birth of Enoch's son Methuselah from the end of his earthly life. The closest in comparison is Noah's 450 years. As a result, the full life span of Enoch is far and away the lowest; in fact, his nearest competitor (Lamech) lived 412 years longer. The brevity of his stay on earth is accented to an even greater degree by the fact that he is sandwiched between the two longest-lived members: his father, Jared, lived to be 962, and his son Methuselah died at 969 years.

The position that he holds and the numbers assigned to him are, then, conspicuous ways in which the writer calls attention to Enoch, but he does so in others as well. Frequently, ancient genealogies appear to be uninspiring lists of names that are presented in stereotypical, patriarchal language: a became the father of b, b became the father of c, etc. The priestly genealogy in Gen. 5 is organized around a different set of typical expressions. For the antediluvian patriarchs one finds these basic elements:

a. When a had lived n years
b. he became the father of b
c. after fathering b he lived nn years and had other sons and daughters
d. so all the days of a were nnn
e. and he died.

When the compiler of the genealogy wished to underscore the importance of a character, he altered the set pattern to a slight extent. For example, in the case of Adam, the son whom he begets is said to be "in

---

but at least for these two genealogies it is more plausible to suppose that P changed the order of J than to hold the opposite. What would be the point of eliminating two names from the P list and switching Enoch and Mahalalel, if J had worked with the earlier P list? For the change in order, see also Kvanvig, *Roots of Apocalyptic*, 45, although he believes two changes occurred: Enoch moved from fifth to seventh, and Mahalalel (Mehujael) and Jared (Irad) had their order reversed. But the latter could be the simple result of switching Enoch and Mahalalel (Mehujael).

his likeness, according to his image" — a phrase that reminds one of the priestly statement about the creation of humanity (Gen. 1:26, in which the order is: image/likeness) and of the paragraph that opens Gen. 5 (vv. 1–2). It is hardly surprising that the first man and his son receive special attention, nor is it unexpected that the last and tenth person, Noah, also breaks the genealogical mold. For Noah's birth the writer does not content himself with saying that Lamech became the father of Noah, as he had for all the others after the first birth; rather, he calls attention to Noah's unusual significance by writing: "When Lamech had lived one hundred eighty-two years, he became the father of a son; he named him Noah, saying, 'Out of the ground that the Lord has cursed this one shall bring us relief from our work and from the toil of our hands' " (5:28–29).[5]

Besides underscoring the import enjoyed by the first and last links in the chain, the priestly writer has also forced the reader to turn his attention to the seventh member — that is, to Enoch. Note which parts of the pattern he uses and which he alters.

a. When **a** had lived **n** years	a. When Enoch had lived sixty-five years
b. he became the father of **b**	b. he became the father of Methuselah
c. after fathering **b** he lived **nn** years and had other sons and daughters	c. after fathering Methuselah he *walked with God* three hundred years and had other sons and daughters
d. so all the days of **a** were **nnn**	d. so all the days of Enoch were three hundred sixty-five years
e. and he died.	e. Enoch *walked with God; then he was no more, because God took him.*

As the lists show, there are two points at which Enoch's section differs from the pattern: the added notice that he walked with God for the three hundred years during which he had other sons and daughters; and the

---

5. The etymology of Noah's name, which is not technically correct but apparently calls attention to his success in planting a vineyard after the flood, should be attributed to the J writer. This is the only place in the genealogy of Gen. 5 in which the deity is referred to as "Lord," not "God."

replacement of "he died" by a second statement that he walked with God plus a notice that "he was no more," for God had taken him. Consequently, there was something unusual about Enoch during most of his earthly sojourn, and he was unique at the end of it as well.

Why did the priestly editor put Enoch in seventh position and credit him with unusual numbers of years for the different segments of his life on earth? Also, what did he mean by the expressions "walked with God" and "he was no more, because God took him"? For at least partial answers to both questions one must look to Akkadian sources to discover the background from which the editor has compiled his genealogy in Gen. 5.

B. MESOPOTAMIAN TRADITIONS ABOUT THE SEVENTH KING

Akkadian sources about the earliest days of humanity ought to be promising ones to check because it is evident that they influenced the priestly editor when he wrote his account of creation in Gen. 1:1–2:4a and his story of the flood in Gen. 6–9. If he used such sources or traditions for these two major sections, it is not unreasonable to think that he also did so in Gen. 5 — the only other contribution that he made to the first nine chapters of Genesis. In the nineteenth century, when the myth entitled *Enuma elish* was found and deciphered, scholars perceived a marked resemblance between the order in which the young god Marduk created the universe and the one according to which God fashions it in Gen. 1:1–2:4a. Other features of the two accounts are massively different (polytheism vs. monotheism for one), but with all the discrepancies the shared order is unmistakable. The most startling convergence of stories, however, became evident when the biblical story about the flood was put side by side with the eleventh tablet of the *Epic of Gilgamesh*. There the similarites were not only in the general order of the narrative but also in specific details such as the dispatching of birds by the flood heroes at the same juncture. If the priestly writer drew inspiration from Mesopotamian accounts of creation and the flood, perhaps he did for his genealogy in Gen. 5 as well. The fact that the last member of the list of long-lived prediluvians is Noah, whose story so strongly resembles the one about Utnapishtim in Gilgamesh XI, adds to the likelihood that borrowing from this source may indeed have occurred.

The comparative sources to which scholars have turned in their analyses of Gen. 5 are first and foremost the various versions of the pre-flood king list.[6] These lists were copied over an immense range of years: the oldest comes from before 1500 B.C.E. and the latest from 165 B.C.E. They exist in different languages and display discrepant numbers of kings and years for their reigns. One feature of these lists is the extraordinarily long reigns that are attributed to the monarchs: the lowest total is a 3,600-year reign, and the highest is one of 72,000 years. That is, the king list and the genealogy of Gen. 5 share the trait of crediting large numbers of years to their members, although the long lives of the Genesis patriarchs are trifling in comparison to the long reigns of the Mesopotamian kings. Moreover, in two versions of the king list—the earliest copy and one of the latest—there are ten kings, the last of whom is the hero of the flood. The same is the case, of course, in Gen. 5, in which Noah occupies position number 10 in the genealogy.

Besides these similarities of character and structure, the two antediluvian lists share another feature: some copies of the king list place in the seventh position a monarch who displays a number of traits that remind one of Enoch, the seventh biblical patriarch in the Gen. 5 genealogy (not the one in Gen. 4). That king is named Enmenduranna or Enmeduranki, and he is the seventh in one very early (Weld-Blundell 444) and two relatively late (Berossus, Uruk) copies of the king list. Elsewhere he figures in eighth or sixth position. Consequently, in some versions of the list, which vary greatly in date and hence cannot be reflections of a temporary glitch, Enmeduranki appears just where Enoch does in Gen. 5. That fact alone, however, could be dismissed as accidental, were it not the case that the two individuals also share a surprising number of traits. This emerges from a study of the texts in which this Enmeduranki figures.

First, all versions of the king list that name the city over which a monarch ruled locate Enmeduranki in the ancient Sumerian city of Sippar. Sippar was the city of the sun god (Utu was his Sumerian name, Shamash the Akkadian one) who was worshiped in the great temple called Ebabbarra. The god with whom Sippar was associated reminds one of Enoch in that his unusual age at removal—365 years—is the equivalent in years of the number of days in a solar year. That is, it may be that Enoch's low total of years offers not so much a chronological statement as a reflection, however indirect, of Enmeduranki's ties with the sun god.

---

6. For a summary of the data from the versions of the king list, see Vander-Kam, *Enoch and the Growth of an Apocalyptic Tradition*, CBQMS 16 (Washington, D.C.: Catholic Biblical Association of America, 1984), 33–38.

Second, two Akkadian texts show clearly that Enmeduranki entered a special relationship with the major deities of the Mesopotamian pantheon. The first of these compositions, which comes from Asshurbanipal's libraries, reads as follows:

Shamash in Ebabbarra [appointed] Enmeduranki [king of Sippar], the beloved of Anu, Enlil [and Ea]. Shamash and Adad [brought him in] to their assembly, Shamash and Adad [honoured him], Shamash and Adad [set him] on a large throne of gold, they showed him how to observe oil on water, a mystery of Anu [Enlil and Ea], they gave him the tablet of the gods, the liver, a secret of heaven and [underworld], they put in his hand the cedar-(rod), beloved of the great gods. (ll. 1–9)[7]

What is of special note here is that Shamash and Adad brought Enmeduranki into their council or assembly. Hence, he had with them a closer association than humans could normally enjoy. While he was in their assembly, the gods taught him various divinatory techniques, which he then, in the sections that follow, relays to other humans. Enmeduranki in this way was regarded as the founder of a guild of diviners—the *baru* priests.

A second and briefer reference to the same primordial king occurs in a first-person statement delivered by a monarch who appears to be Nebuchadnezzar I (1124–1103 B.C.E.). The king refers to himself as: "Distant scion of kingship, seed preserved from before the flood, Offspring of Enmeduranki, king of Sippar, who set up the pure bowl and the cedar-wood (rod), Who sat in the presence of Shamash and Adad, the divine adjudicators."[8] Here again Enmeduranki benefits from intimate association with the two great gods who instructed him in divinatory practices.

C. GEN. 5 IN LIGHT OF THE COMPARATIVE EVIDENCE

These two texts along with the king lists reveal important comparative information regarding the seventh member of the pre-flood genealogy.

---

7. The translations of the two texts about Enmeduranki are taken from W. Lambert, "Enmeduranki and Related Matters," *JCS* 21 (1967): 126–38.
8. Ibid., 126–27.

Both men are said to have had some special relationship with the divine realm: Enoch walked with God, and Enmeduranki was welcomed into the fellowship of the great gods. Moreover, Enoch lived a highly unusual total of 365 years—the same as the number of days in a solar year—while one of the gods with whom Enmeduranki had special communion was the sun deity Shamash. These data alone suggest that the similarities are no coincidence; it seems far more likely that they exist because the biblical writer has exploited yet another Mesopotamian tradition in his presentation of the seventh man. The conclusion appears natural that the priestly writer moved Enoch to seventh place in his genealogy to reflect what some forms of the Mesopotamian list said about the seventh king.

Not everyone accepts this conclusion, even among critical scholars of the Bible. There is not only the problem of the relative dates of the J and P sources already mentioned, but some aspects of the king lists have also led no less an authority than C. Westermann to deny that the P genealogy was based on the Mesopotamian lists of the antediluvian kings—or so it seems. In his commentary on Genesis, Westermann, after noting that earlier scholars had asserted a strong relationship between Gen. 5 and the king lists, argues that almost all has changed because of the discovery of cuneiform texts that embody the lists. Before 1923 experts had to rely on Berossus's Greek list, and on that basis they had found a number of parallels in names between the lists. Westermann draws several conclusions from the newer evidence, among which is this one:

> It has been established likewise that the number of kings before the flood in the older lists is eight, not ten. The dominance of the number ten in Weld-Blundell 62 . . . goes back to the insertion into the second place in this list of the city Larsa with two kings, which does not occur in any other list. The list of Berossus comes to ten by means of two demonstrable elaborations. Later the number ten became as it were a norm for genealogies of kings; . . . But not even the number eight is certain. Though the great majority of lists contain the name Ziusudra as the king in the time of the flood, it is lacking in some.[9]

He sums up the matter by writing: "The old Babylonian list of primeval kings can no longer then be regarded as a parallel to Gen. 5. . . . Whatever parallels remain, such as the remarkable numbers, the number ten,

---

9. Westermann, *Genesis 1–11*, 350.

9

the last name on the list, are to be explained from later stages of the tradition history, and exclude one from regarding the Old Babylonian king list in its original form as the basis of Gen. 5."[10] The hedging phrase "in its original form" is noteworthy. Those who assert a relationship between the two lists need not claim that P, like a modern textual critic, refused to be content with any but the oldest, most original form of the text he could find. If any text of the king list has ten members, then its very existence means it was possible that P somehow knew of that sort of tradition—whatever the original shape of the tradition might have been. That is, if it is true to assert, as Westermann does, that Gen. 5 was not modeled on the original form of the king list, it does not follow from this that it was not patterned on some later version of it.

Moreover, Westermann does not pay adequate attention to the parallels between Enoch and Enmeduranki. His comment is again worth quoting because it is so surprising:

> Before the discovery of the cuneiform texts, one had seen the prototype of Enoch in the seventh king of the list of Berossos, Evedoranchos = Enmeduranki. It was said of him that he was taken up into the company of Shamash and Ramman and was inducted into the secrets of heaven and earth. Since the new discoveries have shown that the parallel between the series of ten in Berossos and Gen. 5 is no longer tenable, one can no longer maintain a dependence of what is said of Enoch in Gen. 5 on the seventh king in Berossos. . . . One can only point in general to a theme that occurs often in the myths of Israel's neighbors, that a certain person is especially near to God or is taken up to God or the gods. One would be more inclined to admit a parallel to Adapa, the first of "the seven sages," of whom it is said that he was taken away and given wisdom, being entrusted with the divine secrets.[11]

It was noted earlier that Westermann has hardly given adequate reason for dismissing the parallels between Gen. 5 and the king lists. In light of those unmistakable similarities and the intriguing set of traits shared by Enoch and Enmeduranki, it is difficult to avoid the conclusion that it was precisely on traditions about the seventh king that the priestly editor drew.

---

10. Ibid., 351.
11. Ibid., 358.

10

Returning to the text of Gen. 5, we can come to a fuller understanding of the Enoch paragraph if we recall the surviving evidence about Enmeduranki.

1. Gen. 5:18: "When Jared had lived one hundred sixty-two years he became the father of Enoch." Though it is not a part of the Enoch pericope per se, the initial mention of Enoch sets his exact chronological position after the creation of Adam. If one combines all of the relevant numbers in Gen. 5:3–18, the result is that, according to the Masoretic (i.e., the traditional Hebrew text of the Bible) chronology, he was born in the year 632. It is not obvious what significance this number has, but the person responsible for the genealogy implies that all of his ancestors were still alive at this point. Adam lived to be 930 years of age. Hence, he lived during the first 298 years of Enoch's earthly life. When the text goes on to say that it was Enoch, and apparently not Adam, Seth, etc., who walked with God, the writer may be hinting that there was something superior about the religious life of this seventh man. If we add Enoch's 365 years to the 632 that elapsed until his birth, he disappeared in the year 997, just three years short of 1000. All of this is true of the Masoretic system; other chronologies will be examined later in this study.

2. The name Enoch (*ḥanôk*): While names such as Adam and Jared are clearly related to familiar Hebrew words, the meaning of *Enoch* is disputed. In Gen. 4:17 the Enoch of the J list is associated with the first city: "Cain knew his wife, and she conceived and bore Enoch; and he built a city, and named it Enoch after his son Enoch." It may be that the author is here exploiting the Hebrew root *ḥnk* in its sense "to dedicate" (cf. Deut. 20:5; 1 Kings 8:63; 2 Chron. 7:5). But in Gen. 5:18 and 21–24 nothing is said about a city or anything else involving a dedication, unless one is supposed to conclude that Enoch himself is the one dedicated (to God). Another suggestion is that the name is related to a word that means something like "retainer, vassal."[12] Experts who favor this derivation often refer to Gen. 14:14, in which Abram, on learning that Lot had been captured by the four invading kings, "led forth his trained men *ḥanîkîm*], born in his house, three hundred eighteen of them, and went in pursuit as far as Dan." On this explanation Enoch would be a retainer of God, one constantly at his service. P. Grelot has argued that

---

12. For references to the scholars who have held this view, see ibid., 327. Westermann here fails to note that W. F. Albright also explained the name in this fashion ("The Babylonian Matter in the Predeuteronomic Primeval History [JE] in Gen 1–11," *JBL* 58 [1939]: 96); but see p. 357, on which he does mention Albright's theory.

the meaning intended by P is *wisdom, understanding;* in support he appeals to Arabic and Ethiopic cognates that have meanings of this sort.[13] Nevertheless, there are no Hebrew cognates that express this sense, and Grelot may be guilty of reading later traditions about Enoch back into the text of Genesis. If the editor wished to evoke any meaning for his readers, it is likely that "dedicate" is the one intended.

3. The Enoch paragraph begins as the others do with the notice of his becoming a father at a certain age—the very low one of sixty-five in his case (like Mahalalel in 5:15).

4. The first unusual feature—replacement[14] of the expected "Enoch lived after the birth of Methuselah 300 years" by the first reference to his walking with God—is worth examining a little more closely. The key expression, regularly translated "Enoch walked with God," involves, besides Enoch's name, an expressive verb and a prepositional phrase. The verb *wayyithallek* seems to entail more than just "walking." Enoch and Noah are the only scriptural characters who are said to have walked in this sense. The verb has Enoch as subject in 5:22 and 24 and Noah in 6:9: "These are the descendants of Noah. Noah was a righteous man, blameless in his generation; Noah walked with God." In Noah's case the context seems to be supplying more information about the meaning of "walked with God." Also, the editor has playfully established a link between the two men in the way in which he has phrased the statement about Noah: in the expression *hthlk nh* (Noah walked) the last three consonants spell the name *hnk* in reverse.[15] Westermann adduces 1 Sam. 25:15–16 to elucidate the meaning of the verb and preposition: "Yet the men were very good to us, and we suffered no harm, and we never missed anything when we were in the fields, as long as we were with them [*hithallaknu 'ittam*]." That is, "it describes friendly everyday conduct with regard to one's neighbors."[16] Or, to put it in other words, for Enoch and Noah it connotes " 'intimate companionship' . . . with God."[17] The fact that this is said about Enoch alone in the Gen. 5 list may imply that it was not true of the others.

---

13. "La légende d'Hénoch dans les apocryphes et dans la Bible: origine et signification," *RSR* 46 (1958): 186.

14. It is in fact a replacement in the MT; in some later versions it is prefixed to the notice about his living 300 years after Methuselah's birth and bearing sons and daughters (see Westermann, *Genesis 1–11*, 347).

15. As noted by J. Sasson, "Word-Play in Gen 6:8–9," *CBQ* 37 (1975): 166.

16. Westermann, *Genesis 1–11*, 358.

17. F. J. Helfmeyer, "*Halakh,*" *TDOT* 3.394.

Though the commentators find in the special verb used with Enoch an indication of his extraordinary relationship with God, one should be careful about reading from the full expression a notion of this sort. The text says that Enoch enjoyed this continuing association with *ha-ʾelohîm* (the *ʾelohîm*). Admittedly, this is a common way of referring to God in the Hebrew Bible, and in both instances in the Enoch paragraph in which he is said to have walked with God the form with the definite article is used. However, in the concluding statement—"then he was no more, because God took him" (v. 24)—the word for "God" is *ʾelohîm*, that is, it lacks the definite article. This is a clue that the priestly writer meant to distinguish between *ha-ʾelohîm* with whom Enoch had ongoing fellowship and the deity who removed him after 365 years. It has often been observed that in a number of other biblical passages the definite form *ha-ʾelohîm* refers not to God himself but, rather, to angels (see Ps. 8:6; 82:1, 6; 97:7; 138:1); this may well be the intended meaning in Gen. 5:22 and 24. It should be noted, too, that at this juncture the text says that Enoch's walk occurred during the three hundred years between Methuselah's birth and the end of his earthly life. It says nothing about what happened after those years.

5. The notice about Enoch's final age of 365 years matches the statements at this point in the other paragraphs of Gen. 5; it is different only in the sense that the number is by far the lowest. It has already been pointed out that 365 at least suggests solar associations, and this connection is confirmed by the close parallels between Enoch and Enmeduranki, the devotee of the solar god Shamash in Sippar.

6. Where the genealogical form dictates the words "and he died," one finds three unexpected clauses in the Enoch paragraph. The first ("Enoch walked with God" [the *ʾelohîm*]) appears for the second time. Commentators tend to miss the significance of the double reference to his continual association with *ha-ʾelohîm*. The editor does not appear to be summarizing here; rather, he is emphasizing that Enoch's walk with *ha-ʾelohîm* took place after his 365-year life as well as during it. The end of his stay on earth did not mean the end of this communion.

7. The final two clauses in the Enoch pericope report that "then he was no more, because God took him." What they mean is not explained, but the suggestive words hold forth real possibilities for elaboration.

Gen. 5:21–24 appears to be the oldest surviving instance of the Enoch tradition. The growth from that root was to be greatly disproportionate to its modest size. Whole books were to be written, and numerous references were later to be made to them by Jewish, Christian, and Muslim writers. There is reason to believe that much of the subsequent material about Enoch derives from careful and expansionary interpretation of the four verses and their context in Genesis, which are extraordinarily suggestive and enigmatic. It does seem unlikely, however, that all of even the earliest subsequent writings about Enoch arose from this modest base. It may be that Gen. 5 is just a small dose of what Jewish tradents had to tell about him in the postexilic period and that if all ancient Judean literature had survived we would have been able to read much more about him. But it has not, with the result that we are reduced to guessing.

It is plausible that those Jewish people who lived in Babylonian and other eastern territories heard stories about characters such as Enmeduranki and adapted them to their native traditions about Enoch. Those Jews, too, who lived elsewhere in the great empires may well have heard similar material and shaped it as they desired. It is highly likely that something like this happened in the centuries between the writing of Gen. 5 and the earliest of the postbiblical texts about Enoch or that it had already happened in the time before and around when the priestly part of the Pentateuch was written. Otherwise, it would be difficult to account for the explosion of Enochic literature that begins no later than the third century B.C.E.

The next several chapters provide a chronological survey of the sources for the expanding Enoch tradition. It begins with a series of texts that may be assigned to the third century B.C.E. and continues to the first century B.C.E. At that point the nature of the material seems to change: books of Enoch are rarely written; instead, the older ones are cited and interpreted by Jewish and Christian writers for a variety of purposes. Before turning to them, however, we should study what may be the earliest extant interpretation of Gen. 5:21–24 — the Greek translation of Genesis.

D. THE GREEK TRANSLATION OF GEN. 5:21–24

There is insufficient evidence for determining which of the Enochic texts is the second oldest after Gen. 5:21–24. It is convenient, however, to use the Greek translation of Genesis as the next in line. There is good reason for believing that the Old Greek translation of the Pentateuch was made in the third century. One of the strongest arguments is the fact that it is cited already by approximately the end of that century. A certain Demetrius, a Jewish author who wrote in the last part of the third century, used it: "The LXX serves as his only source, and his knowledge of its contents is detailed and exact."[18] The *Letter of Aristeas*, the tradi-

---

18. C. R. Holladay, *Fragments from Hellenistic Jewish Authors*, vol. 1: *Historians*, SBLTT Pseudepigrapha Series 10 (Chico, Calif.: Scholars Press, 1983), 52.

tional story about the Greek translation of the Pentateuch, places it during the reign of Ptolemy II Philadelphus (283–42). Too much of what the letter says is legendary and apologetic to take its claims at historical face value, but it may not be far off the mark for the date when at least the Pentateuch was rendered into Greek, as the example of Demetrius shows.

The Greek translation of the Enochic pericope follows the Hebrew text very closely but deviates from it in several interesting ways. A literal rendering of the Greek follows:

5:21 And Enoch lived **165** years and became the father of Methuselah. 22 **Now** Enoch **pleased God** after he became the father of Methuselah for **200** years and he became the father of sons and daughters. 23 And all the days of Enoch were 365 years. 24 And Enoch **pleased God,** and he was not **found** because **God removed** him.

Armin Schmitt has detailed the points at which the the Greek translation, the Septuagint (LXX), which normally stands in the closest relation to the Hebrew text in Genesis, dispenses with a literal translation of the original for the Enoch verses.[19] Schmitt examined the differences between the Hebrew and the Greek to determine whether specific tendencies and motives of the translator can be detected behind the changes. He notes that several of the deviations are of no consequence (e.g., the word chosen for the conjunction in v. 22) or may be attributed to the dictates of Greek syntax (expressing the word *year* only once in age formulas rather than twice, as in Hebrew).

For Schmitt the significant departures are: (1) the two instances in which "Enoch pleased God" (vv. 22, 24) stand where "Enoch walked with God" appears in the Hebrew; (2) "he was not found" instead of "he was not" (v. 24); and (3) "God removed him" in place of "God took him" (v. 24). For the first case Schmitt adduces several other passages in which the LXX translates the Hebrew form "he walked" with the same Greek verb "he pleased"; but he adds others in which the Greek offers a literal rendering. For him, cases such as Gen. 5:22 and 24 evidence a "spiritualizing tendency in the LXX. The literal rendering of these phrases would easily have aroused the impression among Greek readers as though En-

---

19. "Die Angaben über Henoch Gen 5, 21–24 in der LXX," in *Wort, Lied und Gottesspruch: Beiträge zur Septuaginta. Festschrift für Joseph Ziegler,* edited by J. Schreiner, Forschung zur Bibel 1 (Würzburg: Echter Verlag, 1972), 161–69.

15

och 'walked with God' in a literal sense."[20] As for the expression "he was not found" for "he was not," he notes that "not finding" is characteristic of a number of Greek stories about removals of individuals from one place to another. Once the character is removed, others search for him but find nary a trace. The translator of Gen. 5:24 may, then, have adopted this equivalent because of his familiarity with such removal stories. Finally, the expression for removal or transfer rather than "God took him" is more difficult. The Greek verb in question is never used for removals in the stories just mentioned, although synonyms are. Possibly our verb, too, was employed and the examples have perished. The expressions for not being found and for removal could have been selected to remind Greek readers of such accounts about transfers of individuals, just as Enoch was transferred from one mode or place to another.

Schmitt did not notice, however, that another difference separates the Greek from the Hebrew. Earlier it was pointed out that, in the Hebrew, when Enoch walks he walks with the *'elohîm* (possibly meaning the angels) in both cases, but the one who took him is called *'elohîm* (God). The Greek translator leveled out that important distinction by rendering in all three cases with *the God*, its standard translation of *'elohîm* and *the 'elohîm*. By doing so, the translator deprived readers who had access only to the Greek of any chance of observing and interpreting the significant difference found in the Hebrew text.

---

20. Ibid., 164.

16

CHAPTER 2

THE EARLIEST
ENOCHIC BOOKLETS

A. THE ASTRONOMICAL BOOK (*1 ENOCH* 72–82)

Sometime after the final editor completed the Book of Genesis, booklets centering on Enoch began to appear. This chapter examines the two
most ancient ones: the Astronomical Book (AB) and the Book of the
Watchers (BW).

The AB is an Enochic text that may date, like the Greek translation of
Genesis, from the third century B.C.E. It is the first extrabiblical documentation for Enoch and includes far more information than Gen. 5:21–
24 afforded. The eleven chapters of the AB assume or reproduce the data
of Gen. 5, but they virtually explode one aspect of it: whereas Gen. 5:23,
in assigning Enoch the highly unusual number of 365 years, hinted at
some astronomical associations with him (something the LXX in no way
changed), *1 Enoch* 72–82 present extended heavenly revelations that deal
almost exclusively with astronomical matters and assert that all of them
were disclosed to Enoch by an angel. It would be difficult to maintain
that this exponential increase in astronomical material was purely an exegetical inference from the number 365 in Gen. 5:23; surely something
more would be needed to connect him not only with the solar year
(which may be the intent of his age of 365) but also with the moon and
related phenomena. Either there was much more material about Enoch
when P wrote Gen. 5 — material that the editor chose not to reproduce —
or major developments occurred between the sixth and third centuries.
Perhaps both took place.

A third-century date for the AB is now widely accepted by scholars,
although there is room for debate about it. The primary argument in
favor of a time of composition no later than the third century arises from
one of the four copies of the AB found among the Dead Sea Scrolls.
Milik dates its script to the end of the third or beginning of the second
century.[1] Since there is no reason for thinking that the manuscript is the

---

1. *The Books of Enoch: Aramaic Fragments of Qumrân Cave 4* (Oxford: Clarendon,
1976), 7, 273–74.

original, the paleographical dating suggests that the book was written at an earlier time. If the earliest copy does come from about 200 B.C.E., then the third century is a likely date for the work unless it was written at a still earlier time. That possibility should not be excluded, but it is preferable to be on the cautious side and accept a third-century time of writing for the AB.

There is no need to present all the information found in the AB; it should suffice to summarize what it has to say about the situation in Enoch's life and about astronomical and related matters.

1. ENOCH'S SITUATION

The introductory verse of the AB supplies many essential details for understanding the book.

The book of the Motion of the Luminaries of the Heaven, how each one of them stands in relation to their number, to their powers and their times, of their names and their origins and their months, as the holy angel Uriel, who is their leader, showed to me when he was with me. And he showed to me their whole description as they are, and for the years of the World to eternity, until the creation will be made anew to last forever. (72:1; see also 74:2, 75:3)[2]

While the astronomical content of the composition is placed in the first and emphatic position, it is also evident that the AB is not being touted as a purely empirical, scientific treatise. On the contrary, the numerous astronomical theories and details are packaged as revelations from an angel named Uriel to an unnamed person identified here only as "me." The angelic name Uriel is most appropriate for one who functions as the leader of the heavenly luminaries, since it means "God is my light." The name does not occur in connection with an angel in the Hebrew Bible. Uriel does not dictate the words of the composition to the recipient; the verb used is *showed*. As the sequel indicates, he leads the "me" on a tour of the heavens so that his teachings are reinforced by firsthand acquaintance.

---

2. The translation is that of O. Neugebauer, himself a great expert in ancient astronomical texts. It is found in M. Black, *The Book of Enoch or I Enoch: A New English Edition*, SVTP 7 (Leiden: Brill, 1985).

Naturally, the reader of *1 Enoch* knows that the recipient of Uriel's demonstrations is Enoch, but for whatever reason the writer does not divulge his identity until 76:14: "And thus (the description of) the twelve gates in the four (quarters) of heaven is completed; and I have shown to you, my son Methuselah, all their laws, (and all their) calamities and benefactions." A quick check of the genealogy in Gen. 5 reveals that Methuselah's father is Enoch. A similar allusion figures in *1 Enoch* 79:1. That is, for the first eight chapters of the AB the writer does not mention Enoch by name. Only in 80:1 is the point clarified beyond a doubt: "And in these days the angel Uriel spoke to me and said to me: see, I have shown to you, O Enoch, everything and I have revealed to you, everything to be seen under the sun, the moon and everything about those who guide the stars in the heaven and all who turn (back) their works, (and about) their times and their places of exit (i.e. the gates)." Later there is another direct reference to Enoch (81:1), and there is also an attempt to align the chronology of the AB with that of Genesis in *1 Enoch* 81:5–10, in which three (or seven) angels return Enoch to his house and command him to tell Methuselah and his children what has been revealed to him. This is to take one year; then in the second year the angels will take (cf. Gen. 5:24) Enoch from them. There may be an interesting implication of the chronology: if Enoch spent his last year with his family, then when he returned from his sojourn with the angels he was 364—a highly suggestive age for an individual to whom the workings of the 364-day calendar have been disclosed.

It may be that the material in *1 Enoch* 80:2–82:3 is a supplement to the original part of the AB.[3] This is the only section that addresses other topics such as the final wickedness and the deformation of the created order. If these chapters are an addition, they disclose the work of an editor who is trying to tie the material more directly to Gen. 5. It is obvious from the work of this editor that he understood Enoch's time with Uriel and the other three (or seven) angels to have happened before his final removal. That is, the astronomical revelations took place during the three hundred years that Enoch "walked with the *'elohîm*" (Gen. 5:22), after the birth of his first son, Methuselah, but before his final departure from the earth. It hardly needs to be said that the writer understood Genesis's *ha-'elohîm* to mean "angels."

---

3. For the evidence, see VanderKam, *Enoch and the Growth of an Apocalyptic Tradition*, 78–79, 106–7.

19

2. THE CONTENTS OF THE AB

The booklet addresses a range of astronomical and other apparently related topics. The shape in which it left the author's hand is no longer entirely clear, but the contents of the original are really not in doubt. The shape of the original work is a problem because we have so little of it and because only a limited amount of material from the various stages of its subsequent textual journey have survived. The author penned it in the Aramaic language. This conclusion had been suggested at an early time in the modern study of *1 Enoch*, and discovery of four Aramaic copies of the AB in Qumran cave 4 makes it a virtual certainty. Nevertheless, from the Aramaic version only small fragments are now available, nothing resembling a complete text. A copy of the Aramaic AB was at some point translated into Greek; from this Greek version only a few scraps have been found. From Greek it was rendered into Ethiopic. Only in various Ethiopic copies is the complete work preserved, but it is rather different from what is known of the Aramaic original.

The textual situation, somewhat simplified, is this. The Ethiopic version opens with an introductory section (72:1), which leads into a longer unit that describes the law of the sun for a solar year of 364 days (72:2–32). This is the earliest reference to a solar calendar of this length, but the number of days in one year falls one short of matching the number of years in Enoch's life. Earlier it was suggested that the return of Enoch to the earth for one year before his final removal (*1 Enoch* 81:5–10) entailed that he was 364 years of age when the angelic revelations to him about the sun were completed. The writer then turns to the law of the moon, which he calls the smaller luminary (as in Gen. 1:16), and its movements relative to the sun (chap. 73). But the account of the lunar courses is not nearly so complete as that of the sun in chapter 72. In fact, the Ethiopic text describes the amount of the lunar surface which is illuminated for just the first two days of a month (it increases by $1/14$ each day). Similar material follows in 74:1–9, while in the remainder of the chapter calculations for solar and lunar years are recorded. Chapter 75 begins with statements about the four extra days in the solar year (one at the end of each quarter) and concludes with comments about gates in heaven for the sun, moon, winds, and heat. This topic is continued in chapter 76 in which twelve gates—three in each of the cardinal points—for the winds are treated. Geographical concerns dominate chapter 77, which depicts the four quarters of the earth, seven exceptionally high mountains, seven rivers, and seven large islands. Chapter 78 lists names for the sun and moon, but most of the chapter is devoted to the increasing and decreasing illumination of the moon on successive days in a full lunar month and the relationship between its movements and those of the sun. The reader also learns how many days are in the lunar months (29 or 30) and in half of a lunar year (177). Chapter 79 sounds like the last one in a booklet in that it again touches (briefly) on the sun and moon and the heavenly gates. To this point the arrangement is:

sun
moon
moon (and sun)
four extra days
gates
geography
moon
summary

With *1 Enoch* 80:2 a noticeable change occurs. The subject becomes the future days of the sinners and how nature—including the sun, moon, and stars—will fail to follow its normal course: "And the entire law of the stars will be closed to the sinners, and the thoughts of those who dwell upon the earth will go astray over them, and they will turn from all their ways and will go astray, and will think them gods" (80:7). Chapter 81 tells how Enoch read from the "book of the tablets of heaven . . . all the deeds of men, and all who will be born of flesh on the earth for the generations of eternity" (81:2). The angels finally return the patriarch to his home, where he is to instruct his offspring for one year. Upon completion of that year they would take him from them (note how the writer avoids saying that God would take him). His words to Methuselah, his command that he keep his father's books, begin the final chapter:

> And now, my son Methuselah, all these things I recount to you and write down for you; *I have revealed everything to you* and have given you books about all these things. Keep, my son Methuselah, the books from the hand of your father, that you may pass (them) on to the generations of eternity. I have given wisdom to you and to your children, and to those who will be your children, that they may give (it) to their children for all the generations for ever—this wisdom (which is) beyond their thoughts. (81:1–2)

Enoch warns about the sin of not reckoning the additional four days in the calendar of the solar year (82:4–6). But then, strangely, the last chapter concludes with another section about the stars and their angelic leaders. Although one is told that the astral leaders and the four seasons over which they preside will be treated, only two are, and the AB ends.

What do the Aramaic fragments indicate about the original order and contents of the book? Was it always so oddly arranged? Apparently not. Milik reports that the thirty-six fragments that remain from the first Qumran manuscript "contain only the 'synchronistic calendar,' i.e. the writer's 'synchronizing' of the movements of the sun and moon."[4] He considers *1 Enoch* 73:1–74:9 to be a "résumé" of this synchronic calendar. Parts of the same synchronic arrangement appear on manuscript *b*, which continues with material from *1 Enoch* 76–79 and 82. He proposes that the original AB began with an introductory chapter, such as *1 Enoch* 72, and that the next item was this synchronistic calendar. That calendar took the full form it has in the Qumran manuscripts — that is, a schematic account of the relative positions of sun and moon throughout an entire year (it would have filled approximately twenty-seven columns) — not the highly truncated shape it now has in the Ethiopic version. It contained information of this kind:

> And it shines during night nine of this (month) with four [sevenths] and a half. And then it sets and enters (the gate). During this night the sun begins again to move away through [its] sections [(i.e., of the first gate) and to set] through these (sections). And then the moon sets and enters the fifth gate and it wanes during the rest of this night by [two] sevenths and a half. And it waxes during this day up to five sevenths, and its light is equivalent exactly (?) to five sevenths. [And then it emerges] from the fifth gate [and it keeps, during the rest of this day, two sevenths. (MS *b*, 7 iii.4–8)[5]

The other Qumran copies show, with manuscript *b*, that the Aramaic original included at least chapters 76–79 and 82. Copy *d* probably supplies some of the text now missing from the abbreviated ending of the Ethiopic in chapter 82. It may be an accident, but it is significant that the unusual, anomalous material — 80:2–82:3 — is not attested on the Qumran fragments.

With this in mind, we may sketch what were the contents of the astronomical revelations claimed for Enoch:

---

4. *Books of Enoch*, 273.
5. Ibid., 281.

1. A solar year of 364 days, divided into 4 seasons with 91 days each, and 12 months, with 8 having 30 days each and the third, sixth, ninth, and twelfth having 31 days each. The sun in its annual course rises from 6 gates in the east and sets in 6 gates in the west. The variation of daylight and darkness during the days at the solstices is 2:1. The chief error in regard to the solar calendar is that people forget to add the 4 extra days.[6]

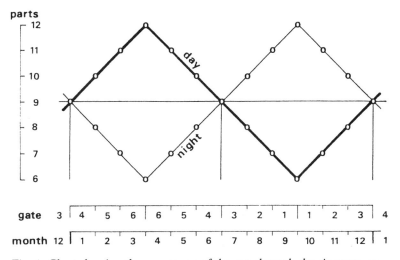

Fig. 1. Chart showing the movement of the sun through the six gates, according to AB. From O. Neuberger, appendix A, "The 'Astronomical' Chapters of the Ethiopic Enoch (72–80.1 and 82.4–20)," in M. Black, *The Book of Enoch or 1 Enoch: A New English Edition*, SVTP (Leiden: E. J. Brill, 1985).

2. A lunar year of 354 days. The movements of the moon and sun are correlated, but 10 extra days are needed to bring a lunar year into harmony with the solar year (354 + 10 = 364). Six of the lunar months have 30 days, and 6 have 29. The lunar surface is dark before the new moon and has $1/14$ of its surface lighted for each day of its waxing; it loses $1/14$ for each day of its waning. The light of the moon is $1/7$ that of the sun.[7]

3. The revelations include information about the various kinds of heavenly gates—for example, those for the sun and moon and those for the winds.

---

6. See O. Neugebauer in Black, *Book of Enoch*, 393–94.
7. See ibid., 400.

Months	1	2	3	4	5	6	7	8	9	10	11	12	1	Months
Gates														**Gates**
4	2													4
5	2	2												5
6	8	8	4	4										6
5	2	2	2	2	2									5
4	1	1	2	2	1	2								4
3	1	1	1	1	1	1	2							3
2	2	2	2	2	2	2	2	2						2
1	8	7	8	7	8	7	8	7	4	4				1
2	2	2	2	2	2	2	2	2	2	2	2			2
3	1	1	1	1	1	1	1	1	2	2	1	2		3
4	1	1	2	2	1	1	1	1	1	1	1		2	4
5		2	2	2	2	2	2	2	2	2	2	2	2	5
6			4	4	8	8	8	8	8	7	8	8	8	6
5					2	2	2	2	2	2	2	2	2	5
4						1	1	1	1	1	1	1	1	4
3							1	2	2	2	1	1	1	3
2								1	2	2	2	2	2	2
1									4	4	8	7	8	1
2											2	2	2	2
3												1	1	3
4													1	4
Days	30	29	30	29	30	29	30	29	30	29	30	29	30	**Days**

Fig. 2. Chart showing the movement of the moon through the six gates, according to AB. From O. Neuberger, appendix A, "The 'Astronomical' Chapters of the Ethiopic Enoch (72–80.1 and 82.4–20)," in M. Black, *The Book of Enoch or 1 Enoch: A New English Edition*, SVTP (Leiden: E. J. Brill, 1985).

4. Geographical topics are also presented. These involve the major points on the earth, usually seven to a category. Though these subjects may not seem related to the dominant one of astronomy, a comparison of the BW with related astronomical/astrological material from Mesopotamia shows that the two belong together. For divinatory purposes the sky was divided into areas, and the earth was as well: depending on which region of the sky was the spot at which an astrological omen was observed, a certain sector of the earth was purported to be affected by it.[8]

It should be stressed that the writer does not evaluate solar and lunar calendars; he simply presents schematic accounts of both, using numbered months (he never names them) and correlates them. Moreover, he makes no attempt to bring them into a Jewish cultic context. That is, he does not

---

8. See VanderKam, *Enoch and the Growth of an Apocalyptic Tradition*, 98–99.

tie the festival cycle to either calendar, nor does he connect the rotations of the priestly groups with them. The calendrical accounts are straightforward, objective descriptions with nothing distinctively Jewish about them. Thus, we search in vain for any reference to the sabbath in the AB.

It is also worth noting that the AB, from its inception, may have had both a theological and eschatological element. First, it presents itself as the holy angel Uriel's disclosure to Enoch of information not accessible to any others. In other words, what Enoch sees, hears, and relates to his children has the stamp of divine authenticity. It should also be recalled that the opening verse, 72:1, claims that Uriel showed Enoch "all their regulations exactly as they are, for each year of the world and for ever, until the new creation shall be made which will last for ever." The revealed laws will be operative until the new creation. The writer therefore knows of a theory by which time is divided into eras. Moreover, all of the laws are revealed by an angel, and, indeed, nature is governed and run by angels on behalf of God (cf. 80:1). Enoch's tour has reminded scholars of the guided tour experienced by the prophet Ezekiel in Ezek. 40–48. There an angel shows the prophet around the new temple and also details for him the new geography of the holy land. It may be significant that the writer is persistent in his concern with what he understood to be astronomical entities and that he does not mention some themes that will later become standard Enoch fare, such as the story about the watchers.

B. THE BOOK OF THE WATCHERS

The composite book which goes under the name The Book of the Watchers (BW) is found in *1 Enoch* 1–36. It contains several major divisions, each of which may have a different author: 1. an introduction announcing judgment (chap. 1); 2. chapters about the lawfulness of nature and the unlawfulness of humanity (2–5); 3. a unit centering on the angelic watchers, their sin, and their fate (6–16, 6–11, and 12–16 seem to be distinguishable sections; Enoch appears only in the latter); 4. a first cosmic journey (17–19); 5. a second cosmic journey (20–36). The book in its full form seems to be one of the oldest Enochic compositions. Passages from most of its chapters have turned up on six different copies from Qumran cave 4, and Milik dates the oldest of them (MS *a*) to the first half of the second century B.C.E.[9] It is reasonable to conclude, there-

---

9. *Books of Enoch*, 5.

fore, that the book was in existence by ca. 200 B.C.E. The final chapters of the BW (33–36) show that the author of this section knew the AB. The BW introduces a range of new topics into the Enochic tradition while resuming some that had already become part of it. The BW has a more sustained, complex relationship with the biblical text than does the AB.

1. ENOCH'S SITUATION

There is reason to believe that for the BW the many revelations that Enoch receives come to him during his first sojourn with the angels (i.e., the first "he walked with the *ʾelohîm*" in Gen. 5:22). The opening words of the booklet, and thus of the entire collection known as *1 Enoch*, identify Enoch and his situation:

> The words of blessing of Enoch according to which he blessed the chosen and righteous who must be present on the day of distress (which is appointed) for the removal of all the wicked and impious. And Enoch answered and said: (there was) a righteous man whose eyes were opened by the Lord, and he saw a holy vision in the heavens which the angels showed to me. And I heard everything from them, and I understood what I saw, but not for this generation, but for a distant generation which will come. Concerning the chosen I spoke, and I uttered a parable concerning them. . . . (1:1–3a)

The text continues with a classic description of a theophany. Enoch predicts that God will appear on Sinai with his hosts to administer punishment to the wicked, among whom are a group called "the watchers" (1:5), while the righteous will enjoy peace with him. The New Testament Epistle of Jude quotes from the final verse of this chapter: "And behold! He comes with ten thousand holy ones to execute judgement upon them, and to destroy the impious, and to contend with all flesh concerning everything which the sinners and the impious have done and wrought against him" (1:9; see Jude 14–15).

There are intriguing features in the description of Enoch and the words that he utters. First, his words are termed a blessing, as is Moses' speech in Deut. 33, but he is primarily presented in language that recalls the descriptions of the diviner Balaam in Numbers 22–24. For example, Balaam took up his parable (Num. 23–24 employ the phrase seven times), his eyes were opened (22:31, 23:3–4, 15–16), he saw a vision of God (24:4, 15), and spoke of a distant future (24:14, 17). It seems odd that a Jewish writer would present his hero in language dripping with reminders of the diviner who tried to curse Israel, but the author did just that, and he did so at the most visible place in his book. He may have recognized that Enoch's associations with divinatory subjects (such as astronomy/astrology) brought him into the same sphere as Balaam, however differently the two carried out their functions.

The AB had a few expressions that could be called eschatological (there are more in the sections that were added later); the BW marks the first literary representation of Enoch as intimately involved with the latter days. The reader is prepared for this by the remark that he blesses "the chosen and righteous who must be present on the day of distress" (1:1) but more fully by Enoch's declaration: "And I heard everything from them, and I understood what I saw, but not for this generation, but for a distant generation which will come" (1:2). That initial impression is strengthened by the theophany that follows in 1:3b–9. The Lord *will* come down upon Sinai with his hosts and terrify all, including the watchers. There will be cosmic upheaval, and all will be judged. Enoch is predicting the final judgment here, although much of what he says could as well apply to the flood, which still lay in the future in his lifetime. But the prediction that "the earth will sink and everything that is on the earth will be destroyed, and there will be judgement upon all, and upon all the righteous" may be directed to the second judgment, not the first (i.e., the flood). As we will see, in other passages in the BW Enoch addresses the latter days, especially the judgment that will befall the wicked.

Enoch quickly changes, however, from visionary of the latter days to a preacher of righteousness in chapters 2–5. There he invites people to consider nature—whether the luminaries in the sky, seasons, or trees—and to notice that "all his [God's] works serve him and do not change, but as God has decreed, so everything is done" (5:2). Here he appeals to the theme familiar from the AB that natural phenomena operate according to unchanging laws. People, too, like the elements of nature, have been given laws by their Creator; they, however, fail to obey them: "But you have not persevered, nor observed the law of the Lord. But you have transgressed, and have spoken proud and hard words with your unclean mouth against his majesty. You hard of heart! You will not have peace!" (5:4). He warns that the wicked will become the object of an eternal curse, while the righteous will have light, peace, joy, and wisdom: "they will complete the number of the days of their life, and their life will grow in peace, and the years of their joy will increase in gladness and in eternal peace all the days of their life" (5:9b). Enoch's moral exhortations will become a regular feature in later texts such as the Epistle of Enoch.

The immensely important section about the angels who descended and mated with women (chaps. 6–11) will be treated later, but, as Enoch does not appear in them, we may skip over them for a moment. The ancient patriarch reappears at the beginning of chapter 12; he then occupies center stage for the remaining parts of the booklet. *1 Enoch* 12:1–2 use some fairly familiar language in describing Enoch—in fact, the first verbal echo of Gen. 5:21–24 in the BW: "And before everything Enoch had been hidden, and none of the sons of men knew where he was hidden, or where he was, or what had happened. And all his doings (were) with the Holy Ones and with the Watchers in his days." These verses could be considered an interpretation of Gen. 5:24, especially of the words "Enoch walked with the *'elohîm*; then he was no more, because God took him." In the Greek translation the phrasing for the latter two clauses was "and he was not found because God removed him." But in the sequel in *1 Enoch* the patriarch is on earth, "by the waters of Dan in Dan which is south-west of Hermon" (13:7); and the present scene is said to be "before everything," that is, before the descent of the watchers and its consequences. They came down, according to *1 Enoch* 6:6, in the days of Enoch's father, Jared (a pun on the name Jared, which is related to the Hebrew for "come down"). So, we may again be dealing with Enoch during his initial stay with the angels.

In chapters 12–16 Enoch plays an intriguing and suggestive role: though he is a human being, he serves as an intermediary between angelic groups. He brings to the evil watchers, who sinned with women and thereby unleashed all manner of evil on the earth, the announcement that they will have no peace.

> . . . the Watchers [the good ones] called to me, Enoch the scribe, and said to me: "Enoch, scribe of righteousness, go, inform the Watchers of heaven who have left the high heaven and the holy eternal place, and have corrupted themselves with the women, and have done as the sons of men do, and have taken wives for themselves, and have become completely corrupt on the earth. They will have on earth neither peace nor forgiveness of sin. . . ." (12:3b–5)

Enoch, then, has become a scribe and a messenger for celestial angels, and the group to which he is to relay the message consists of other angels, now fallen from heaven and grace.

Once he delivers the condemnatory message the fallen watchers commission him to write out their petition to receive forgiveness for what they have done.

> Then I went and spoke to them all together, and they were all afraid; fear and trembling seized them. And they asked me to write out for them the record of a petition that they might receive forgiveness, and to take the record of their petition up to the Lord in heaven. For they (themselves) were not able from then on to speak, and they did not raise their eyes to heaven out of shame for their sins for which they had been condemned. And then I wrote out the record of their petition and their supplication in regard to their spirits and the deeds of each one of them, and in regard to what they asked, (namely) that they should obtain absolution and forebearance. (13:3–6)

The picture here is remarkable: Enoch, a man, evokes fear and trembling from angels when he approaches—a reaction more appropriate for an appearance of a divine being (see 1:5). Moreover, he, in his human condition, is to bear their message to the Lord because their sin meant they could no longer do so themselves (see also 14:5). Enoch clearly outranks these angels and is their superior in virtue. Enoch later sees in a vision that he should reprove the watchers, and this he does (13:7–10). As he narrates to them the contents of his vision, Enoch reports yet another extraordinary experience: his ascent to the heavenly throne room and thus to the presence of God himself (while the angelic watchers were prohibited forever from entering heaven). The particulars of that account will be discussed later, but once he is in the very presence of God he is addressed:

> And until then I had a covering on my face, as I trembled. And the Lord called me with his own mouth and said to me: "Come hither, Enoch, to my holy word." And he lifted me up and brought me near to the door. And I looked, with my face down.
> And he answered me and said to me with his voice: "Hear! Do not be afraid, Enoch, (you) righteous man and scribe of righteousness. Come hither and hear my voice. And go, say to the Watchers of heaven who sent you to petition on their behalf: 'You ought to petition on behalf of men, not men on behalf of you.'" (14:24–15:2)

From the mouth of God, Enoch then hears words of judgment for the watchers and predictions about their influence and doom. The second half of the BW consists of two journeys on which angels conduct Enoch ("And they took me . . ." [17:1]) through the universe — a scene reminiscent of the AB. He narrates these in the first person, and a frequent expression is "I saw." One of the items that he sees on different occasions is the place(s) at which various beings will be or will be punished, including the watchers (18:13, 19:1–2). In 19:1 the angel Uriel speaks to Enoch about the "spirits of the angels who were promiscuous with women" and their coming punishment. After the first of his travels Enoch highlights the superiority of his knowledge: "And I, Enoch, alone saw the sight, the ends of everything; and no man has seen what I have seen" (19:3).

After an interlude in chapter 20 which names seven "holy angels who keep watch" (20:1), Enoch resumes his journey. The second travelogue includes more examples of dialogue between Enoch and Uriel (or Raphael, Raguel, Michael) regarding the identity and meaning of the places they see. Generally, the places and explanations center on the final judgment and the spots at which different categories of beings are held until it happens. Enoch even sees an extraordinary mountain in the middle of a group of seven mountains, among which was the tree of life. Michael explains: "This high mountain which you saw, whose summit is like the throne of the Lord, is the throne where the Holy and Great One, the Lord of Glory, the Eternal King, will sit when he comes down to visit the earth for good" (25:3; see 24:3). The tree will give life to the chosen after the judgment. At times Enoch responds in praise of God for what he sees and hears: "Then I blessed the Lord of Glory, and said: 'Blessed be my Lord, the Lord of Glory and Righteousness, who rules everything for ever' " (22:14; cf. 25:7). Enoch's travels even bring him to the Garden of Righteousness and the tree of wisdom (32:3). So, with the tree of life, the garden, and the tree of wisdom, he experiences the major features of the scene in Gen. 3.

Beginning with 33:2 and continuing to 36:3 Enoch's report becomes a résumé of the AB's teachings about gates in heaven for the stars and winds. His tour in these chapters takes him to the ends of the earth in all four directions (actually, to the ends of the heavens in the east). The angel Uriel is again his guide. The BW concludes with a blessing:

And when I saw, I blessed, and I will always bless the Lord of Glory who has made great and glorious wonders that he might show the greatness of this work to his angels and to the souls of men, that they might praise his work, and that all his creatures might see the work of his power and praise the great work of his hands and bless him for ever. (36:4)

2. THE CONTENTS OF THE BW

No other document in the early Enochic tradition proved more important for later use and adaptation than the BW. In it Enoch assumes several roles that were either only hinted at before or were not present at all in the Enochic tradition known to us.

As already shown, Enoch is placed before the reader in *1 Enoch* 1:1–3a as a visionary who speaks of days far off, and the theophany that follows immediately on this introduction focuses on God's descent to earth for universal judgment on the evil.

The short section in chapters 2–5 also has a heavy eschatological emphasis, but in it Enoch functions more as a preacher of righteous behavior—of fidelity to the laws that the Lord had established for humanity, just as God had set principles by which natural phenomena are governed.

a. *1 ENOCH* 6–11.[10]   The most significant element—a novel one in the tradition—is the story of the angels who descended and the consequences of their actions (*1 Enoch* 6–11). That new theme is elaborated at considerable length and becomes the leitmotiv of the Enochic tradition. It should now be examined in some detail, and that examination will be more helpful if the text of *1 Enoch* is compared with the sections of Genesis to which it is related.[11] The translations in this section are not quoted from another source but are very literal renderings designed to bring out the points at which the two texts agree and disagree.

The opening words of *1 Enoch* 6 are clearly drawn from Gen. 6.

Gen. 6:1–2	*1 Enoch* 6:1–2
And it was when the sons of mankind began to become numerous	And it was when the sons of mankind became numerous, in those

---

10. The analysis of *1 Enoch* 6–16 is deeply indebted to the detailed study of D. Dimant, "The 'Fallen Angels' in the Dead Sea Scrolls and in the Apocryphal and Pseudepigraphic Books Related to Them" (Ph.D. diss., Hebrew University of Jerusalem, 1974 [in Hebrew]).

11. The next paragraphs are dependent to some extent on VanderKam, "Biblical Interpretation in *1 Enoch* and *Jubilees*," in *The Pseudepigrapha and Early Biblical Interpretation*, edited by J. H. Charlesworth and C. A. Evans, JSP Supplements 14/Studies in Scripture in Early Judaism and Christianity 2 (Sheffield: Sheffield Academic Press, 1993), 103–7.

on the face of the earth, and
daughters were born to them, and
the sons of the ᵓelohîm saw the
daughters of mankind that they
were beautiful,

days beautiful and lovely daughters
were born to them, and the angels,
the sons of heaven, saw them and
desired them, and they said among
themselves, "Come on, let's choose
for ourselves wives from the sons
of mankind and let's have sons for
ourselves."

One point that is obvious from the comparison is that the writer of *1
Enoch* 6:1–2 has seen in the word "ᵓelohîm" in Gen. 5:22, 24 a reference
to angels, just as was done in the AB: he reads opposite "the ᵓelohîm" two
expressions, "the angels, the sons of heaven." So the expositors of the
Enoch tradition were consistent in interpreting the word ᵓelohîm introduced by the definite article as a designation for the angels. It should
also be evident that the author accents the lustful nature of the angels'
decision: humanity produced not just beautiful but beautiful and lovely
daughters. The angels not only saw them, but they desired them as well.
They took wives in order to be able to father sons. Already in 6:2 the
author, by having the angels discuss the matter with one another, shows
that their action was deliberate. They knew exactly what they were doing: they formed a plan, and, as the sequel relates, they carried it out.

After these closely parallel lines, the texts diverge. Gen. 6:3 contains
the Lord's decree that his spirit would not remain (?) in mankind forever,
since they were flesh; rather, their days would be 120 years. These words
may play a role later in *1 Enoch* but not here. *1 Enoch* 6:3–8 is vastly
different. This section is devoted to a discussion that takes place between
the lustful angels who wanted to become fathers. We learn that their
leader, named Shemihazah, wanted to insure that the group was unified
in its intentions:

"I fear that you may not wish this deed to be done, and (that) I
alone will pay for this great sin." And they all answered him and
said: "Let us all swear an oath, and bind one another with curses
not to alter this plan, but to carry out this plan effectively." They
all swore together and all bound one another with curses to it. And
they were in all two hundred, and they came down [in the days of
Jared on][12] this summit of Mount Hermon. And they called the

---

12. As the Aramaic and one of the Greek versions indicate, the correct reading
here is "in the days of Jared on"; in Knibb's translation, which is based

mountain Hermon, because on it they swore and bound one another with curses.

We again learn of the conscious transgression of the watchers: Shemihazah calls what they are going to do "this great sin," and all of them bind themselves with oath and curse to perform it. Clearly, the guilt lies with them, not with the women after whom they lust or with any other being. The text centers on a set of word plays: the watchers who have sworn to carry out their plan descend in the days of Jared (the name is related to the word for "descend") and touch the earth on Mount Hermon (the name is related to the word for "swearing an oath").

The two hundred angels who descended on their own volition were led by twenty chiefs, all of whom are named in *1 Enoch* 6:7. The list is interesting for those who study the ancient Jewish beliefs about angels, but for our purposes a more important point is that a substantial percentage of them have names that have astronomical or astrological significance or at least relate to the sorts of concerns found in the AB. The names in their Aramaic forms are: Ramshiel (evening of God?; or Ramtʾel [burning heat of God?]);[13] Kokhavʾel (star of God); Raʿamʾel (thunder of God); Ziqiʾel (lightning flash of God); Baraqʾel (lightning of God); Matarʾel (rain of God); Ananʾel (cloud of God); Satavʾel (winter of God); Shamshiʾel (sun of God); and Sahriʾel (moon of God).[14] The connection of all of them with God is explicit, but they will teach humankind information (suggested by their names) which they were not supposed to communicate to them. This is curious, because Uriel had told Enoch about astronomical and meteorological matters. Apparently, that was a licit transmission; the present one is illicit.

Once the writer of *1 Enoch* 6–11 has presented the angelic oath and their names, he returns to the biblical text.

Gen. 6	1 Enoch 7
and they took for themselves wives from all whom they chose. [6:3 is next]	and they took for themselves wives and each one chose one for himself. And they began to come in to

largely on one Ethiopic manuscript, we find "on Ardis which is" and a footnote that gives the correct reading.
13. See Milik, *Books of Enoch*, 153.
14. Milik (*Books of Enoch*, 151–53) and Knibb (*Ethiopic Book of Enoch*, 2.70–71) provide charts that give the forms of the names in the different witnesses. Not all of them are certain.

The *nephîlîm* were on the earth in in those days, and also after this when (?) the sons of the *'elohîm* came in to the

daughters of mankind and they gave birth for them. They were the *gibborîm* who were from eternity, the men of the name

them, and they became promiscuous with them. And they taught them charms and spells, and showed to them the cutting of roots and trees. [7:2] And they became pregnant and gave birth to great giants, and the height of each one was 3000 cubits.

As can be seen, *1 Enoch* 7:1 expands freely on Gen. 6:2, but by the end of the verse the reader is aware of significant additions. The text continues to emphasize the evil of the angels' actions: "and they began to come in to them, and they became promiscuous with them." The Greek texts here employ a verb meaning "defile": the angels, in their sexual contact with women, defile themselves.[15] The notion of defilement, which seems more likely in the context, conjures up various biblical passages that speak of sexual or cultic defilement or impurity. The bizarre marriages that produce some sort of impurity are not further described at this point.

The writer also highlights a new element vis-à-vis the biblical text: the angels taught their mates forbidden arts—"they taught them charms and spells, and showed to them the cutting of roots and trees." The instruction that is introduced in this highly negative setting concerns magical and medicinal lore. The statement in 7:2 provides an interpretation of the final sentence of Gen. 6:4 by explaining "the *gibborîm* who were from eternity, the men of the name," as "great giants, and the height of each one was 3,000 cubits." Genesis's reference to those "who were from eternity" may have suggested to the expositor that supernatural, possibly immortal beings were involved in the episode. It is heavenly ones who live eternally, not human beings. It should be noted that the understanding of *gibborîm* in *1 Enoch* 7:2 as giants agrees with the interpretation found in the LXX. The Greek Genesis translates both *nephîlîm* and *gibborîm* as *hoi gigantes* (the giants).

After *1 Enoch* 7:1 the instructional motif is dropped for a short time while the narrative returns to the theme of the angels-women marriages.

And they became pregnant and bore large giants, and their height (was) three thousand cubits. These devoured all the toil of men,

---

15. See Knibb, *Ethiopic Book of Enoch*, 2.76–77.

until men were unable to sustain them. And the giants turned against them in order to devour men. And they began to sin against birds, and against animals, and against reptiles and against fish, and they devoured one another's flesh and drank the blood from it. Then the earth complained about the lawless ones. (7:3–6; note that most of these categories of animals are included within the beings that are to be destroyed in Gen. 6:7)

The offspring of the marriages, in which one of the spouses was supernatural, were beings of almost unimaginable size—3,000 cubits, that is, 4,500 feet tall. Not surprisingly, there were inadequate provisions for supporting their massive appetites, and they soon began devouring anything they could find, including themselves. Not only did they become cannibals; they also consumed blood—a matter that is strongly forbidden in Genesis after the flood ended (9:4). The uncontrolled evil here pictured clearly violates all norms; there is no question that such supernaturally powerful evil needed to be met with supernatural punishment. The point of the story is to impress on the reader the impossible situation that obtained when the giants came on the scene. They violated the most basic human laws—the so-called Noachic laws[16]—and had to be stopped through appropriate punishment. As the human population was in no condition to exercise that function, judgment would have to come from above, from the world in which the fallen angels had previously lived within their assigned bounds. It is no wonder that "the earth complained about the lawless ones." The divine-human marriages had resulted not in superior humans—demigods—but, instead, in hideous, lawless, uncontrollable giants.

The narrative again switches motifs at the beginning of chapter 8, in which the teaching theme of *1 Enoch* 7:1 returns. *1 Enoch* 8:1–3 supplies a list of angels and the arts that each one taught, not just to the women but to humanity in general. The first to appear and the one who receives the brunt of the blame and space is Asael. He "taught men to make swords, and daggers, and shields and breastplates. And he showed them 'the metals,'[17] and the art of making them: bracelets, and ornaments, and the art of making up the eyes and of beautifying the eyelids, and the most precious and choice stones, and all (kinds of) coloured dyes. *And the world was changed.* And there was great impiety and much fornication, and they went astray and all their ways became corrupt" (8:1–2). At this

---

16. So Dimant, " 'Fallen Angels,' " 49–56.
17. See Knibb, *Ethiopic Book of Enoch,* 2.80.

point, where Gen. 6:5 and 11–12 (the complete evil and corruption on the earth) underlie the text, Asael for the first time assumes a position of evil prominence among the fallen angels. In the list in *1 Enoch* 6:7 an angel with a similar name was the tenth of the twenty leaders. Possibly, the same one is intended. But here and in some other passages he becomes the arch-fiend in the field of education, a far more important character than the preceding material would have led us to expect. Whatever the exact wording of parts of the verse may be, there is no mistaking the assertion that he taught the manufacture of armaments and of cosmetics. This latter theme, feminine adornment introduced by an evil angel, was to become prominent in the writings of some early Christian authors, such as Tertullian.

It is worth stressing that the writer of these chapters in *1 Enoch* continues to follow the biblical text in a loose way. One reads in the New Revised Standard Version for Gen. 6:11: "Now the earth was corrupt in God's sight, and the earth was filled with violence." However, careful exegetes such as our author would again have noted that the Bible uses "the *'elohîm'*; in consistent fashion he understood this to be not a reference to God, as in the NRSV, but as a name for angels. Hence, the verse said that "the earth was corrupt before the angels, and the earth was filled with violence." To explain this connection of the angels and corruption, the author has used the watcher story about the supernatural infusion of evil and violence on the earth. It should also be noted that Asael teaches humanity, not just the woman he chose to marry. The fact that he taught people to *make* things may be a play on the meaning of his name: God has made. Perhaps one may sum up his curriculum as taking good things that God has made (literally: Asael) and transforming them into instruments of violence and seduction.

The second angel seems, according to the first copy from Qumran, to have been *Shemihazah*, although his name was badly distorted in the textual tradition (*Amezarak*, in the Ethiopic version). After him come a number of other angels, each with his pedagogical area of specialization. *1 Enoch* 8:3 says that Shemihazah "taught all those who cast spells and cut roots, *[Hermoni* ?; Ethiopic: *Armaros]* the release of spells, and Barakiel astrologers, and Kokabel portents, and Tamiel taught astrology, and Asradel taught the path of the moon." The Aramaic fragments suggest that the list of names may not be correct: the names Zeq'el, Artoqoph, Shamshiel, and Sahriel — three of which (the first, third, and fourth) are related to astronomical phenomena — once also appeared in it. The names, in both lists (i.e., Aramaic and Ethiopic), are related to the one in *1 Enoch* 6:7 and connect the angel names with what they taught: medicinal, magical, and astrological information that humanity did not know before this.

These are forbidden arts, negative subjects; in the opinion of the author they should never have been taught to humanity. They are techniques that angels might be expected to understand, but they play only a negative role in human life. It may be, as mentioned, that the list is an elaboration of the vague scriptural references to human evil, that every inclination of humanity's mind was toward wickedness, and that the earth became corrupt because all people corrupted their path before the angels (6:5, 12).

After conveying this information, the writer again displays his penchant for intertwining the different themes by returning to the motif of violence: "And at the destruction of men they cried out, and their voice reached heaven" (8:4; cf. Gen. 4:10). It may be that Gen. 6:13 (the earth was filled with violence) lies behind the verse. One of the Greek versions of *1 Enoch* renders the first part of the verse as "and men began to decrease on the earth," a reading possibly supported in part by the first Aramaic manuscript. If it is the correct reading, it contrasts with Gen. 6:1 = *1 Enoch* 6:1, in which the multiplication of mankind was mentioned.

Once the author has introduced the two themes of violent, gigantic offspring and illicit teaching (a novelty relative to the biblical base), the writer turns to the provisions that God made for punishing these evils (just as Gen. 6:13 does). *1 Enoch* 9:1 reports that four angels "looked down from heaven and saw the mass of blood that was being shed on the earth and all the iniquity that was being done on the earth." Judging from the Aramaic evidence, two of the angels were Michael and Raphael; a third was perhaps Sariel and the fourth possibly Uriel. The earthly cries reach heaven: humans petition the celestial angels, the ones who, unlike the others, had remained in their proper dwelling, to bring their suit before the Most High. There is a notable difference at this point relative to the biblical presentation. There the one who sees the evil on earth (no blood is mentioned) is God himself (Gen. 6:5, 12); in *1 Enoch* the angels are the ones who see, and, as the sequel and general context indicate, the cry for help comes to the angels from humans, who have been sorely tried by the giants (see 8:4; 9:3, 9–10). Thus, the heavenly angels learn of the calamity in two ways: they observe it from heaven, and they receive the cries of oppressed humanity. They become the intermediaries who take the pleas and bring them before God. The angels deliver humanity's legal case to God.

It may seem odd, but, when the angels bring the suit to God, they begin with praise of him as omnipotent creator, sustainer, and true watcher of the world (9:4b). He is then told, as if he does not know, to look at what is happening on the earth. What the sinful angels had tried to do secretly cannot be hidden from God. The suit itself names just two angels as defendants: Asael and Shemihazah, in that order. The charge against Asael (Azazel) comes as something of a surprise in light of his limited role in the story to date: "See then what Azazel has done, how he has taught all iniquity on the earth and revealed the eternal secrets which were made in heaven" (9:6). The magnitude of the charge against him is striking. *1 Enoch* 8:1–2 had named him, listed what he taught, and hinted at the wide-ranging results. His association with instruction continues: he has taught all iniquity on the earth and revealed eternal secrets (secrets of the world?). The indictment of Shemihazah rehearses the dominant story: he "has made known spells, (he) to whom you gave authority to rule over those who are with him. And they went in to the daughters of men [Gen. 6:4] together, and lay with those women, and became unclean, and revealed to them these sins. And the women bore giants, and thereby the whole earth has been filled with blood and iniquity" (9:7–9). *Blood and iniquity* stand where Genesis has *violence.* Shemihazah, then, is punished as leader of the angels who mated with women, suffered defilement through the act, and became fathers of giants who shed blood. There is also the note about revealing, perhaps an allusion to 8:3.

In response to the angels' (?) question "What ought we to do with them about this?" (9:11), the Most High himself makes his first speech in the story. He dispatched four angels on four separate missions to address the events that had transpired (the deity himself does not deal directly with humanity).

1. Uriel (?): The first angel's name is not clear from the evidence. The Ethiopic text has Arsyalalyur, which must be wrong, while one of the Greek versions has Uriel, a far more likely name and one that may lie behind at least part of the corrupt Ethiopic spelling. His commission was to announce the flood to the son of Lamech (= Noah, whose name is not mentioned, except in one of the Greek versions): "Say to him in my name 'Hide yourself,' and reveal to him the end which is coming, for the whole earth will be destroyed, and a deluge is about to come on all the earth, and what is in it will be destroyed. And now teach him that he may escape, and (that) his offspring may survive for the whole earth [or: for all the generations of the world]" (10:2–3). Through angelic mediation Noah receives commands similar to the ones that God gives him in Gen. 6:13. The word *end* comes from Gen. 6:13, as does the notion that God will destroy the whole earth (cf. also 6:17). Angelic contact with Noah may be exegetically based: Gen. 6:9 says that Noah, like

38

Enoch, walked with "the *ʾelohîm,*" that is, with the angels. It is interesting that the ark is not named, nor is the covenant that is to be
made between God and Noah. His children are, however, included
in verse 3 (cf. Gen. 6:18), and the last words of the verse may give
an eschatological twist to the command.

2. Raphael: The primacy of Asael and the gravity of what he had done
make him the first of the angels to receive punishment. This second
assignment fell to Raphael (10:4–8): he was to bind Asael. The fate
of this leading angel was to be twofold. First, Raphael was to bind
him hand and foot and throw him into the darkness, which is further defined as being in a hole in Dudael.[18] There he was to remain
until the day of judgment, when he will be tossed into a fire. His
sentence, then, involves an immediate and an ultimate side, much
as the flood itself was an immediate response to evil (the first *end*)
and the final judgment would be the definitive answer (the second
end). His indictment reads: "And the whole earth has been ruined
[cf. Gen. 6:11] by the teaching of the works [recall the meaning of
his name] of Azazel, and against him write down all sin" (10:8).
From such remarks one begins to suspect that there was once a
more extensive Asael story that was abbreviated when it was spliced
into the Shemihazah version in *1 Enoch* 6–11. Asael, contrary to the
meaning of his name, seems to have undone what God had made
(cf. Gen. 6:6, 8, in which the Lord regrets making humanity). The
name Raphael ("God has healed"), too, has significance in the context: he is ordered to restore the earth that the angels have ruined.

3. Gabriel (10:9–10): The third angel is commissioned to proceed not
against one of the first-generation sinners but, rather, against their
children. The terms employed for the second generation highlight
the impropriety of the marriages that produced them: the sons of
the watchers are called bastards, reprobates, sons of fornicators.
The writer heaps up critical categories to dispel any lingering doubt
that the marriages in and of themselves were harmless. The method
used to destroy the offspring—that is, the giants—is a battle of mutual annihilation. As a result, they are not to have long lives (10:9b–
10): ". . . for they will not have length of days. And they will all
petition you, but their fathers will gain nothing in respect of them,
for they hope for eternal life, and that each of them will live for five

---

18. See ibid. (2.87) for the debates about the meaning of the word; it may relate
Asael to Lev. 16, in which in verses 21–22 Targum Pseudo-Jonathan calls
the place to which the goat for *Azazel* was led *bet haduri* or *bet hadudi.*

hundred years [Noah's age when his sons were born (Gen. 5:32)]." The angelic fathers wanted their sons to be immortal (or close to it) as they were, but their wish was to be denied. The children would die in internecine strife. This motif of denied longevity, noted only briefly here, becomes more central in *1 Enoch* 12–16.

4. Michael: The fourth angel handles Shemihazah and his associates. Their punishment is connected with what Gabriel was to effect: the imprisonment of these angels was to begin after they had witnessed the battle in which their sons slaughtered one another. Again the marriages themselves are faulted: these angels "have associated with the women to corrupt themselves with them in all their uncleanness" (10:11; note v. 15: "destroy all the souls of lust"). These angels are to be bound for seventy generations beneath the hills. In this way the former residents of heaven reach the opposite end of the cosmos. But their sentence, like that of Asael, has a second stage: when the day of judgment comes, they will be transported to a fiery abyss, where they will remain forever. Michael is thus to destroy all wrong from the earth.

The relatively short but involved account of the watchers' sin concludes with a picture of eschatological bliss that will accrue to the righteous. As it now stands in the text, it seems to be a continuation of Michael's commission. The righteous are here termed "the plant of righteousness and truth" (Ethiopic) or "plant of truth" (Aramaic). All the righteous, who must be Noah's descendants alone, are to escape (the verb in the Aramaic text), "and will live until they beget thousands, and all the days of their youth and their *old age* ([Aramaic] they will fulfil in peace" (10:17). So, having children will continue, but then it will occur in the proper way. Righteousness is to replace the iniquity for which the watchers were responsible. The eschatological section speaks of two kinds of planting: the people who serve God and a fertile earth (cf. Hos. 2). Then "all the sons of men shall be righteous, and all the nations shall serve and bless me, and all shall worship me. And the earth will be cleansed from all corruption, and from all sin, and from all wrath, and from all torment; and I will not again send a flood upon it for all generations forever" (10:21–22). The last clause returns us to Genesis and reminds us that this whole story is an elaboration of the biblical base. At the end of the scriptural account the Lord promises never again to send a flood on the earth to punish sinful humanity; rather, seed time and harvest will always continue (Gen. 8:21–22). The blissful picture of the new age ends in the short eleventh chapter of *1 Enoch*. It talks of blessings from above for humanity and of the eternal unity of peace and truth.

This lengthy study of the watcher story in *1 Enoch* 6–11 has shown that there are different forms of the myth interwoven with one another. If the BW dates to the third century, then the sources of its different stories would be even earlier. Another conclusion that may be drawn is that from beginning to end some sort of relationship with Gen. 6–9 is maintained, at times taking the form of quotations or near quotations and at others having only a loose verbal or thematic connection. For some parts there is no clear biblical precedent. Since the evidence for the biblical connection has already been presented, no more need be said here about it. The variant forms of the story deserve more attention.

Scholars long ago noticed that there were at least two watcher stories embedded in *1 Enoch* 6–11. The one centers on Shemihazah and his colleagues, the other on Asael. In the surviving forms of the text, the Shemihazah version dominates. It appears first and last: the descent to earth under his leadership opens chapter 6, and his punishment concludes the narrative sections in chapter 10. The passages that are often assigned to a Shemihazah version are: 6:1–8; 7:1abc, 2–5; 9:7–10; and 10:11–16a. The Asael passages, in which the theme of teaching is prominent, are fewer: 8:1–2; 9:6; and 10:4–6 and 8. There are, however, a few other lines that present vestiges of what may be a third version: 7:1de and 8:3 tell of several angels who taught illicit arts. These traces may reflect an intermediate version between the other two in which a *group* of angels do the teaching.[19]

While there are signs that point to separable sources for the versions of the watcher story, they are now incorporated into one. That one literary entity serves as a comprehensive explanation for the magnitude that antediluvian evil attained. It stands as an attempt to explain how it was that wickedness had become so widespread and muscular before the flood; in so doing, it also supplies the reason why God was more than justified in sending that flood. Genesis notes that corruption and violence were widespread and that human thoughts were constantly evil, but it does not explain how that had come about. According to *1 Enoch*, polluted contacts between angels and women led to two results: giants who brought violence and rapacity to new depths; and human acquisition of forbidden lore. These results created conditions that demanded not only the extraordinary verdict of the flood but also special provisions to punish the angels, who were not, as immortal beings, vulnerable to being destroyed by a flood.

---

19. This is the conclusion of Dimant, " 'Fallen Angels,' " 52–65.

The story does, however, raise some questions. One has to do with who exactly is punished by the deluge. The stories make it clear that the angels—the original culprits—were not affected by the flood. As heavenly beings, they lived eternally. They could be imprisoned but not killed. Also, the hybrid offspring of the impure marriages—the giants—are unlikely candidates for punishment by the flood. They were sentenced to kill one another in battle while their fathers were spectators; there is no hint in the stories that any of them were to survive the carnage. In some versions of the story innocent humanity did not deserve to be obliterated by the deluge because its members were merely the victims of angelic and gigantic abuse. The Asael version of the story suggests how it was that almost all of humanity was rightfully eliminated by the flood: Asael taught humans, and through what he taught they made the entire earth corrupt: "there was great impiety and much fornication, and they went astray, and all their ways became corrupt" (8:2). The flood becomes, as it were, the fifth response to the prediluvian situation: the four angels were sent to Noah, Asael, the angels, and Shemihazah and his associates. The only group not affected by their instructions were the evil majority of humanity, who met their end in the flood.

The full-fledged myth about the descent of the angels, although it seems bizarre today, became for many Jewish and Christian groups a credible, indeed authoritative, account for the exponential growth of evil in antediluvian days. The flood was not a capricious act, and human sinfulness did not grow to epic proportions simply through the unfortunate influence and consequences of Adam and Eve's regrettable decision. Eating forbidden fruit and fratricide were not sufficient as explanations for the violence and sin before the flood. Evil grew so powerful because it had received a supernatural boost. God's several responses were measured and appropriate.

As it now stands, the story in *1 Enoch* 6–11 could explain the situation in the days leading up to the flood, but a more pressing concern for readers in the Hellenistic era would have been the continuation of monstrous evil in the postdiluvian age. *1 Enoch* 6–11 does not really address that problem, although there are hints about it (see the Greek versions of *1 Enoch* 10:14, in which post-flood sinners are tied and burned with Shemihazah). The next section of the book, chapters 12–16, deals directly with this issue.

b. *1 ENOCH* 12–16.   At the outset these chapters confront the reader with an important distinction from the preceding ones: in them Enoch takes center stage, while he never appeared or was even mentioned in chapters 6–11. According to the chronology that underlies

1 Enoch 6–11, Enoch would have lived on earth during at least some of the events. The angels had descended in the days of Jared, Enoch's father, and the flood is announced near the end of the section, in chapter 10. Nevertheless, the focus of the text on the angelic sins did not permit mention of Enoch, whose relations with these watchers began after they had carried out their evil deeds.

Like *1 Enoch* 6–11, chapters 12–16 begin with a fairly close citation of a biblical passage. Soon, however, the text departs from that base and develops in an independent direction. At times it is difficult to follow the progress of the story in these chapters, but through narrative and summaries a remarkable tale is told. Here we find a strong accent on transgressing boundaries that God had put in place at the creation. Crossing from the upper to the lower world, as the angels did, is emphatically condemned; crossing from the lower to the upper realm is the path followed by the hero, Enoch. In these chapters Enoch, a mere human, assumes the former place of the sinful angels, while they take the posture of humanity.

The opening words of chapter 12 are fairly closely modeled on Gen. 5:22 and 24.

Gen. 5:22 Enoch walked with the *'elohîm* after the birth of Methuselah three hundred years and had other sons and daughters. 5:24 Enoch walked with the *'elohîm;* then he was no more, because God took him.

1 Enoch 12:1 And before everything [literally: all these things] Enoch had been hidden, and none of the sons of men knew where he was hidden, or where he was, or what had happened. 12:2 And all his doings (were) with the Holy Ones and with the Watchers in his days.

It seems that the words from the biblical verses which refer to two sojourns by Enoch with the angels have been combined but that the point in Enoch's life is during his first stay with the *'elohîm.* That is, the writer of *1 Enoch* 12:1–2 modeled his account about the first stay of Enoch with the angels on the more complete description that the Bible gives for the second one. Thus, "Enoch had been hidden" explains what was meant by "and he was not found," which is the wording of Gen. 5:24 in the LXX. "And none of the sons of men knew where he was hidden, or where he was, or what had happened" probably further explicates the biblical phrase. "And all his doings (were) with the Holy Ones and with the Watchers in his days" rephrases and expands the idea of his walking with the *'elohîm.*

The opening phrase "before all these things" ties the new section to the previous one. An editor aware of the Genesis chronology would have known that Enoch was no longer a resident of the earth when Noah learned of the flood. Hence, the present story had to fit at an earlier period than the one that had been reached at the end of the account in chapters 6–11. Moreover, the story in chapters 12–16 presupposes that the angels have not yet received their definitive verdicts. Hence, the action is to be imagined as taking place before the events of chapter 10. R. H. Charles correctly recognized that Enoch was still an inhabitant of the earth in these chapters and that he had not therefore experienced his final translation.[20] Rather, he is now associating with the heavenly angels during his three-hundred-year stay with them, when he is approached by the angels who had sinned and descended in the days of Enoch's father, Jared.

The account opens with Enoch pointedly blessing the great God, something the angels had not done and could no longer do. As he blesses, the faithful angels, who are also called watchers, ask Enoch the scribe to serve as an intermediary between them and the sinful angels. He was the logical candidate to exercise this function, since he was in close communion with the heavenly angels but was still a resident of the earth, where the fallen angels awaited their punishments. Chapters 12–16 show that Enoch goes back and forth between the company of both kinds of angels. Gen. 5:22, as our author understood it, also indicates that there were times when Enoch was on furlough from angelic society: he continued to have sons and daughters during these three hundred years. Enoch, like the sinful angels, was one who crossed boundaries, but he, unlike them, retained the ability to retrace his steps. The angels, once they had committed themselves to the life of flesh and blood, lost the ability to return.

The remainder of chapter 12 gives the story of this section from the viewpoint of the heavenly angels. They enlist the services of a scribe because legal documents must be drawn up (cf. 14:1). The resulting indictment provides a clear statement about what the writer considered to be the greatest sins the watchers had committed (12:4):

1. They "have left the high heaven and the holy eternal place."[21]

20. *The Book of Enoch or 1 Enoch* (Oxford: Clarendon, 1912), 27–28.
21. Knibb (*Ethiopic Book of Enoch*, 2.92) thinks that the word *place* resulted through a copyist's error and that *covenant* was the original reading. J. Crenshaw (pers. comm.) raises the interesting possibility that in this section of *1*

2. They "have corrupted [defiled] themselves with women, and have done as the sons of men do, and have taken wives for themselves, and have become completely corrupt on the earth."

The fact that their leaving heaven figures first establishes a theme, one merely noted in chapters 6–11, that transgressing the celestial-terrestrial divide constituted the original sin of the watchers. The second criticism — their defilement through marriages — is closely related to the first: they conducted themselves in a way befitting human beings, not in a manner appropriate to immortal residents of heaven.

The punishment announced by the heavenly watchers on their erstwhile colleagues reminds one of what Michael was commissioned to do to Shemihazah and his band (10:11–16a): "They will have on earth neither peace nor forgiveness of sin for they will not rejoice in their sons. The slaughter of their beloved ones they will see, and over the destruction of their sons they will lament and petition forever. But they will have neither mercy nor peace" (12:5–6). As they could not return to heaven, their fate would be found on the earth, where they would experience nothing positive. They would even be deprived of seeing their dear children (who do not seem very much like the rapacious giants of earlier chapters) live long lives. In fact, they themselves would witness their deaths but still find no compassion from above.

Enoch carries out his assignment. He approaches the watchers in two stages. Initially, he goes to Asael, who again assumes the leading role, or at least the first place. He is to have no peace but is to be bound and granted no requests. As in *1 Enoch* 6–11, he is associated with teaching and condemned for the instructing he had done: "because of the wrong which you have taught, and because of all the works of blasphemy and wrong and sin which you have shown to the sons of men" (13:2). His sentence recalls in part the one Raphael was told to execute on him in 10:4–8 (note esp. the binding and the phrase in 10:8: "the whole earth has been ruined by the teaching of the works of Azazel").

Enoch next proceeds to all the angels together — apparently a group that does not include Asael (13:3–6). The extraordinary reversal of roles that dominates chapters 12–16 becomes especially visible here: "Then I

Enoch we have an anticipation of rabbinic use of *place* as a substitute for *God.* The same could be said about the terms *heaven, holy,* and *eternal.* For a summary of the rabbinic evidence, see E. E. Urbach, *The Sages: The World and Wisdom of the Rabbis of the Talmud* (Cambridge and London: Harvard University Press, 1987), 66–79.

went and spoke to them all together, and they were all afraid; fear and trembling seized them" (13:3). A human should tremble before angels; here the reverse occurs (cf. 1:5, in which the watchers shake in terror when God appears for judgment). In a further exchange of roles the angels request that Enoch serve as an emissary between them and the Lord—another task that angels should do for people. Enoch agrees to write out their petition for forgiveness (and possibly for length of life for their sons)[22] and to bring it before the Lord, since shame prevented the angels from bringing it. The reader already knows that their petition will be unsuccessful. Chapter 12 contained the reply of the heavenly angels, and Enoch had told Asael. The petition in 13:3–6 brings us back to a step before the one taken in chapter 12.

The flashback continues in the sequel in which Enoch, in the first person, tells the circumstances in which he received the official rejection of the angels' requests. He relates that he went to the waters of Dan, located southwest of Mount Hermon, the peak on which the angels had first touched earth at the beginning of their misadventures. As Enoch read out the petition, he fell asleep. A dream and visions came to him as he slept: "I saw a vision of wrath, (namely) that I should speak to the sons of heaven and reprove them" (13:8; for "sons of heaven" as a designation for the angels, see 6:2; cf. 13:10, 14:3). There is irony in Enoch, a son of the earth, reproving "sons of heaven." Enoch communicates this message to the angels, who were weeping in a place called ʾAbilin (ones who weep [13:9]). As in chapter 6, their actions have etymological significance.

Chapter 14 then contains a fuller account of the visionary experience: "This book (is) the word of righteousness and of reproof for the Watchers who (are) from eternity, as the Holy and Great One commanded in that vision." In other words, the flashback or rehearsing of what had been told before continues here. The later installment fills in details not present in the first presentation. The repeated use of this technique suggests that the older critics, such as Charles, were incorrect to rearrange the text to fit a chronological progression. The author seems intentionally to have organized the material in a step-forward/step-back sequence. Here we learn again that Enoch is reproving heavenly beings (14:3), that their petition had been rejected (14:4), and that God himself is the source of the criticism (14:1; cf. v. 2).

As he addresses the watchers, Enoch again reads out their eternal indictment: no return to heaven, destruction of their sons, being

---

22. See Knibb, *Ethiopic Book of Enoch*, 2.94.

tied forever in the earth. But these items serve as a prelude to a new and remarkable element. In 14:8–16:4 we discover the extraordinary circumstances in which Enoch had received the now familiar condemnation of the watchers. In his vision he had ascended to the heavenly throne room, or temple! His visionary journey comes in response to the watchers' plea that he bring their petition before the Lord in heaven (13:4). Enoch does this in a literal sense and, in so doing, accomplishes something never claimed for biblical visionaries. Micaiah ben Imlah, Isaiah, and Ezekiel (and Daniel at a later time) saw the divine surroundings, but they did not ascend. Enoch ascends to catch sight of God's palace.

His autobiographical vision report is replete with biblical allusions. The sorts of natural phenomena that Enoch had observed in the AB here transport him into heaven from his earthly place by the waters of Dan. "Behold clouds called me in the vision, and mist called me, and the path of the stars and flashes of lightning hastened me and drove me, and in the vision winds caused me to fly and hastened me and lifted me up into heaven" (14:8). The celestial structures that he sees are made of what appear to be impossible combinations of cold and hot elements.

Enoch encounters a wall and two houses, and all three make him tremble with fear (14:9, 13, 24). The second house is said to be immeasurably larger and more splendid than the first. The wall was made of hailstone and was surrounded by fire. The houses have these features:

house 1 (14:10–13)	house 2 (14:15–23)
walls are built of hailstones	walls are tongues of fire
floor is made of snow	floor is made of fire
roof is like path of stars, lighting, with cherubim	roof is of lightning, path of stars, burning fire

That is, the two, except for the roof, are exact opposites in the temperature of their elements. Enoch goes on to say that a fire blazed around the hailstone walls of the first house, whose door was somehow ablaze. It was hot as fire and cold as snow. The second house contains God's throne, which looked like ice and was bright as the sun. Here the cherubim are mentioned in connection with the second house, as they were in the first. From beneath that icy throne flowed rivers of fire, and a sea of fire surrounded it. Innumerable angels attended the enthroned deity, who was dressed in very bright clothing.

Though none of the attendants around God's throne was able to come near him (14:22), "the Lord called me with his own mouth and said to me: 'Come hither, Enoch, to my holy word [Greek: hear my word].'[23] And he lifted me up and brought me near to the door. And I looked away with my face down" (14:24–25). The divine command accords Enoch a privilege no other angel had. The sinful watchers were unable to enter heaven, while the celestial angels could not enter God's immediate presence. Enoch did both.

The purpose of the first-person vision report is not primarily to regale the curious reader with details about what heaven is like but, more particularly, to provide the awesome, terrifying setting for the announcement of God's verdict on the angels who had descended. They had left these spectacular environs, drawn downward by lust. The Lord chooses to avail himself of Enoch's scribal services. He assures him that he is not to be afraid, despite the frightening place in which he finds himself. The message of God is to the point:

1. Enoch is doing for the watchers what angels should do for humanity.
2. The angels have done what humans were meant to do by taking wives, an act that rendered them impure. Procreation had been instituted because humans were not immortal. The eternal angels, however, had no need of reproduction, since they lacked the necessary limitation of mortality. It should be added that God's indictment may give a different viewpoint on the nature of the impurity that the angels contracted. One of the Greek witnesses (Panopolitanus) suggests that they had intercourse when the women were menstruating (15:4); the Ethiopic version may represent a miscopying of the correct text (*ba-diba 'anest* = on the women [Ethiopic]; *ba-dama 'anest* = in the blood of the women [Greek]).
3. The Lord says that the "giants who were born from body and flesh will be called evil spirits upon the earth, and on the earth will be their dwelling" (15:8). Later it appears that these spirits are not the giants themselves but, rather, ghosts that emerge from the bodies of the dead giants (15:11–16:1). The result is that, although the watchers are to be imprisoned and the giants are to be killed, their evil influence will live on through the work of these spirits or demons. In this way the continued, post-diluvian existence of evil can be explained.

---

23. Could the strange reading have arisen through confusion of Hebrew *dabar* (word) and *debir* (inner room of the sanctuary)? The problem with this simple solution is that these chapters were written in Aramaic.

4. God then repeats the indictment of the watchers by condemning them for their teachings: "You were in heaven, but (its) secrets had not yet been revealed to you and a worthless mystery you knew. This you made known to the women in the hardness of your hearts, and through this mystery the women and men cause evil to increase on the earth." (16:3)

Chapters 12–16 set forth the form of the watcher story with which Enoch was first associated. Shemihazah is never mentioned in these chapters; only Asael and the other teaching angels figure in it. This does not mean that the descent from heaven and the birth of the giants were not a part of the story; on the contrary, both are mentioned. The concerns are somewhat different, however, than they are in parts of chapters 6–11. Here the instructional wickedness of the angels receives the accent; there the violence and consumption of the giants played a larger role. Yet, whatever the emphases, Enoch is always associated with some form of the watcher story after this. His thus becomes a name that is tied with an alternate or, perhaps more accurately, a supplementary story about how evil became so rampant in the pre-flood days and how it continues after the deluge.

c. ENOCH'S COSMIC JOURNEYS (*1 ENOCH* 17–36). The AB showed that one type of information divulged to Enoch by the angels was cosmological. Uriel led him on a tour on which he saw the sun, moon, stars, winds, and regions of the world; the angel also explained to him the laws that governed the several phenomena. In the second half of the BW, Enoch appears in a similar capacity. *1 Enoch* 17–36, excepting chapter 20, present two journeys or perhaps two versions of the same trip throughout the universe.[24] This time, however, he does so as part of a literary tradition that includes the watcher story; those angels had played no role in the AB.

The connection between *1 Enoch* 17–36 and the preceding chapters is not clear. Although small pieces of these chapters have survived on two of the Qumran manuscripts (*c* and *e*), the transition from chapter 16 to chapter 17 is not preserved among them. The wording of 17:1 makes it quite likely that it does not begin an independent composition, since the subject of the first verb is a pronoun: "And they took me to a place. . . ." A reasonable guess regarding the antecedent of *they* would be the

---

24. R. H. Charles (*Book of Enoch*, xlviii) lists these parallels between 17–19 and 21–36: 18:6–9 is a doublet of 24:1–3, and 18:11 and 21:7–10; 18:12–16, and 21:1–6 are related in a similar way.

angels, as Enoch is in their company in the following chapters. Prior to this point in the BW, however, Enoch has had no angelic guides. It is possible that these chapters belong with a text like the AB. In fact, *1 Enoch* 33–36 give a summary of the AB. Another and perhaps more likely suggestion is that *they* refers to the winds and other natural phenomena that carried Enoch to heaven in 14:8. The same verb is used in both places (14:8, 17:1). Also, the angels lead Enoch; they do not lift him up, as happens here. If this is true, then chapters 17–36 are meant to be the continuation of the action that begins in chapter 14. There the winds lifted Enoch vertically into heaven; here they carry him horizontally to remote and exotic spots in the universe. Moreover, in these chapters Enoch speaks in the first person, as he has since 12:3. This formal trait also ties 17–36 to the preceding chapters (although it was found in the AB as well).

One way in which chapters 17–19 are unusual in the Enochic tradition to this point is in their use of Greek mythological geography. Charles maintained that they "are full of Greek elements. We have references in 17:5, 6, to the Pyriphlegethon, Styx, Acheron and Cocytus: in 17:5, 7, 8; 18:10, to the Ocean Stream: in 17:6 to Hades in the west."[25] He may be correct that the Greek fiery river and the streams of Hades served as models for Enoch's geography, but it is also likely that the author drew on Mesopotamian and biblical sources for his ideas about what lay at the ends of the earth. Rather than pursuing the question of sources any farther, it will suffice for the present purposes to sketch the contents of these chapters and to place them within an evolving Enochic tradition.

1) 1 Enoch 17–19.   The geographical notices in chapter 17 place Enoch in the extreme west. We read first of a few places that are described briefly (the place of fire, storm, a mountain reaching to heaven, thunder and lightning); later he reports that ". . . they took me to the water of life, as it is called, and to the fire of the west which receives every setting of the sun. And I came to a river of fire whose fire flows like water and pours out into the great sea which (is) towards the west" (17:5–6). He also sees the rivers, the deep, their mouths, the great darkness, and the mountains of darkness.

Chapter 18 begins with Enoch's words about the winds, their storehouses, and how they support the earth and sky by positioning themselves between the two. The winds play a role in the movements of the sun, stars, and clouds. In 18:6 Enoch moves toward the south, where it is hot and where seven mountains containing precious stones were

---

25. *Book of Enoch*, 38.

found. The directional notices in the text indicate that three mountains are aligned along the western and and three along the northern extremes of the earth (in a southerly and easterly direction). The remaining mountain is located in the middle of the other six, that is, at the northwest corner of the world. It is unusual in that it "reached to heaven, like the throne of the Lord . . ." (18:8). Enoch also views places beyond the end of the earth: a chasm with fiery pillars of impressive size, and a place where there was "neither the firmament of heaven above it, nor the foundation of earth below it; there was no water on it, and no birds, but it was a desert place" (18:12).

All of these elements are preliminaries to the remaining words, in which one reads about the significance of these places that lie beyond what anyone has ever seen or experienced. Enoch finally engages an un-named angel in dialogue—the first concrete clue that he remains in angelic company. This angel explains the significance of the terrifying place that Enoch has just seen: it is the prison of "the stars of heaven and the host of heaven" (v. 14). They had not obeyed the Lord "from the beginning of their rising because they did not come out at their proper times" (v. 15). They were to remain in their prison until "the consummation of their sin in the year of mystery" (v. 16).[26] The disobedient stars are a new element in the tradition, one that sits uneasily alongside the Enochic theme of the regularity of nature.[27]

1 Enoch 19 returns us to more familiar concepts in the tradition. Here the angel Uriel, who had been his guide in the AB, explains to Enoch that what appears to be this same terrible place is also a prison for certain guilty parties attached to the watcher story.

> The spirits of the angels who were promiscuous with the women will stand here; and they, assuming many forms, made men unclean and will lead men astray so that they sacrifice to demons as gods— (that is,) *until the great judgement day* on which they will be judged so that an end will be made of them. And their wives, having led astray the angels of heaven, will become [Sirens]. (19:1–2)

This is a version of the angel story that has traits we have not seen before. The guilty ones are called the spirits of the promiscuous angels

---

26. *Mystery* appears to be a mistake for *ten thousand*. See Knibb, *Ethiopic Book of Enoch*, 2.106, following Charles.
27. As Charles (*Book of Enoch*, 42) notes, the notion of the disobedient stars is reflected in Jude 13.

(they are not imprisoned here), and they are charged with the sin of leading people astray. The tenses in the Ethiopic text convey the impression that they have done so and will continue in their sin. The angels had done wrong, but the prison was for their spirits, who were the malevolent agents. The giants are not even mentioned in this context. These spirits accomplish their purpose by taking various shapes (some later forms of the story, such as the Pseudo-Clementine *Homilies*, will repeat this idea) and thus inducing people to worship idols in different forms. Moreover, for the first time we encounter the notion that the women were to blame: they led the angels of heaven astray, and they will become Sirens.[28]

The final verse of chapter 19 gives Enoch's summary of his stunning experiences: "And I, Enoch, alone saw the sight, the ends of everything; and no man has seen what I have seen" (19:3). His travels and what he has learned on them put Enoch in a class by himself.

2) **1 Enoch 20.** Wedged between the two travel sections in the BW (17–19, 21–36) is a list of "the holy angels who keep watch" (20:1). They are for the most part familiar names, and to each of them the writer adds a short description of the entities that the angel supervises. It comes as no surprise in a touring context to find that the first angel is Uriel. The Ethiopic form of the list includes six names, while one of the Greek texts has seven which is probably the more original number.

1. Uriel: He is appointed over the thunder and tremors (Ethiopic) or over the world and Tartarus (Greek). The terms in the Ethiopic text may have resulted from mistakes.[29] The Greek version seems a more apt characterization of his role in *1 Enoch*.
2. Raphael: He is placed over the spirits of men. In 9:1 he is listed third.
3. Raguel: According to the preserved texts, he is the one who wreaks vengeance on the world and on the lights. The more original wording may have been somthing like: "tends the world of the luminaries."[30]
4. Michael: He is in charge of the best part of humanity, in charge of the nation. Here again there is a textual problem: the Greek has

---

28. The Ethiopic text has *peaceful ones*, which, as commentators have noted, reflects a misreading of the Greek term for *sirens*.
29. See Charles, *Book of Enoch,* 43; Knibb (*Ethiopic Book of Enoch*, 2.107) does not accept his explanations.
30. Black (*Book of Enoch*, 163) prefers "hosts of the luminaries."

him supervising the best of the people and chaos. See also Dan. 10:13 and 21 and 12:1, in which Michael is the angel set over Israel. Michael is listed first in 9:1.

5. Sariel (Greek): The Ethiopic texts say that Saraqael is responsible for the spirits of men who cause the spirits to sin (Greek: who sin in the spirit). Commentators often find the text corrupt; perhaps he is over the spirits who make people sin.[31] He is listed second in 9:1.

6. Gabriel: He oversees the serpents, the garden, and the cherubim. This clear allusion to the Eden story should be noted. In the second journey account there are numerous references to the first chapters of Genesis. Gabriel is listed fourth in 9:1.

7. Remiel: He is the angel who is over those who rise (a play on his name). He figures in the Greek version, not in the Ethiopic.[32]

The list of seven angels stands in some relationship with the material that follows, but the correspondence with the present shape of chapters 21–36 is not exact. Uriel, who had spoken to Enoch in chapter 19 (and in the AB), appears first (chap. 21), and angels 2–4 follow in order (Raphael in chap. 22, Raguel in chap. 23, and Michael in chaps. 24–25). At that point, rather than continuing with the last three angels, the author has Enoch conversing with Uriel in chapter 27 and Raphael in chapter 32 and then reverting to Uriel in chapter 33 (33–36 are the chapters that parallel the content of the AB).

3) 1 Enoch 21–36. The second travelogue begins with several sections that parallel, to one degree or another, the one in chapters 17–19:

18:6–9 and 24:1–3
18:11 and 21:7–10
18:12–16 and 21:1–6

That is, most of chapter 18 recurs in chapter 21 and the first verses of chapter 24. These chapters sandwich chapters 22, which centers on a new topic (the abode of the souls of the dead), and 23, which describes a perpetually blazing fire. Chapters 24–27 revolve around imagery of the Garden of Eden and the Jerusalem area. Enoch's travels continue in chapters 28–32 with a tour of the east, and chapters 33–36 summarize a number of topics treated in the AB. These are presented in connection

---

31. Ibid.
32. See Charles, *Book of Enoch*, 44.

with Enoch's journey to the four cardinal points of the earth (there are gates at each of these). In the next paragraph primary attention will be paid to just two of the topics: the chambers for the souls of the dead in *1 Enoch* 22 and the Eden-Jerusalem section in 24–27.

a) *1 Enoch* 22.   Enoch is still in the extreme west according to 22:1 and the general context. An angel who is later identified with Raphael (unless this is still Uriel) shows him "a large and high mountain." In it were four hollow places (Greek). Raphael explains to Enoch that the hollow places are gathering points for the souls of the different classes of humanity; they remain in these places at least until the great judgment day. Before the depictions of the places begins, the reader receives an unusual introduction to what seems to be the first of the hollow places. He sees a spirit (the Greek has correctly retained the singular) whose cries of complaint reached heaven. Raphael, who is over the spirits of men (according to 20:3), says that the spirit belongs to Abel, whom his brother Cain had killed (22:5–7). Those cries will continue until Cain's descendants are destroyed from the face of the earth (see Gen. 4:10–11). This reference is another indication that the writer has the first chapters of Genesis in mind as he composes his work.

The text is not always easy to follow, with the result that the nature of one of the places is not clear. A question from Enoch introduces the enumeration of the chambers: "Then I asked about him and about the judgement on all and I said: 'Why is one separated from another?' And he answered me and said to me: 'These three (places) were made in order that they might separate the spirits of the dead' " (22:8–9). Despite the number *three* in the angel's reply, the Greek text clearly distinguishes four places by repeating "and thus" before each of them.

1. "And thus the souls of the righteous have been separated; this is the spring of water (and) on it (is) the light" (22:9). Righteous Abel serves as an example of the sorts of souls found in this chamber.
2. "Likewise [literally: and thus] (a place) has been created for sinners when they die and are buried in the earth and judgement has not come upon them during their life. And here their souls will be separated for this great torment, until the great day of judgement . . ." (vv. 10–11).
3. "And thus (a place) has been separated for the souls of those who complain and give information about (their) destruction, when they were killed in the days of the sinners" (v. 12).
4. "Thus [= and thus] (a place) has been created for the souls of men who are not righteous, but sinners, accomplished in wrongdoing, and with the wrongdoers will be their lot. But their souls will not

be killed on the day of judgement, nor will they rise from here" (v. 13). The last clause suggests that the author is aware of a belief in a resurrection of sorts.

The third place is the difficult one. Are its inhabitants righteous or evil? It makes good sense to read the verse as referring to righteous individuals such as Abel; in fact, they are described as complaining, just as he is.[33] Yet the Greek text of 22:2 says that three of the places are dark and one light, not two. Hence, it would be reasonable to include the third place in the three dark ones, since the place of the righteous is said to be the place of light in verse 9. Charles, who mentioned the idea that there were two places for the good and two for the evil, concluded that the one in verse 12 (he takes 12–13 together as describing one place) is "for sinners who suffered in this life, and therefore incur a less penalty in Sheol." In the context, and in view of 22:2, it seems more likely that verse 12 presents the second chamber for the souls of the wicked. It contains the spirits of people who were evil but lost their lives "in the days of the sinners."

It is less important to sort out the exact configuration of the chambers than to observe that the antediluvian Enoch sees the places in which all classes of souls experience their eternal fate (nothing is said about any type of soul emerging from the chambers at the judgment). The eternal home of souls is a geographical fact, not an item of faith. Eschatology has here been built into the universe; rewards and punishments are already in place. The very existence of these places evokes a blessing from Enoch (a recurring theme in chaps. 21–36) for "the Lord of Glory and Righteousness, who rules everything for ever" (v. 14). The Aramaic fragment also has Enoch calling God the judge, an obviously appropriate title in the context.

b) *1 Enoch* 24–27.   After the short chapter 23 – in which Raguel, who has to do with the luminaries (according to 20:4), explains a continual fire, which has something to do with the heavenly lights[34] – the fascinating section about the tree of life and the middle of the earth begins. Michael is Enoch's angelic companion in these chapters. What is said of him in chapter 20 is appropriate for the second part of this section – that having to do with Jerusalem and environs, since he is in charge of the best part of mankind – but chapter 20 would also

---

33. See ibid., 46; Knibb, *Ethiopic Book of Enoch*, 2.111.
34. See Charles, *Book of Enoch*, 51; Knibb, *Ethiopic Book of Enoch*, 2.112, for the textual problems.

have led us to expect Gabriel (over serpents, garden, and cherubim) to preside over at least the part of these chapters that reminds one of Eden.

The first sight for Enoch in the northwest (24:1–3) is a mountain of fire from which he sees a set of seven magnificent mountains—presumably the ones he had viewed in 18:6–9. They were made of precious stones, and the seventh is in the middle, while three are toward the east and three toward the south. The preferred text indicates that this seventh mountain is higher than the others and that it resembled a throne. Fragrant trees encircled the thronelike mountain. One of them caught Enoch's attention ("Beautiful to look at and pleasant [are] its leaves, and its fruit delightful in appearance" [see Gen. 2:9, 3:6]), so he asked about it. Michael's answer gives more information than he had requested. He reports that the mountain is the place to which God will descend and be enthroned for the great judgment. The tree he identifies as the tree of life, but it is not for everyone: "From its fruit life will be given to the chosen; toward the north it will be planted, in a holy place, by the house of the Lord, the Eternal King. Then they will rejoice with joy and be glad in the holy (place); they will each draw the fragrance of it into their bones, and they will live a long life on earth, as your fathers lived, and in their days sorrow and pain and toil and punishment will not touch them" (25:5–6). The future will be a literal return to the conditions of the first people. The contrast is striking, however. In Gen. 3:3 the woman told the serpent: " 'but God said, "You shall not eat of the fruit of the tree that is in the middle of the garden, nor shall you touch it, or you shall die" ' " [cf. 3:22]. Here the angel says: "And this beautiful fragrant tree—and no (creature of) flesh has authority to touch it until the great judgement" (25:4). At that time the chosen will obtain access to the tree and its powers of vitality, thus reversing what the first pair had experienced. Once more the sights and their meaning elicit praise from Enoch (v. 7).

As with the description of Michael's (and Gabriel's) responsibilities in chapter 20, so in chapters 24–25 the primeval biblical stories are on the writer's mind. Yet his gaze is directed primarily not toward the most distant past but, rather, to the future. Paradoxically, the phenomena associated with origins in the Bible are the ones that Enoch sees as part of the last times. The tree, the long lives of the ancestors, and the rule about touching all remind us of Gen. 2–5. The fact that this tree is in the northwest is of some interest in view of Genesis's clear placement of the garden in the east (2:8). Moreover, the terse text of Genesis has been enriched in *1 Enoch* 24–25 by addition of imagery from Ezekiel 28:13–14. There the prophecy says about the king of Tyre:

You were in Eden, the Garden of God;
every precious stone was your covering,
[nine kinds are listed].
With an anointed cherub as guardian I placed you;
you were on the holy mountain of God;
you walked among the stones of fire.

From Ezekiel the author has taken the stone imagery, the mountain, and the reference to stones of fire. In light of so much Eden imagery from at least two biblical passages, it is curious that the place is not called either "Eden" or "garden." That designation is saved for the garden of righteousness in the east (32:3). In addition, the text mentions that the tree will be planted (or transplanted) "in a holy place by the house of the Lord, the Eternal King" (25:5). Charles understood this to mean that it would be transplanted in Jerusalem, possibly the new Jerusalem.[35] The Ethiopic text mentions the north as the place where the fruit from the tree will be given to the elect, but it is likely that *north* is a mistake for *food*.[36]

At last in 26:1 Enoch leaves the west/northwest and travels to "the middle of the earth." Both the general location and the details of the description in the sequel help to identify the place as Jerusalem and its vicinity. In naming it the middle of the earth, Enoch again borrows from Ezekiel (5:5, 38:12) who refers to Jerusalem as the navel of the earth (see *Jub.* 8:12, 19).[37] He sees "a holy mountain, and under the mountain, to the east of it, (there was) water, and it flowed towards the south" (v. 2). The emphasis here is on how well watered the place is, and in this respect the writer may have been influenced by Ezekiel 47:1–2:

Then he brought me back to the entrance of the temple; there, water was flowing from below the threshold of the temple toward the east (for the temple faced east); and the water was flowing down from below the south end of the threshold of the temple, south of the altar. Then he brought me out by way of the north gate, and led me around on the outside to the outer gate that faces toward the east; and the water was coming out on the south side. (see also vv. 3–12)

---

35. Charles, *Book of Enoch*, 53.
36. See ibid.; Black, *Book of Enoch*, 171. Confusion between the Greek words for "north" (*borran*) and "food" (*boran*) could have occurred very easily.
37. For these and other references, see Charles, *Book of Enoch*, 54.

The prophecy of Zechariah contains similar imagery about the future: "On that day living waters shall flow out from Jerusalem, half of them to the eastern sea and half of them to the western sea; it shall continue in summer as in winter" (14:8; see also Ps. 46:4).[38]

Other mountains, rocky ravines, and valleys appear before Enoch, and, as he marvels at them, he asks the meaning of the verdant land and the accursed valley in the middle (27:1). Uriel[39] clarifies the matter for him:

This accursed valley is for those who are cursed for ever; here will be gathered together all who speak with their mouths against the Lord words that are not fitting and say hard things about his glory. Here they will gather them together, and here (will be) their place of judgement [Greek: dwelling place]. And in the last days there will be the spectacle of the righteous judgement upon them before the righteous for ever, for evermore; here the merciful will bless the Lord of Glory, the Eternal King. And in the days of the judgement on them they will bless him on account of (his) mercy, according as he has assigned to them (their lot). (27:2–4)

The righteous, thus, witness the judgment of the wicked whose principal sin is their speaking improperly against God (as does the little horn in Dan 7:8, 11, 20, 25; cf. 1 Enoch 1:9 in the Aramaic and Greek versions; 5:4). The whole scene once more fills Enoch with blessing and praise for God.

c) 1 Enoch 28–36.   After seeing the holy city, Enoch's travels take him eastward (Ethiopic) toward the desert, which, although it was a desert, was full of trees and supplied with gushing water. Ezekiel 47:1–12, with its picture of a river running from the temple to the Dead Sea, is clearly the inspiration for the image in Enoch. Enoch continues toward the Orient and sees a variety of aromatic trees (29–31). At some point well to the east he looks northward (32:1), where, as he had in the northwest, he spots seven mountains. Still farther eastward, after passing over a place of darkness (the texts are difficult here), he reached what is

---

38. The prophecy of Joel combines features that appear in Ezekiel and Zechariah regarding a miraculous river that flows from the temple: "In that day the mountains shall drip sweet wine, the hills shall flow with milk, and all the stream beds of Judah shall flow with water; a fountain shall come forth from the house of the Lord and water the Wadi Shittim" (3:18 [English]; 4:18 [Hebrew]).

39. Raphael in Knibb's translation follows a poorly attested variant.

termed "the Garden of Righteousness" (32:3: "paradise of truth," in Aramaic). This paradise contained, among its many trees, "the tree of wisdom from which they eat and know great wisdom" (v. 3). The Eden language is unmistakable and explicit here, and the tree of wisdom is obviously "the tree of the knowledge of good and evil" (Gen. 2:9), which was also one of the many trees in the garden. The fact that the garden lies in the east reflects the geography of the biblical paradise (Gen. 2:8). Naturally, Enoch inquired about the tree and just as naturally he received an angelic reply (Raphael): "This is the tree of wisdom from which your old father and your aged mother, who were before you, ate and learnt wisdom; and their eyes were opened, and they knew that they were naked, and they were driven from the garden" (32:6). The author echoes Genesis in saying that the tree of knowledge produced added knowledge for the first couple (Gen. 3:7, 22: "See, the man has become like one of us, knowing good and evil").

The two trees—of life and of the knowledge of good and evil—which Genesis puts in the same easterly garden are separated from one another in *1 Enoch* by what appears to be a vast distance. It is strange that the writer does not expand on this point. He merely alludes to the Gen. 2–3 story and adds no clarifying words. Black writes about the doubling of places where the trees were found: "They are, no doubt, an inevitable consequence of the 'conflation' of two traditions, the oriental locating paradise in the east and the hellenistic which places Elysium in the west."[40]

The grand tour concludes in chapters 33–36 with Enoch circumnavigating the globe. First, he goes as far to the east as possible (33:1–3), where he sees the gates from which the stars come. The topic is drawn from the AB, and, naturally, Uriel here serves as Enoch's guide. He then proceeds to the extreme north (34:1), where he views the gates from which the cold winds blow. His journey next takes him to the far west (35), where he finds more gates, and a trip to the deep south follows (more gates). He finally returns to the extreme east. As we might expect by this time, the sights induced Enoch to bless and praise the great God who had made them all and showed his greatness to angels and spirits so that they (unlike the angels who descended) could praise him forever (36:4).

---

40. *Book of Enoch*, 179.

CHAPTER 3

SECOND-CENTURY
ENOCHIC BOOKLETS

A. INTRODUCTION

One of the more memorable roles assumed by Enoch in second-temple texts is that of a seer who received visions about the course of world history, from beginning to end. The AB already contained some indications that suggested an eschatological theme in the Enochic tradition. Its laws, it will be recalled, were to operate until the new creation. In the BW concern with the end time, especially with the final judgment, comes emphatically to the fore. The booklet begins with the appearance of God for the judgment, while the watcher sections and the travelogues are replete with eschatological language and concepts. It also offers a hint about the span of time which separated the events of Enoch's earthly career from the day of judgment. *1 Enoch* 10:12 quotes the Lord's order to Michael that he bind Shemihazah and his colleagues "for seventy generations under the hills of the earth until the day of their judgement and of their consummation, until the judgement which is for all eternity is accomplished" (an Aramaic fragment preserves parts of the verse, including the number 70).[1] The suggestive number 70 entails a heptadic division of history—one that will recur in the tradition. Nevertheless, neither the AB nor the BW sets forth a dream or vision in which Enoch sees in considerable detail the events that will transpire from his time until the end. The revelations given to him are predominantly of natural phenomena (the AB and large parts of the BW [2–5, 17–19, 21–36]) or of celestial geography and architecture (*1 Enoch* 14), not of subsequent history.

It is very likely that the AB and the BW were written in the third century B.C.E. and that the material contained in them was formulated to address issues that the writers took to be pressing or worthy of comment in their day. Precious little is known about the course of Jewish history during that century and virtually nothing about the controversies that

---

1. Milik, *Books of Enoch*, 175–76.

exercised the religious groups. But in neither of these compositions did the authors see fit to provide a "prediction" of what would transpire in sacred history. It seems that changed historical circumstances served as the catalyst that impelled writers in the Enochic tradition to adopt this form for the presentation of their message.

That change in the historical situation may have been the rise of an aggressive Hellenizing movement in Judea in the early second century B.C.E. It is generally recognized today that Greek influences had been a part of Near Eastern life for centuries before this. Greek trade and culture had made their presence felt throughout the Levant long before the second century rolled around. Also, it is apparent that with the campaigns of Alexander and the rise of the Hellenistic monarchies, Jewish residents of Palestine came into even closer and more constant contact with Greek political structures, education, language, and religion. The Ptolemies in Egypt controlled Palestine for approximately one hundred years (roughly 300–200), and the Seleucids, centered in Syria, ruled them thereafter. Thus, by 175 there had been a long history of Greek influence, in one form or another, on Jewish people.

The sources indicate, however, that the situation in Jerusalem and Judea took a new turn in approximately 175 B.C.E. At that time Jason, a brother of the reigning high priest Onias III, purchased the right to hold the high priesthood from the new Seleucid king, Antiochus IV (175–64). Armed with the authority of the office and eager to bring Judea into the larger culture, Jason instituted reforms that struck the author of 2 Maccabees as blasphemous.

> Jason the brother of Onias obtained the high priesthood by corruption, promising the king at an interview three hundred sixty talents of silver, and from another source of revenue eighty talents. In addition to this he promised to pay one hundred fifty more if permission were given to establish by his authority a gymnasium and a body of youth for it, and to enroll the people of Jerusalem as citizens of Antioch. When the king assented and Jason came to office, he at once shifted his compatriots over to the Greek way of life. (2 Macc. 4:7–10)

The writer goes on to explain that this reform movement involved setting aside former royal concessions to the Jewish customs: "he destroyed the lawful ways of living and introduced new customs contrary to the law" (4:11)—building a gymnasium, wearing some Greek apparel, and instituting games that attracted priests away from their service at the altar (4:11–15). After providing this list, the writer declares: "For this reason heavy disaster overtook them, and those whose ways of living they admired and wished to imitate completely became their enemies and punished them. It is no light thing to show irreverence to the divine laws—a fact that later events will make clear" (4:16–17).

1 Maccabees does not deal with these events in the detail found in 2 Maccabees, but it adds an intriguing paragraph about the significance of the new movement:

> In those days certain renegades came out from Israel and misled many, saying, "Let us go and make a covenant with the Gentiles around us, for since we separated from them many disasters have come upon us." This proposal pleased them, and some of the people eagerly went to the king, who authorized them to observe the ordinances of the Gentiles. So they built a gymnasium in Jerusalem, according to Gentile custom, and removed the marks of circumcision, and abandoned the holy covenant. They joined with the Gentiles and sold themselves to do evil. (1 Macc. 1:11–15)

Some years later the king, in response to revolts against his representatives in Jerusalem, banned the practice of Judaism and replaced the ancient temple cult of Yahweh with one of a pagan nature. This ban gave rise to the famous Maccabean revolt (after 166), which eventually restored the ancestral religion in the temple and won a measure of independence for the Jewish people in and near Jerusalem.

Around the time of the Hellenistic reforms in Jerusalem, the Seleucid prohibition of Jewish religious practices, and the Maccabean revolt, the first Jewish historical apocalypses made their appearance. These are the Apocalypse of Weeks (*1 Enoch* 93:1–10, 91:11–17), the visions in Dan. 7–12, and the Animal Apocalypse (*1 Enoch* 85–90). J. Collins has formulated a widely used definition of the genre *apocalypse:* "a genre of revelatory literature with a narrative framework, in which a revelation is mediated by an otherworldly being to a human recipient, disclosing a transcendent reality which is both temporal, insofar as it envisages eschatological salvation, and spatial insofar as it involves another, supernatural world."[2] It seems reasonable to suppose that a writer who opted to clothe his narrative in the dress of a historical apocalypse meant to convey to his readers that the course of history and its conclusion were not only

---

2. "Introduction: Towards the Morphology of a Genre," in *Apocalypse: The Morphology of a Genre*, edited by J. Collins, *Semeia* 14 (1979): 9. Collins now accepts an amendment that clarifies the purpose: an apocalypse "is intended to interpret present earthly circumstances in the light of the supernaturalworld and of

known to God but also predetermined and controlled by him. The general procedure of the apocalyptic authors is clear: they place the revelations they describe in an early time, say, in the time of Enoch before the flood, one far in the past when they actually wrote; "predict" events between then and their time; and, finally, in fact, forecast the end of history and the last judgment. In the cases of the three early historical apocalypses listed, the writers were kind enough to leave sufficient clues so that their own time can be detected from their "predictions." For the Apocalypse of Weeks that time of composition appears to have been shortly before 167 B.C.E., while Daniel's visions may be dated to the time of the Maccabean revolt (ca. 165) and the Animal Apocalypse perhaps a couple of years later. Each one of these works is an artistic, scholarly tour de force, the product of a learned author. The Enochic historical apocalypses should now be studied for the portrait they paint of Enoch himself and for the developments in the tradition displayed in them. It is in these texts that for the first time writers in the Enoch tradition manifest their familiarity with and their use of the full biblical story line.

B. THE APOCALYPSE OF WEEKS
(*1 ENOCH* 93:1–10, 91:11–17)

The Apocalypse of Weeks is a short composition that divides all of history into a series of units called "weeks." The survey in the apocalypse stretches from earliest times before the flood to the different stages of the final judgment and beyond. Through an accident at some point in the history of copying the section of *1 Enoch* in which it occurs, the Apocalypse of Weeks was divided unnaturally into two parts: weeks 1–7 are described in *1 Enoch* 93:3–10, while weeks 8–10 are located in 91:11–17. It was obvious to commentators that something had gone wrong so that this backwards arrangement resulted; the Aramaic fragments from Qumran cave 4 not only confirm that this was the case but also demonstrate that the entire Apocalypse of Weeks belongs in *1 Enoch* 93, not in chapter 91. According to the way in which Milik reconstructs the sixth manuscript of Enoch, the material appears in this sequence:

---

the future, and to influence both the understanding and behaviour of the audience by means of divine authority" ("Genre, Ideology and Social Movements in Jewish Apocalypticism," in *Mysteries and Revelations: Apocalyptic Studies since the Uppsala Colloquium,* edited by J. J. Collins and J. H. Charlesworth, JSP Supplement Series 9 [Sheffield: Sheffield Academic Press, 1991], 19).

1 ii 13–26: *1 Enoch* 91:10 + 18–19; 92:1–2
1 iii 15–25: *1 Enoch* 92:5–93:4
1 iv 11–26: *1 Enoch* 93:9–10 + 91:11–17
1 v 14–26: *1 Enoch* 93:11–94:2.[3]

The short apocalypse[4] opens in a way that reminds one of the first verses in the entire book—*1 Enoch* 1:1–3a. It reads this way:

Ethiopic	Aramaic[5]
And after this Enoch began to speak from the books. And Enoch said: "Concerning the sons of righteousness and concerning the chosen of the world and concerning the plant of righteousness and uprightness I will speak these things to you and make (them) known to you, my children, I Enoch, according to that which appeared to me in the heavenly vision, and (which) I know from the words of the holy angels and understand from the tablets of heaven. And Enoch then began to speak from the books and said. . . .	E]noch [took up] his discourse, saying [ ] from a plant of truth [ ] my [s]ons. I Enoch, [I] have been shown [ ] a word of Watchers and Holy Ones I have known everything [And Enoch took up his discourse ag[ain] and said. . . .

The Aramaic version, which appears to follow the same repetitive line of development as the Ethiopic, highlights the fact that Enoch's speech is again described, as in *1 Enoch* 1:2, in language that imitates the Balaam oracles in Numbers 22–24. The Ethiopic translation lacks this more colorful expression and simply has Enoch beginning to speak. Both versions preserve the setting for Enoch's account: his sons are gathered around him, while he discloses to them what has happened and will occur. This is in line with 91:1–3, the first verses in the Epistle of Enoch (EE). There

---

3. Milik, *Books of Enoch*, 247.
4. The following analysis is indebted to the results presented in VanderKam, "Studies in the Apocalypse of Weeks (*1 Enoch* 93:1–10; 91:11–17)," *CBQ* 46 (1984): 511–23.
5. Adapted from Milik, *Books of Enoch*, 264.

Enoch orders Methuselah, his eldest son, to summon his brothers and other relatives so that "I may show to you everything that will come upon you for ever" (91:1). The testamentary setting adds a certain gravity and wisdom to Enoch's words. He is near the end of his earthly sojourn and wishes to teach his children what he has learned from celestial sources. In this way the EE and the Apocalypse of Weeks have the same setting as the one chapter 81 gives to the AB.

The two versions also reveal the sources from which Enoch drew his survey of events, past, present, and future. The fuller Ethiopic text mentions first that he speaks "from the books," which are not further specified. Both versions mention something that appeared or was shown to Enoch, and they refer to a message from angels. The Ethiopic also names "the tablets of heaven" for which the Aramaic is not extant (it does have part of the verb *read*, suggesting that it also mentioned the tablets). This multiplication of heavenly sources, written and visual, buttresses the patriarch's words with the greatest possible authority: while his last words would in themselves carry great weight, they are now underscored by the authority of unimpeachable sources. His words can unquestionably be trusted.

The characterizations of the ten weeks that form the core of the apocalypse are very brief and have been arranged in an artful and symmetrical fashion. The patterns that are most evident section off different parts of the description into major units.

First, the sentences about weeks 1 and 10 are the only ones in which the author mentions something that is the *seventh* in a sequence.

Ethiopic	Aramaic
"I was born the seventh in the first week, while justice and righteousness still lasted.	"I [Enoch], the seventh I [was born in the] first [Week], and until my time justice was sti[ll enduring.]

Here Enoch rehearses the familiar fact that he is the seventh member in the antediluvian genealogy of Gen. 5. There are problems with rendering the second part of the sentence: "The Ethiopic might also be translated: 'While judgement and righteousness held back.' In this case the judgement will be the judgement of the flood."[6] Otherwise, he may be alluding to the time before the sin of the angels grew to monstrous proportions. It is noteworthy that the sin of Adam and Eve in Gen. 3 receives no mention. This is typical of the Enoch tradition, in which the

---

6. Knibb, *Ethiopic Book of Enoch*, 2.224.

story connected with human sin is the watcher tale, not the incident in the Garden of Eden.

The line for the tenth week (91:15) reads in this way:

Ethiopic	Aramaic[7]
And after this in the tenth week, in the seventh part, there will be the eternal judgement which will be executed on the watchers, and the great eternal heaven which will spring from the midst of the angels.	And a[fter [seven]th part the eternal judgment and the fixed time of the great judgment [

The fact that these two weeks, 1 and 10, and only these contain a reference to a seventh entity invites the reader to search for more parallels between them. The creation of the world, although it is not mentioned, would fall in the first week, while the sequel to the sentence about week 10 makes explicit mention of the first and second creations: "And the first heaven will vanish and pass away, and a new heaven will appear, and all the powers of heaven will shine for ever with sevenfold (light)" (91:16; several of the words are preserved in Aramaic, including both references to "heaven," the passing away of the old, and the shining of the lights).[8] It is also worth remembering that, according to the watcher myth in *1 Enoch* 6–11, the angels descended in the days of Enoch's father, Jared (the meaning of whose name suggested the connection; 6:6). That is, they came down to earth during the first week in the scheme found in the Apocalypse of Weeks. *1 Enoch* 91:15 in the Ethiopic version mentions the judgment on the watchers in the tenth week. Whether the Aramaic held a reference to the doom of the watchers is not clear, as a part of the text in which it might have appeared is lost.[9] Hence, the first and tenth weeks are parallel to one another in several ways: the sentences about them are the only ones that mention a seventh item, and they have related contents: old and new creation and, perhaps implicitly, descent of the watchers and punishment of them. These two sections function as brackets around the remaining numbered weeks in the survey of history.

---

7. Adapted from Milik, *Books of Enoch*, 267.
8. Ibid., 266–67.
9. Milik considers the allusion in the Ethiopic version to the watchers as a gloss on the words "from the midst of the angels" (ibid., 269).

Since weeks 1 and 10 are related, it is reasonable to expect that weeks 2 and 9 may be as well. And this proves to be the case. The parallel item shared by the two descriptive statements is a worldwide judgment and destruction of evil humans (not angels).

93:4 (Ethiopic)	91:14 (Ethiopic)
And after me in the second week great wickedness will arise, and deceit will have sprung up; and in it there will be the first end, and in it a man will be saved. And after it has ended, iniquity will grow, and he will make a law for the sinners.	And after this in the ninth week the righteous judgement will be revealed to the whole world, and all the deeds of the impious will vanish from the whole earth; and the world will be written down for destruction, and all men will look to the path of uprightness.

The second week is a time when evil grows; the Aramaic uses the term *violence*,[10] which figures prominently in Gen. 6 when it speaks of the time before the flood. *1 Enoch* 93:4 refers to the flood as "the first end" and notes that a righteous man will survive; 91:14 mentions "the righteous judgement," at which time "all the deeds of the impious will vanish . . . and the world will be written down for destruction" (the Aramaic has the wicked being tossed into a pit).[11] The watcher myth had clearly distinguished between the punishment meted out to the angels, the giants, and humanity; the Apocalypse of Weeks continues that distinction by having humanity, not the other two kinds of beings, perish in the flood. *1 Enoch* 93:4 extends the second week to a point sometime after the flood ("After it has ended" refers to the flood, not the week). During that time wickedness will again increase but "a law for the sinners"—apparently the Noachic laws, the laws applicable to all humanity, not just the chosen line of Shem—is also imposed. Perhaps it is according to this law that the righteous judgment is conducted in week 9.

The lines about weeks 3 and 8 also mirror each other to a certain extent. The words *righteous* and *righteousness* are common in the Apocalypse of Weeks, but they are heavily concentrated in these sentences:

93:5	91:12–13
And after this in the third week, at its end, a man will be chosen as the	And after this there will be another week, the eighth, that of righteous-

---

10. Ibid., 264.
11. Ibid., 266–67.

plant of righteous judgement; and after him will come the plant of righteousness for ever.

ness, and a sword will be given to it that *the righteous judgement* may be executed on those who do wrong, and the sinners will be handed over into the hands of the righteous. And at its end they will acquire houses [Aramaic: riches] because of their righteousness, and a house will be built for the great king *in glory* for ever.

Almost all of 91:12–13 survives in Aramaic. It provides a similar text, but where Ethiopic has "a sword will be given to it," Aramaic gives "[a sword] shall be giv[en] to all the righteous."[12] In other words, it has yet another reference to "righteous." The sentence about the third week describes the election of Abra(ha)m, the ancestor of the chosen people. He comes on the scene toward the end of the period in question. Then, in week 8, the first one that deals with the judgment, the righteous descendants of Abraham execute judgment on the wicked. At that time there will be a reversal, it appears: the righteous will be the ones with the wealth, not the wicked. Although there is great emphasis in these two sections on righteousness, the closest parallel to the language of the eternal plant of righteousness actually comes in the second part of the section about week 7.

It may be that the cryptic summaries of weeks 4 and 7 are parallel in content. Week 4 speaks about the revelation of "a law for all generations" (93:6), while of week 7 we read: "And at its end the chosen righteous from the eternal plant of righteousness will be chosen, to whom will be given sevenfold teaching concerning his whole creation" (93:10). (Chap. 93, v. 11, which is not part of the Apocalypse of Weeks, asks: "For is there any man who can hear the voice of the Holy One, and not be disturbed?"—a line that reminds one of the Sinai revelation.) Thus, there are revelations to the righteous in both of these weeks: the law on Sinai, apparently to the entire "plant of righteousness," and sevenfold wisdom to a smaller, chosen group from among the "eternal plant of righteousness." It may be significant that nothing is said, however indirectly, about Moses himself.

Finally, weeks 5 and 6 may be considered a unit because they center on a house:

---

12. Adapted from ibid., 266.

93:7

And after this in the fifth week, at its end, a house of glory and of sovereignty will be built for ever.

93:8

And after this in the sixth week all those who live in it (will be) blinded, and the hearts of all, lacking wisdom, will sink into impiety. And in it a man will ascend; and at its end the house of sovereignty will be burnt with fire, and in it the whole race of the chosen root will be scattered.

It may be significant that Elijah, Enoch's colleague in being removed while alive from the earth, does receive explicit notice—the first individual to receive this honor since Abraham. The "house of sovereignty" is probably the davidic kingdom (note "all those who live in it," in v. 8), which came to an end of sorts in the Babylonian exile. The reference to it as an "eternal house" is drawn from 2 Sam. 7:11, 13, and 16.

A series of parallels, therefore, connects the weeks, beginning with the first and last and continuing, with greater or less clarity, to the middle pair of weeks. The result is that there is a three-part judgment at the end corresponding to the events of the first three weeks. There are, however, other ways in which the author has created an artistically interlocking survey of all historical periods.

Specifically, those ways have to do with the wording of the lines about weeks 3 through 8, the central section of the apocalypse. Each of these units, and these alone mention the end of each week as the point at which an important event takes place or a key character appears. So, for example, in week 3 one reads: "And after this in the third week, at its end, a man will be chosen as the plant of righteous judgement. . . ." However, not all of the sections include the "weekend" in the same place. The sentences about weeks 3–5 refer to it near the beginning; and it always follows the words "and after this, in the *x*th week." The writer identifies no event or person before this reference to the weekend. The situation is different for the sections about weeks 6–8. In them the weekend is mentioned at a later point in the sentence and after a significant event has been noted. Also, in each of these three cases another significant event follows the mention of "end." The facts that the writer highlights the end of each of these six weeks and that he also refers to a seventh phenomenon in weeks 1 and 10 demonstrate that for him crucial historical events take place at the end of weeks, not at their beginnings or middles. This feature may have followed from the fact that the author adopted a scheme of weeks: as the sabbath, the last day of the week, is the most significant day of the seven, so in the great week units of history the major events and people belong at the weekends. The sabbatical principle that underlies the learned and artistic author's presentation reminds one of other apocalyptic schemes. Dan. 9 is a well-known example. In it Daniel reads Jeremiah's prophecy about the seventy years that Jerusalem will lie desolate, and he learns that the seventy years are actually to be understood as seventy weeks of years. As we will see, a similar scheme surfaces in the Animal Apocalypse of *1 Enoch* 85–90. But the heavy stress that the Apocalypse of Weeks lays on the number 7 (the revelation about the weeks of history is given to the seventh man, the last day of the seven in a week is underscored, the chosen receive sevenfold wisdom) suggests most strongly that for him the decisive week was the seventh one and that the event mentioned at the end of it was most important: "And at its end the chosen righteous from the eternal plant of righteousness will be chosen, to whom will be given sevenfold teaching concerning his whole creation" (93:10). There is every reason to believe that the writer is here describing in cryptic language the rise of his community, the one to whom true wisdom, such as that found in the Apocalypse of Weeks (and the AB and BW, chaps. 17–19, 21–36), was granted. The fact that the end of the seventh week—the forty-ninth day—is the one accented reminds the attentive reader of the biblical legislation regarding the sabbatical years and the jubilee. The latter is either the year after a forty-nine-year period or is the forty-nine-year period itself. Whichever reading of Lev. 25 our author followed, he structured his apocalypse in such a way that the themes of freedom and acquisition of land would spring to the mind of the reader when he heard the end of the seventh week. Freedom lay just ahead for the author's party.

C. THE APOCALYPSE IN *1 ENOCH* 83–84 AND THE ANIMAL APOCALYPSE (*1 ENOCH* 85–90)

1. THE APOCALYPSE IN *1 ENOCH* 83–84

Before turning to the lengthy Animal Apocalypse in *1 Enoch* 85–90, it will be convenient to consider quickly the other apocalypse with which it is connected in the Enochic Book of Dreams (BD; *1 Enoch* 83–90). The first section of this booklet offers the setting in which Enoch received his revelations. He is pictured as relating two visions to his son Methuselah:

> Two visions I saw before I took a wife, and neither one was like
> the other. For the first time when I learnt the art of writing, and
> for the second time before I took your mother, I saw a terrible
> vision; and concerning them I made supplication to the Lord. I had
> lain down in the house of my grandfather Malalel, (when) I saw in
> a vision. . . . (83:2–3)

Whatever may be the full significance of the fact that the editorial framework puts these two visions before Enoch became a husband, we may
infer that he saw them before he was sixty-five years of age, that is, his
age when his first son Methuselah was born (Gen. 5:21). These apocalyptic visions, then, belong early in the biography of Enoch, while the
revelations in the AB clearly fit near the end of his terrestrial days. Perhaps a chronological point is being made: Enoch's career in visions began
while he was young—young enough to be in his grandfather's house and
not in his own. Then already he had been singled out as worthy to receive the "terrible" visions that came to him. It is interesting that the
initial vision appeared when he learned how to write; his new skill gave
him the means for recording what he saw (see 83:10) and thus preserving
it for posterity. The vision itself is short enough to quote in full:

> (when) I saw in a vision (how) heaven was thrown down and re-
> moved, and it fell upon the earth. And when it fell upon the earth,
> I saw how the earth was swallowed up in a great abyss, and moun-
> tains were suspended on mountains, and hills sank down upon hills,
> and tall trees were torn up by their roots, and were thrown down,
> and sank into the abyss. (83:3–4)

This is the extent of what the young Enoch sees. It seems that the terse,
cryptic description deals with the impending flood, when "all the foun-
tains of the great deep burst forth, and the windows of the heavens were
opened" (Gen. 7:11), and "the waters swelled so mightily on the earth
that all the high mountains under the whole heaven were covered" (7:19).
The interpretative words that follow the vision account point in the same
direction. Enoch cried out that the earth was destroyed. Once he had
recounted the dream vision to his grandfather, Malalel declared: "A terrible thing you have seen, my son! Your dream-vision concerns the secrets
of all the sin of the earth; it is about to sink into the abyss, and be utterly
destroyed. And now, my son, rise and make supplication to the Lord of
Glory—for you are faithful—that a remnant may be left on the earth,
and that he may not wipe out the whole earth" (83:7–8). The older man

71

accepts the authenticity of Enoch's experience and understands what it betokens. He also lets us know how virtuous Enoch is already at his tender age: he is faithful, one who should supplicate the Lord for the sake of a human remnant. Enoch followed his grandfather's advice and also, since he could write, recorded the words of his prayer (83:10).

Enoch receives reassurance when he goes outside after this troubling experience. He sees the phenomena that were to become so large a part of his experience. He looks at the sky, sees the sun, moon, and stars following their accustomed paths and patterns, and praises "the Lord of Judgement," "for he makes the sun come out from the windows of the east, so that it ascends and rises on the face of heaven, and sets out and goes in the path which has been shown to it" (83:11). Here we find the theme expressed in *1 Enoch* 2–5, that nature operates according to divine law, while humans so thoroughly violate the divine will that great punishment upon them is required.

The next chapter is entirely given over to Enoch's address to God. Perhaps the repeated references to speaking in 84:1 explain the otherwise puzzling appearance of the obscure Malalel in this section: his name means "God has spoken." He blesses and praises God as Lord of creation, king of kings, and ruler over all. In this chapter the angels make an appearance: "And now the angels of your heaven are doing wrong, and your anger rests upon the flesh of men until the day of the great judgement" (84:4). He then pleads for the survival of his posterity on the earth. Evil human beings are to be wiped out, "but the flesh of righteousness and uprightness establish as a seed-bearing plant for ever" (84:6). This is the prayer of the one who terms himself the Lord's servant.

2. THE ANIMAL APOCALYPSE (*1 ENOCH* 85–90)

The lengthy Animal Apocalypse[13] follows without a break, other than the introductory notice "And after this I saw another dream, and I will

---

13. For important studies of the Animal Apocalypse that have influenced the presentation here, see Dimant, "History according to the Vision of the Animals (Ethiopic Enoch 85–90)," *Jerusalem Studies in the Thought of Israel* 2 (1982): 18–37 (in Hebrew); eadem, "Jerusalem and the Temple in the Animal Apocalypse (*Ethiopic Enoch,* 85–90) in Light of the Views of the Sect of the Judean Wilderness," *Shenaton* 5–6 (1982): 177–93 (in Hebrew); and P. Tiller, *A Commentary on the Animal Apocalypse of* I Enoch, SBLEJL 4 (Atlanta: Scholars Press, 1993). See also VanderKam, *Enoch and the Growth of an Apocalyptic Tradition,* 160–70.

show it all to you, my son" (85:1). Hence, the testamentary setting remains throughout the BD. Even though the visions had come at early points in Enoch's life, he relates their contents to Methuselah at a much later time.

The Animal Apocalypse derives its name from the abundant use of animal imagery in the vision. In it people and nations are represented as animals and birds, while angels or individuals who take on angel-like characteristics appear as human beings.[14] The narrative covers all of biblical history and beyond, again through the final judgment. Thus, the Apocalypse of Weeks and the Animal Apocalypse share the trait of covering all of history including the final assize.

The general character of the presentation can be understood by quoting the first few lines of the survey that Enoch tells to his son. "Before I took your mother Edna, I saw in a vision on my bed, and behold, a bull came out of the earth, and that bull was white; and after it a heifer came out and with the heifer *came two bullocks*, and one of them was black, and the other red" (85:3). A reader of the Bible would immediately recognize in the bull who came out from the earth Adam who was taken from the ground (Gen. 2:7, 3:19). The white color of the bull is the author's way of expressing an evaluation: Adam is a positive figure in his scheme of things. The heifer who came out after the bull is, of course, Eve, whose birth follows that of the man in Gen. 2. The two bullocks or offspring of the bull and heifer are, then, Cain and Abel. The color of the older, who is mentioned first, evidences his character. Cain is a negative character, while Abel, who does very little in the Bible, has a red color, which seems to fall between white and black.[15]

The Apocalypse continues in this vein throughout biblical history. Chapter 85, which opens the unit, is devoted entirely to the story of Adam, Eve, and their descendants. Cain's killing of Abel is noted, as is the birth of Seth, who is a white bull like his father. In fact, he seems to

---

14. For a survey identifying the sundry animals in the Animal Apocalypse, see Tiller, *Commentary on the Animal Apocalypse*, 28–36. There are, of course, other cases in which animal imagery is used for characters, whether divine or human: the god El, for example, is regularly termed "the bull" in Ugaritic texts; the empires of Daniel 7 are represented as varied unusual animals (see also Dan. 8). Also, in Gen. 16:12 the angel tells Hagar that her son Ishmael will be "a wild ass of a man" (cf. Judg. 14:18).

15. A number of biblical passages use colors in similar evaluative ways. For example, in Ps. 51:7 the poet says: "Purge me with hyssop, and I shall be clean; wash me, and I shall be whiter than snow." Cf. Isa. 1:18; Dan. 7:9; Rev. 17:4, 19:8, etc.

be more important than his father because he becomes "a large white bull" (85:9). The writer clearly establishes two contrasting lines of humanity from the first family: Cain and the other children of Adam and Eve (cf. Gen. 5:4) are black, but Seth and his children are white. This strong distinction may articulate what is stated by the two separate genealogies of Cain and Seth in Gen. 4 and 5. One episode that is not expressed in any form in the fable is the story of the Fall in Gen. 3. The fact that the author omits this incident shows that thinkers in the Enoch tradition placed little emphasis on the Gen. 3 story for explaining the growth of sin on the earth. The first sin is the murder of Abel, and the narrative of the serpent, the temptation, and the fruit finds no place in this Apocalypse. It is safe to say the writer knew about it, but he chose not to symbolize it.

What does assume a prominent place in the Animal Apocalypse, however, is the story of the angels who sinned. The relative amount of space given to the Gen. 3 account (no mention) and the watcher story (more than virtually any other episode) underscores the fact that in the Enoch tradition Gen. 6:1–4, not Gen. 3, was the primary narrative about sin. Chapters 86–88 center on the watcher topic, and chapter 89, verses 1– 9, tell the story of the flood. The intriguing element in the symbolic retelling of the watcher myth for the evolving Enochic tradition is that it differs somewhat in detail from the versions found in *1 Enoch* 6–11, although the same basic message is conveyed.

> And again I looked with my eyes as I was sleeping, and I saw heaven above, and behold, a star fell from heaven, and it arose and ate and pastured amongst those bulls. And after this I saw the large and black bulls, and behold, all of them changed their pens and their pastures and their heifers, and they began to moan, *one after another.* And again I saw in the vision and looked at heaven, and behold, I saw many stars, how they came down and were thrown down from heaven to that first star, and amongst those heifers and bulls; they were with them, pasturing amongst them. And I looked at them and saw, and behold, all of them let out their private parts like horses and began to mount the cows of the bulls, and they all became pregnant and bore elephants and camels and asses. (86:1–4)

Beneath the symbols it is easy to recognize the contours of the watcher story, but the differences from the presentation in chapters 6–11 are also readily observable. The angels, unlike what happens elsewhere in the Apocalypse, are not said to be humans but are, rather, stars. It may be that the BW already speaks of some angels in this way (see 18:13–16,

21:3–6). The angels, who are neither like the other dwellers of the heavens nor entirely like people, are placed into a separate category to mark their distinctiveness. That they should be stars is a fitting metaphor for their heavenly origins, but the text is explicit in terming them "fallen stars" (86:1, 3).

It is immediately noteworthy that the story begins with just one star that fell from heaven and lived among the bulls. This appears to be Asael, who is the protagonist of one version of the story in *1 Enoch* 6–11. He is pictured as eating and living with "those bulls," who are not further specified. Chapter 86, verse 2, however, makes it clear that "the large and the black bulls" were the ones affected by the presence of the lone fallen star: they changed their pens and pastures and began moaning after one another. Perhaps the language of change reflects what is said in *1 Enoch* 8 in connection with Asael alone and his teaching about armaments and ornamentation: "*And the world was changed*. And there was great impiety and much fornication, and they went astray, and all their ways became corrupt" (8:1–2).[16] That is, in connection with Asael we find both change and fornication, the two items that chapter 86 associates with the first star. If the character is Asael, then the writer is working with a form of the watcher story in which he alone is first in time; only later do others join him. But the author has made an extra effort to incorporate his reading of the angel story into the flow of biblical history. The baleful influence of Asael was felt by all the bulls—both the large ones, who would be Seth's descendants (see 85:9), and the black bulls, who must be Cain's offspring (86:2).[17]

Once Asael has caused a revolution accompanied by sexual immorality, he is joined by other stars—many stars that were cast from heaven to join the first star (86:3). They, too, enter human society, but what is noted about them is their sexual behavior: "They let out their private parts like horses [a type of animal that has not yet appeared in the fable but which is an eloquent if negative symbol] and began to mount the cows of the bulls . . ." (86:4). The theme of intermarriage is associated with Shemihazah and his band in *1 Enoch* 6–11. The offspring of these mixed unions were elephants, camels, and asses—animals unlike either of their parents. At least the elephants suggest the idea of giants, so familiar from the BW. The offspring are apparently the ones of whom the bulls are afraid, and the offspring are also the ones who turn to violence— another theme well-known from the BW. In a curious slip the author

16. For the textual difficulty here, see Knibb, *Ethiopic Book of Enoch*, 2.81.
17. See ibid., 2.197.

momentarily drops his animal imagery in verse 6, when he writes: "And so they began to devour those bulls, and behold, all the sons of the earth began to tremble and shake before them, and to flee." There is no doubt, then, that the bulls are the human beings.

After this the story proceeds in a way analogous to the account in *1 Enoch* 6–11. There is fighting, cannibalism, and the earth consequently cries out. At this point Enoch looks to the sky

> . . . in the vision, and behold, there came from heaven beings who were like white men; and *four* came from that place, and three (others) with *them*. And those three who came out last took hold of me by my hand, and raised me from the generations of the earth, and lifted me on to a high place, and showed me a tower high above the earth, and all the hills were lower. And one said to me: "Remain here until you have seen everything which is coming upon these elephants and camels and asses, and upon the stars, and upon all the bulls. (87:3–4)

Enoch's autobiographical account includes the theme, found initially in *1 Enoch* 10, that four angels bring punishment to the sinners and news of how to escape to Noah. But here, too, the writer ties Enoch in more closely with the story than was the case in the earlier version: here his removal is connected with the time of punishment on the malefactors. The angels who came to take Enoch followed directly on the four who had other missions. The AB knew of three angels who returned Enoch to his family after his tour with Uriel; they allowed him one year before they would take him away permanently (81:5–6). They now take Enoch to "a high place" and show him a tower. In the Animal Apocalypse the word *tower* refers to a temple (see, e.g., 89:50, 66, 73).[18] The suggestion is that Enoch is removed from the earth so that he will not be affected by the flood; the place to which he goes is some sort of sanctuary.

The division of labor among the four angels closely parallels what was said about them in the BW. The first one takes the star that had fallen initially—Asael—binds him, and throws him into an abyss (88:1). The

---

18. The sanctuary tower to which Enoch is raised and the image of a tower for the Jerusalem temples remind one of the Mesopotamian *ziggurats* such as Etemenanki. These towering structures are often thought to be the background for the story about the tower of Babel in Gen. 11:1–9. For a discussion and rejection of such a connection, see Westermann, *Genesis 1–11*, 540–42.

second hands his sword to the elephants, camels, and asses, who kill one another (88:2). The third ties up all the stars that had committed sexual sins and throws them into a chasm (88:3). It should be noted that nothing is said about Shemihazah in this version. The fourth heavenly emissary "went to a *white bull* and taught him a mystery, trembling as he was. He was born a bull, but became a man, and built for himself a large vessel and dwelt on it, and three bulls dwelt with him in that vessel, and they were covered over" (89:1). A flood story follows (89:2–8). The waters of the deluge destroy the bulls (people), elephants, camels, asses, and other animals.

There is no doubt that the four white men who descend from heaven are the angels of *1 Enoch* 10. But, if the equation man = angel in the symbolism of the vision holds, then, according to the Animal Apocalypse, Noah changes at some point from being a man to being an angel. If he was born a bull, then he was not angelic at that time (a point worth noting in view of other stories about Noah's birth).[19] It should also be observed that in the vision Enoch himself is never depicted as a bull; he is always a human being.

The survey then picks up the biblical narrative with the three sons of Noah, each of whom is a bull but of a different color: white, red, and black — the same colors present in the sons of the original family. Perhaps the reappearance of these three colors in one family is not so surprising, since Noah's family played the same role as the first one in beginning life anew after the flood. The line of Shem continues the imagery of the white bull, but the others (apparently) give birth to all sorts of animals and birds — all of them wild and dangerous. This section expresses in symbolic language the many nations that are mentioned in the table of nations in Gen. 10.

The line of white bulls goes from Shem to Abraham and Isaac, but with Jacob a major change in symbolism occurs: "But that bull [Isaac] that was born from it begat a black wild-boar [Esau] and a white sheep [Jacob]; and that wild-boar begat many boars, and that sheep begat twelve sheep" (89:12). From this point on, imagery of sheep and flocks dominates the Apocalypse. The coverage of Genesis concludes with the twelve sons of Jacob, Joseph's stay in Egypt, and the move of Jacob's children to Egypt (nothing is said of Jacob's going there).

It should strike any reader that our author is quite selective in his symbolic retelling of Genesis. Perhaps it is not surprising that he omits the covenant with Noah after the flood, but his failure to repeat the

---

19. See section D on *1 Enoch* 106–7; and *Gen. Apoc.* 2.

covenant with the patriarchs is unexpected. The events selected presumably show what the writer found to be particularly important in Genesis, or at least significant for his concern with the end of time. Judging by the amount of space he devotes to it, there is no doubt that the watcher story (esp. the Asael version) was most meaningful for him. All other episodes in the Book of Genesis could be passed over quickly. This is an approach to the sacred record which would not have been shared by all. If one examines Ben Sira's Praise of the Fathers (Sir. 44–50), his list from Genesis much more nearly reflects the proportions of Genesis itself. The Enoch tradition, however, focuses on the fallen angels and the punishments that their actions required. The rest of the ancient history was minor in comparison with this episode.

A second biblical story that gets lengthy attention from our author is the exodus from Egypt and the wilderness wanderings, or, to put it in another way, the events of Moses' life. Although the Bible devotes much space to these events, the earlier parts of the Enochic tradition would not lead us to expect an honored place for them in the Animal Apocalypse. The Apocalypse of Weeks never mentioned the Egyptian sojourn or the exodus. For the fourth week only the giving of the law is noted (93:6). In the Animal Apocalypse, however, the Egyptian period, the exodus, the crossing of the sea, the revelation of the law, and the wilderness wanderings fill *1 Enoch* 89:14–39. This means that more space is allotted to it than to the watcher story and its implications.

The author calls the Egyptians "wolves," natural enemies of sheep (Israel). After he mentions Israel's numerical growth in Egypt and the Egyptian oppression of Israel, he introduces Moses thus: "But a sheep which had been saved from the wolves fled and escaped to the wild asses" (89:16). Midianites, that is, are symbolized as wild asses. The same verse introduces us to another character—the Lord/owner of the sheep, the symbol for God himself. This is the way in which our writer chooses to express the special relationship between God and Israel which was his special possession. It is easy to follow the familiar story in the next verses, as one reads about Egyptian oppression, the call of Moses and Aaron, the plagues, the exodus, and the miracle at the sea.

1 Enoch 89:28 offers an interesting description of the relationship between God and Israel in the period between the crossing of the sea and the story of Mount Sinai: "But the sheep escaped from that water and went to a desert where there was neither water nor grass; and they began to open their eyes and to see; and I saw the Lord of the sheep pasturing them and giving them water and grass, and that sheep [Moses] going and leading them." The writer must have understood this as an ideal period:

everything seems to be as it should be for the sheep and their owner. He says nothing about the complaints the Israelites brought against Moses in Exod. 16 and 17. Their displeasure in those biblical chapters had to do with food: in chapter 16 their complaints led the Lord to send manna; in chapter 17 they received water from the rock Moses struck with his staff. In the Animal Apocalypse only positive things are said: the owner of the sheep gives them water and grass.

Another new expression—one that plays a prominent role in the Apocalypse—appears in this context: the sheep "began to open their eyes and to see." Such language clearly has something to do with religious fidelity, but it does not signify actually seeing God (the sheep confess they are unable to do so in 89:31). The way in which the writer describes the sin of the golden calf illustrates the point: "And that sheep [Moses] which led them went up to the summit of that rock; and the sheep began to be blinded and to go astray from the path which it had shown to them, but that sheep did not know" (89:32; see also v. 33). Idolatry is represented as blindness; serving the one God is called "seeing." The same is apparent from the story of Israel's religious vacillation in the period of the Judges: "And sometimes their eyes were opened, and sometimes blinded, until another sheep rose up and led them, and brought them all back, and their eyes were opened" (89:41). The Bible does refer to apostasy as blindness and compares knowledge of God and his ways with seeing properly, but more may be involved in this image.[20]

The expression "their eyes were opened" may have something to do with the meaning of the name Israel, which is itself a much disputed point. The name was given first to Jacob in Gen. 32:28 (cf. 35:10), in which his wrestling partner explains it as meaning "you have striven with God and with humans, and have prevailed." Jacob named the place where he had fought him "Peniel, saying, 'For I have seen God face to face, and yet my life is preserved' " (32:30). Though this verse gives one explanation for the meaning of the name, others were suggested in antiquity. One etymology interpreted the name as meaning "a man who sees God."[21] It may be that the writer of the Animal Apocalypse is reflecting this understanding of the name Israel when he characterizes the nation's

20. See Tiller, *Commentary on the Animal Apocalypse*, 292–93, for a review of proposals. He suggests that Exod. 15:25b–26 is the scriptural base, but it says nothing about Israel's eyes.

21. For the references, see L. L. Grabbe, *Etymology in Early Jewish Interpretation: The Hebrew Names in Philo*, BJS 115 (Atlanta: Scholars Press, 1988), 172–73.

worship of God as "seeing." When Israel is truly Israel, it sees God; its religious eyes are opened.[22]

The prominence accorded the exodus and Moses shows that these topics were known to and valued by writers in this tradition. Indeed, Moses becomes the first character since Noah to begin as an animal (a human) and become a man (an angel [89:36]). It remains a fact, however, that no emphasis is placed on the Mosaic law. In the Apocalypse Moses ascends Mount Sinai, but nothing is said about God's revealing or Moses' receiving the law. It simply plays no role for this writer. The spectacular and frightening nature of the Sinai theophany is mentioned, yet the reader never learns about a revelation there. The text does say that after becoming a man he "built a house for the Lord of the sheep, and made all the sheep stand in that house" (89:36). It is tempting to identify this house as the tabernacle, the temporary dwelling of God, but the last words of verse 36 make that interpretation unlikely. Here all of the sheep are in that house; this would not have been true of the tabernacle, where only priestly individuals served. It is more likely, as D. Dimant has argued, that the house here refers to the entire camp of Israel.[23]

The dream vision continues its pursuit of biblical history through the entry into Canaan, "a good and a pleasant and glorious land, and I looked until those sheep were satisfied; and that house (was) in the middle of them in the pleasant land" (89:40). The house here should again refer to a sacred area or city, but in this case it can hardly be Jerusalem which the Israelites did not take until the time of David. Apparently, the writer intends one of the places at which the ark was stationed. The enemies of the sheep (Israel) in the land are said to be "the dogs and the foxes and the wild-boars" who eat the sheep until the owner of the sheep selected a ram (Saul). The sequel shows that the dogs are the Philistines (89:47). Saul was initially successful against them but finally turned against the sheep. Samuel then appoints David, who, like Saul, is termed a ram. The text becomes somewhat unclear in verses 48 and 49, but *1 Enoch* 89:50 reports a significant event: "And that house became large and broad, and

---

22. The expression "their eyes were opened" reminds the reader of Gen. 3, in which the serpent tells the woman that her own and her husband's eyes would be opened and that they would be like God (gods) if they ate the forbidden fruit (3:5). After they ate, "the eyes of both of them were opened, and they knew they were naked" (v. 7). The disappointing result suggests that this passage is not the immediate inspiration for the image in the Animal Apocalypse, in which it has a positive meaning.

23. "Jerusalem and the Temple," 183–87.

for those sheep a high tower was built on that house for the Lord of the sheep; and that house was low, but the tower was raised up and high; and the Lord of the sheep stood on that tower, and they spread a full table before him." We have here a description of Jerusalem's growth and the construction of the temple under Solomon (who is called a "small sheep," in v. 48). From this verse it is evident that the house is the city, while the tower is the temple. The full table in God's presence is the sacrificial cult. It is worth noting that in just eleven verses the author has covered the period from the crossing of the Jordan to the building of the temple.

1 Enoch 89:51–58 move just as quickly through the prophetic age. Apart from general notices the text pauses long enough to record the experience of just one individual: Elijah's career and removal to where Enoch observes history are mentioned in verse 52. Israel's apostasy is described as leaving "the house of the the Lord of the sheep and his tower"; the people's straying is characterized as having their eyes blinded (v. 54). The Lord brought in nations (wild animals) to punish his flock, and he himself is said to have left *their* house and *their* tower. Although Enoch himself intercedes for the sheep, which are being torn apart by wild animals, the owner oddly rejoices in the destruction of his flock. In other words, the Lord of the sheep acts in just the opposite way one would expect a sheep owner to behave.

At *1 Enoch* 89:59 the dominant image of the remaining historical survey is introduced:

And he called seventy shepherds and cast off those sheep that they might pasture them; and he said to the shepherds and to their companions: "Each of you from now on is to pasture the sheep, and do whatever I command you. And I will hand (them) over to you duly numbered and will tell you which of them are to be destroyed, and destroy them." And he handed those sheep over to them. And he called another and said to him: "Observe and see everything that the shepherds do against these sheep, for they will destroy from among them more than I have commanded them. And write down all the excess and destruction which is wrought by the shepherds, how many they destroy at my command, and how many they destroy of their own volition; write down against each shepherd individually all that he destroys. And read out before me exactly how many they destroy of their own volition, and how many are handed over to them for destruction, that this may be a testimony for me against them, that I may know all the deeds of the shepherds, in order to hand them over (for destruction), and may see

81

what they do, whether they abide by my command which I have commanded them, or not. But they must not know (this), and you must not show (this) to them, nor reprove them, but (only) write down against each individual in his time all that the shepherds destroy and bring it all up to me." (89:59–64)

There is a remarkable sort of determinism expressed in this section. The Lord of the sheep punishes his sheep, but he knows that the shepherds, the agents of his anger, will overstep their bounds and kill more than the prescribed number. All of this is to be recorded silently by the unnamed individual so that there will be a written record at the proper time.

Naturally, all of this happens. The period of the seventy shepherds begins before the destruction of the first temple, since the excesses of the shepherds are noted in verses 65–66a and the destruction of Jerusalem and the temple follow ("and they burnt down that tower and demolished that house" [v. 66b]). The age during which the shepherds practice their brutality is, as we expect in an Enochic text, carefully circumscribed. The book prepared by the divinely appointed scribe revealed that the shepherds pastured the sheep for twelve hours (v. 72). At this point the text notes the return of three sheep—seemingly a reference to the return from exile, perhaps under Sheshbazzar, Zerubbabel, and Joshua:

. . . three of those sheep returned and arrived and came and began to build up all that had fallen down from that house; but the wild-boars hindered them so that they could not. And they began again to build, as before, and they raised up that tower, and it was called the high tower; and they began again to place a table before the tower, but all the bread on it (was) unclean and was not pure. (89:72–73)

This negative image of the second temple and its cult may say much about the estrangement the author felt from the official cult and hierarchy of the second temple, which is, of course, pictured in a very positive way in the biblical book of Ezra. In this context we should recall the lack of interest found in the Apocalypse for the law of Moses which contains many cultic prescriptions. According to our text, the impurity of the cult was accompanied by continuing blindness on the part of the sheep, who were in turn punished by the shepherds. Hence, the period of the shepherds began toward the end of the first-temple era and continued into the age of the second sanctuary.

1 Enoch 90:1 mentions that thirty-seven shepherds had carried out their duties on the sheep. The context makes it very likely that this number should be thirty-five. The shepherds' violence against the sheep was increased by attacks from wild animals and predatory birds. In 90:5 there is reference to twenty-three shepherds, bringing the grand total to fifty-eight (this is why the thirty-seven in v. 1 should be thirty-five; twelve *hours* had been mentioned in 89:72). Only at this point, which must be well into the time of the second temple, does a change take place—a change that may have something to do with the author and his assumed community. While the shepherds, animals, and birds are doing their worst, "small lambs were born from those white sheep, and they began to open their eyes, and to see, and to cry to the sheep. But the sheep did not cry to them and did not listen to what they said to them, but were extremely deaf, and their eyes were extremely and excessively blinded" (90:6–7). This new group has the characteristic associated with the true service of God (opened eyes), and the writer credits them with an attempt to call the rest of the nation back to serving him. Directly after this verse is a symbolic reference to what is often interpreted as the death of the high priest Onias in 175 (90:8). If so, this would place the rise of the new group in Israel just before the high priest's death.

The Apocalypse of Weeks devoted three of its ten numbered weeks to stages of the final judgment. It did not, however, provide much detail about the events that preceded it. Here the Animal Apocalypse is much more specific. In 90:9 the author refers to a sheep with a big horn; his appearance is associated with opening of eyes on the part of others. The birds of prey attempted to overpower this horned sheep but were unsuccessful. Even the shepherds tried to exhort the ravens to kill this ram. It fought with them and cried for help. The recording scribe is the one who reassures the ram of assistance from above. At this point one learns that the last group of twelve shepherds had destroyed more than their quota. This is the signal for the Lord of the sheep to act: with a blow from his staff he opens a crack in the earth's surface, and the animals and birds who were attacking the sheep fell into it. In addition (apparently), the sheep received a large sword with which to kill their enemies.

Interpreters of *1 Enoch* have reached agreement that the sheep/ram with the large horn is Judas Maccabeus, who led the Jewish resistance to Seleucid rule from 166 until 161. Milik has argued that the reference to his cry for help and the heavenly assurance of deliverance in 90:13–14 reflect the events surrounding the battle of Bethsur in 164 B.C.E.; he adduces 2 Macc. 11:6–12 in support of his claim.[24] Since this is the last historical event presented in the survey, the time of Judas, perhaps even

---

24. *Books of Enoch*, 44.

the battle of Bethsur, would be the point at which the historical section ends and the predictions begin. That is, the author would have written this text in 164 or shortly thereafter, under the impress of the persecution and victories that the Jews had experienced.[25]

The final judgment has some familiar features. God commands seven good angels to bring that first star before him, that is, Asael. He and the other stars were thrown into a deep place of fire, but interwoven into the account of their punishment is the report of what happens to the seventy shepherds who exceeded the terms of their employment. The scribe who had noted their excesses was to take them and throw them into the same abyss of fire (90:21–25). These two evil entities from the beginning and end of the story are thus associated in their final destiny. Blind sheep (unfaithful Israelites) were also pitched into a similar abyss. The old house (Jerusalem, the holy city) is then folded up and replaced by a new and larger house. The Lord of the sheep took up his place in the middle of this eschatological Jerusalem; there is, however, no reference to a tower—temple—in this context. That is, the new age has no temple. Enoch was led to the appropriate place before the judgment was held, perhaps in the company of Elijah, who had been with him (90:31). This is the first indication that Enoch himself is present at the final judgment, although he seems to do nothing on this occasion. The sheep who had been scattered, the wild animals, and the birds of prey also gathered with the sheep in that capacious house. Not surprisingly, everyone now has eyes opened; all now are able to see (90:35).

The story at the end reverts to the beginning: a white bull is born. No such bull has been mentioned since Isaac. After the first white bull was born, all were transformed into white bulls (90:38). The first white bull is the messiah, who is said here to have been born. At this time Enoch awakens from his long dream, blesses God, but eventually weeps because of what he now knows will happen on the earth (90:39–42).

This great vision that covers all of history begins and ends with the same symbol of white bulls. In this sense the messiah is a second Adam or at least another patriarch. If the white bull of 90:37 and the wild ox of verse 38 are the same, then this figure may be a new Seth rather than a second Adam, because he, like Seth, is said to be large. The rich sym-

---

25. Tiller (*Commentary on the Animal Apocalypse*, 61–79) thinks the battle of Karnaim (1 Macc. 5:40–44; 2 Macc. 12:20–23) in 163 lies behind the language of 90:15. As this verse is part of what he considers an addition (90:13–15), it need not date from when the original text of the Apocalypse was composed. He concludes that the full text was available not far from 163.

bolism that plays so large a part in the dream vision shows, when its sources are investigated, that the writer was familiar not only with the full extent of the biblical story line but also with a range of prophetic literature and themes. It will be useful here to look more closely at the dominant image in the latter part of the Apocalypse—the rule by the seventy shepherds.

The image of the shepherds begins in *1 Enoch* 89:59 and continues until 90:25. The notion of shepherds is obviously related to the figure of sheep, the other major symbol in the Apocalypse. God himself is not the shepherd of his people; he is their Lord or owner.[26] Late in the monarchical period he calls upon shepherds to pasture his sheep but to do so as punishment for the blindness of the sheep. There can be little doubt that for the theme of the seventy shepherds the author of the Animal Apocalypse is indebted primarily to the material in Jer. 25. In the survey itself the writer mentions only one prophet in a way clear enough to identify him (Elijah), but he does allude to a series of God's prophets: "And I saw those sheep again, how they went astray, and walked in many ways, and left that house of theirs; and the Lord of the sheep called some of the sheep and sent them to the sheep, but the sheep began to kill them. . . . And he sent many other sheep to those sheep to testify (to them) and to lament over them" (89:51, 53; the two verses that sandwich the reference to Elijah). Perhaps the mention of "lament over them" is meant to remind us of Jeremiah, the traditional author of the poems in Lamentations. There is nothing more about the prophets in the survey. They are there, but they do not occupy an overly important place in it.

The imagery of the seventy shepherds, however, shows that this author, like other Jewish writers of the time (e.g., of Dan. 9) pondered the meaning of the prophecy in Jer. 25. Even though the writers in the Enochic tradition prefer to focus on the early chapters of Genesis, they were obviously familiar with the other parts of Israel's ancient literature. The device of the seventy shepherds is an interpretation of Jeremiah's enigmatic seventy years. Jer. 25:1 ties his prophecy to the fourth year of the Judean king Jehoiakim, which was the first year of Nebuchadrezzar of

---

26. Obviously, the writer could have referred to the Lord as shepherd of the flock, appealing to such passages as Ps. 23:1 (for comparative evidence for shepherd as a positive image in Mesopotamia and Egypt, see J. W. Vancil, "Sheep, Shepherd," in *ABD* 5.1188–89). He chose to reserve the image of owner, or Lord, of the sheep for God and the symbol of shepherd for those who oppress the sheep. As will be noted, there is a strong biblical basis for a negative image of shepherds. See Jer. 23:1–4; Zech. 10:2–3; 11:3–6, 15–17; 13:7.

Babylon and hence a good year from which to begin a new era (605 B.C.E.). Verses 3–7 of that chapter are Jeremiah's general indictment of the nation for forsaking the Lord and not listening to his prophets — sentiments that remind one of *1 Enoch* 89:51 and 53. The punishment that the Lord decrees upon his people must have served as at least part of the source from which the author of the Animal Apocalypse drew his idea that the Lord would punish Israel through other nations. The people had forsaken the Lord to their own harm (v. 7).

> Therefore thus says the Lord of hosts: Because you have not obeyed my words, I am going to send for all the tribes of the north, says the Lord, even for King Nebuchadrezzar of Babylon, my servant, and I will bring them against this land and its inhabitants, and against all these nations around; I will utterly destroy them, and make them an object of horror and hissing, and an everlasting disgrace. And I will banish from them the sound of mirth and the sound of gladness, the voice of the bridegroom and the voice of the bride, the sound of the millstones and the light of the lamp. This whole land shall become a ruin and a waste, and these nations shall serve the king of Babylon[27] seventy years. Then after seventy years are completed, I will punish the king of Babylon and that nation, the land of the Chaldeans, for their iniquity, says the Lord, making the land an everlasting waste. I will bring upon that land all the words that I have uttered against it, everything written in this book, which Jeremiah prophesied against all the nations. For many nations and great kings shall make slaves of them also; and I will repay them according to their deeds and the work of their hands. (Jer. 25:8–14)

Here we have the same general scenario as in the Animal Apocalypse: Israel sins to its own injury, and God, to punish them, summons the nations, especially the Chaldeans, to chastise them severely for seventy years. That punishment, however, will become too harsh, and the Lord will finally repay in appropriate measure the ones who had exercised his wrath.[28] It should be added that Jer. 25:34–38 calls on shepherds to wail because the

---

27. The LXX does not refer to the Babylonian king and says that Israel will be enslaved among the nations.
28. Isa. 10:5–19 expresses a similar idea. There Assyria, the rod of the Lord's anger against his people, overreaches in its zeal to punish and will itself be punished by the Lord for its excesses.

time of their slaughter has come; there will be no escape. This identification of the leaders of the nations as shepherds appears also in Jer. 6:3.

Besides the general scenario, the prophecy of Jeremiah provides much of the specific imagery as well. The seventy years come immediately to mind. If those seventy years were to begin in approximately 605 B.C.E., they would have ended in 535 B.C.E.—a year quite close to the actual time of the initial return from exile. But, if that were so, then there should have been some clear evidence that the time of Israel's suffering at the hand of the nations had ended then. Reality hardly fit the prophecy. The people did return, rebuilt the temple and city, and resumed life in the land. Yet they remained subject to foreign powers for centuries after this, and conditions in Judea were hardly ideal. These circumstances must have left later expositors in a quandary: the Lord himself had spoken the prophecy to Jeremiah and had even said that all his words to the prophet would come to fruition, but Israel continued to live under foreign domination. In other words, it looked as if God's revelation to Jeremiah had been falsified by historical facts. This was, nevertheless, a conclusion that no pious Jewish expositor could draw. The prophecy could not be false; only the literal interpretation of it could be untrue. Hence, the exegete was called upon to develop a proper exposition of Jeremiah's words so that the true intent of the inspiring God could be divined.

The author of Dan. 9 took up this task and came to the conclusion (with heavenly help) that the prophecy meant not seventy years but, instead, seventy weeks of years. This exegetical move allowed him to save the validity of the prophecy and to read it as if it related to events that would transpire in the future for him (i.e., after about 165 B.C.E.).[29] The scholar who composed the Animal Apocalypse reinterpreted in a different way. He translated the weeks of Jeremiah into seventy periods of rule by seventy shepherds. The figure of shepherds was natural enough in connection with sheep, and the number seventy, drawn from Jer. 25, also coincided with the traditional number of nations in the world—a number based on the table of nations in Gen. 10 (even though the Animal Apocalypse does not indicate seventy at that point in its survey). Deut. 32:8 added another bit of evidence for his case: it seems to have said that the nations each had an angel associated with them (as is clear from one of the Qumran manuscripts). The transposition of *year* into *period of rule by another nation/angel* provided greater flexibility for the author as he attempted to rescue some contemporary relevance and validity for Jere-

---

29. Note that Gabriel, the angel who brings the word to Daniel, is called a "man" in Dan. 9:21, just as angels are called "men" in the Apocalypse.

miah's prophecy. He, like the editor of Jeremiah, set the beginning of the period in question just before the destruction of Jerusalem and the burning of the temple, but, without an explicit basis in the text of Jeremiah, he extended the time when the shepherds (angelic rulers of the seventy nations) exercised dominion to the end of time — explicitly into Maccabean times (i.e., after 166). Thus, he, like the author of Dan. 9, lengthened the period over which Jeremiah's seventy years extended. The years were not to be taken in a literal sense; they were figurative years, pointing to longer periods of time. The age from the rise of Nebuchnezzar to the Maccabean period could be characterized as one of domination by the gentiles. This fact our writer expresses by his graphic image of the seventy vicious shepherds who ruled the flock but treated it brutally. The Apocalypse of Weeks had schematically presented the whole of history and of the judgment as seventy units of time (ten weeks), but the Animal Apocalypse, though it too covers all of history and the eschatological judgment, divides the last phases into seventy periods because it is tied more tightly to the constraints of Jeremiah's prophecy. By rereading Jeremiah in this way, the author could also vindicate the Lord while explaining what were known to be the facts of history. Israel was indeed enduring a long period of foreign rule and oppression; all of this was, however, merely part of the divine plan, and at some time not too far in the future a great change would occur. In fact, the early phases of that change were already evident in the rise of the lambs and Judas Maccabeus' great triumphs over the Seleucids, just when circumstances may have seemed most dire to the faithful observer of Judean affairs. The ram with the great horn was on the scene, and the events of the end lay in the near future. The author's group, the small sheep with opened eyes, were now proclaiming their message and calling on their contemporaries to hear and respond.

The debt of the author to Jer. 25 does not end with the images of the shepherds and the seventy times when they rule. The final battle about which we read in *1 Enoch* 90:18–19 may be related to the sword and judgment that are mentioned in Jer. 25:15–38 (see esp. vv. 16, 27, 29, 31, 38). The book in which God's scribe records the deeds of the shepherds may have been suggested by Jer. 25:13, which refers to a book that contains all the words of Jeremiah on the subject of the seventy-year punishment.[30]

---

30. Tiller (*Commentary on the Animal Apocalypse*, 53–58) finds seven sources for the shepherd image, but some of them, such as "the traditional Mesopotamian metaphor of the shepherd," seem unhelpful.

If one compares the Apocalypse of Weeks and the Animal Apocalypse, it soon becomes apparent that the author of the latter has taken roughly the same material—all of the biblical story line and the end—and has added numerous details to the presentation. He has also opted for a different system of organization. He does not divide all of history into units that are given the same name; rather, he indicates historical epochs through changes in his animal imagery. People are represented as bulls through the time of Isaac; beginning with Jacob he and his descendants appear under the symbol of sheep. This latter image continues to the last judgment, when the primeval bull imagery returns. The chief attempt at periodization comes in the age that begins just before the destruction of Jerusalem, when seventy shepherds or gentile nations rule over the Israelite flock. The conclusion of their reign is an event of the end time. In the Animal Apocalypse, unlike the Apocalypse of Weeks, there is a suggestion that at least some of those who have died will be raised to life: "And all those which had been destroyed and scattered and all the wild animals and all the birds of heaven gathered together in that house, and the Lord of the sheep rejoiced very much because they were all good and had returned to his house" (90:33).

D. THE EPISTLE OF ENOCH (*1 ENOCH* 91–107)

The Apocalypse of Weeks is part of the larger Epistle of Enoch (EE), which is found in *1 Enoch* 91–107. This document may date to roughly the same time as the Apocalypse of Weeks itself, that is, to some point just before the Maccabean revolt. It is a different kind of document from others in the Enochic tradition studied to this point. It shares with the BD and the AB the testamentary setting, since it opens with these words: "And now, my son Methuselah, call to me all your brothers and gather to me all the children of your mother, for a voice calls me, and a spirit has been poured out over me, that I may show to you everything that will come upon you for ever" (91:1). The Apocalypse of Weeks and other material in the EE fulfill the expectations created by these introductory words, but much of the book is more of a preaching document.

In the EE Enoch exhorts the righteous/wise and warns the sinners/ fools. It is clear that as he does so he has the whole scope of history in mind, as was evident in the apocalypses that have been analyzed. For example, *1 Enoch* 91:3–10 contain Enoch's words to his assembled children. He encourages them to practice righteousness and to avoid the unrighteous. He then supplies a motive for this kind of behavior:

For I know that the state of wrongdoing will continue on the earth, and a great punishment will be carried out on the earth, and an end will be made of all iniquity, and it will be cut off at its roots, and its whole edifice will pass away. And iniquity will again be complete on the earth, and all the deeds of iniquity and the deeds of wrong and of wickedness will prevail for a second time. And when iniquity and sin and blasphemy and wrong and all kinds of (evil) deeds increase, and (when) apostasy and wickedness and uncleanness increase, a great punishment will come from heaven upon all these, and the holy Lord will come in anger and in wrath to execute judgement on the earth. In those days wrongdoing will be cut off at its roots, and the roots of iniquity together with deceit will be destroyed from under heaven. And all the idols of the nations will be given up; (their) towers will be burnt in fire, and they will remove them from the whole earth; and they will be thrown down into the judgement of fire and will be destroyed in anger and in the severe judgement which (is) for ever. And the righteous will rise from sleep, and wisdom will rise and will be given to them. (91:5–10)

In these few lines we find a sketch of all history and of the judgment which will bring it to a close. The first punishment to which Enoch refers is the flood. After it, iniquity will again increase, only to be uprooted and destroyed in the second and last judgment. It is of some interest for a text in the Enochic tradition that the watchers and their misdeeds have no place in this scenario. Nothing is said about why evil increases; it just grows. It is also interesting that the righteous rise from sleep in this text—another indication that at least some, here only the righteous, were expected to regain life at the end. The latter paragraphs of the Apocalypse of Weeks follow immediately after this short survey.

The ninty-second chapter may, in its original Aramaic form, refer to Enoch as the wisest of men and judge of the entire earth.[31] It suggests the actual setting toward which Enoch's words are directed: he speaks to an audience experiencing difficult times. He urges them not to be discouraged because the Lord has everything under control, whatever appearances may suggest. "Let not your spirit be saddened because of the times, for the Holy Great One has appointed days for all things. And the righteous man will rise from sleep, will rise, and will walk in the path of righteousness, and all his paths and his journeys (will be) in eternal

---

31. Milik, *Books of Enoch*, 263.

goodness and mercy" (92:2–3). The righteous one will live in eternal light, while sin will be destroyed in darkness (92:4–5).

The first sentences of the Apocalypse of Weeks follow these verses. After the words from the Apocalypse end, there is a curious section that makes one wonder whether there was a debate going on in the Enochic tradition. *1 Enoch* 93:11–14 contain a series of questions to which the answer for one versed in the Enochic tradition might seem obvious; they are, however, not answered. The questions sound rhetorical:

> For is there any man who can hear the voice of the Holy One, and not be disturbed? And who is there who can think his thoughts? And who is there who can look at all the works of heaven? And how should there be anyone who could understand the works of heaven and see *a soul or a spirit* and could tell (about it), or ascend and see all their ends and comprehend them or make (anything) like them? And is there any man who could know what is the breadth and length of the earth? And to whom have *all its measurements* been shown? Or is there any man who could know the length of heaven, and what is its height, and on what it is fixed, and how large is the number of the stars and where all the lights rest?

Once the reader moves beyond the first two questions, the transparent answer to each of them should be "Enoch," who, on his travels with the angels, had seen all the heavenly bodies, all the earth, had been told the laws governing nature, and had seen the fate of all. The series of questions is phrased in a way that reminds one of biblical passages such as Job 38, in which God queries an overwhelmed Job about such matters. There the point is to highlight the vast distance between God and humans.[32] Here, however, one would think that the passage should be meant to praise the surpassing wisdom and knowledge of Enoch himself, the one who knew and understood all these deep matters. Nevertheless, if that is the point, we have to infer it for ourselves; the author does not help us with it. Is he questioning the vast claims made for Enoch's more esoteric knowledge in other booklets (note that, apparently contrary to the watcher-giant story, humanity is responsible for its own sin, according to 98:4)?

---

32. Sirach and *2 Esdras* also pose questions that are impossible to answer and do so for the same reason; on them, see J. Crenshaw, "Impossible Questions, Sayings, and Tasks," in *Gnomic Wisdom*, edited by J. D. Crossan, *Semeia* 17 (Chico, Calif.: Scholars Press, 1980), 19–34.

Chapters 94–105 are filled with Enoch's words to his audience, his group, who are here cast as his children. He offers words of comfort and encouragement for them and commands them to hold fast to his words (94:1–5). Yet he warns and condemns the wicked for their behavior. A noteworthy feature in these chapters, whose contents are often rather unremarkable, is the several groups of woe sayings placed on the lips of Enoch. The statements of woe are addressed to particular sets of evildoers, and the reason for the threat is specified in the latter part of the statement. The sorts of groups who feel the sting of Enoch's wrath and the types of evils for which they are indicted say something about the social location of the author of the EE. They show how he perceives his community (his children) and how he understands others.

The woe sections are in *1 Enoch:*

94:6–10: against those who build iniquity, build houses with sin, the rich

95:4–7: against those who pronounce anathemas that cannot be loosed, who repay neighbors with evil, lying witnesses, those who persecute the righteous

96:4–8: against sinners who are rich, those who devour the finest wheat, drink the best water, trample the humble, drink water all the time, commit iniquity, deceit, blasphemy, the powerful who oppress the righteous

97:7–10: against sinners on the sea and land, those who acquire silver and gold

98:8–99:2: against fools, the stubborn, those who love iniquity, rejoice at their neighbor's troubles, declare the words of the righteous empty, write lying and impious words, who do wrong and praise lying words, who alter words of truth and distort the eternal law [perhaps a reference to the Torah], considering themselves sinless

99:11–15: against those who extend evil to neighbors, lay foundations of sin, build houses with the labor of others, reject the measure and eternal inheritance of the fathers, commit iniquity

100:7–9: against sinners who afflict the righteous on the day of severe trouble, the perverse who plan evil, sinners in word and deed

103:5: against sinners who die in their sin.

If we subtract from these eight woe sections the generic warnings (i.e., those against the wicked, the ones who commit iniquity, and the like), it becomes clear that the writer emphasizes the rich and the ones who oppress the weak and righteous. Perhaps the two—the rich and the oppressors—are the same. Another point that stands out is the lack of proper neighborly behavior. One gets the impression that the writer feels persecuted by stronger, wealthier members of his own nation, his own people. His opponents even have the audacity to distort or change true words for their own ends.

His purpose in denouncing the various classes of sinners is to maintain that, while they may be prospering now, God has a severe punishment planned for them. Oddly enough, the righteous, who are now seemingly the objects of God's anger, will judge the sinners (95:3). Relief for the righteous will come from above (96:1–3), and the sinners will become an object of shame (97:1). Enoch's message is intended to bolster the weakening endurance and hope of the righteous, who have much reason to be discouraged. Their prayers serve as reminders of what the sinners do (99:3). They are, in fact, the blessed because they accept wisdom and the path of the Most High (99:10). It may not seem to be true, but holy angels guard the righteous like the apple of their eyes (100:5). If the righteous sleep for a long time (death), they have no reason to fear; even nature is against the wicked (100:5, 10–13; cf. 102:4). Sinners misunderstand the true nature of the situation: they do not understand the fate of the righteous. "But when you die, the sinners say about you: 'As we die, the righteous have died, and of what use to them were their deeds? Behold, like us they have died in sadness and in darkness, and what advantage do they have over us? From now on we are equal, and what will they receive, and what will they see for ever?' " (102:6–8). In order to answer the charge of the sinners the writer admits that the righteous die and their souls descend to Sheol. But then something unexpected happens: Enoch has read on the heavenly tablets (hence, this is absolutely reliable)

> that all good and joy and honour have been made ready and written down for the spirits of those who have died in righteousness and (that) much good will be given to you in recompense for your toil, and (that) your lot (will be) more excellent than the lot of the living. And the spirits of you who have died in righteousness will live, and their spirits will rejoice and be glad, and the memory of them (will remain) before the Great One for all the generations of eternity. Therefore do not fear their abuse. (103:3–4)

Enoch does not promise a resurrection of bodies but, rather, a spiritual happiness. Indeed, he tells his audience that they will have joy like the angels in heaven (104:4). In language reminiscent of the Qumran *Ho-*

dayot, they will become the associates of the heavenly host (104:6). If they understand the real situation, therefore, the righteous will take courage and persevere through this temporary vale of suffering.

Enoch's role as proclaimer of comfort and warning is more evident in the EE than in any earlier composition within the Enochic tradition. The Apocalypse of Weeks should be seen as part of that same message of encouragement for the battered faithful. Their plight is painful now, but there will be a great reversal when God judges the wicked and gives victory and peace to the righteous.

While most of the EE is given over to such hortatory material, chapters 106–7 are quite different and offer another look at the use to which Enoch's unique experience was put in the tradition. The two chapters are a narrative about the birth of Noah. The questions raised by the appearance of the precocious child called for the special expertise and connections of Enoch. Aspects of the story may be read in two ancient versions: in *1 Enoch* 106–7 and in the Qumran cave 1 text entitled the *Genesis Apocryphon* (cols. 2–5).[33]

Although *1 Enoch* 106–7 now consitute the final part of the EE, they are usually regarded as an originally independent unit.[34] The Aramaic fragments of 4QEnoch[c] now show that, by the last third of the first century B.C.E., chapters 106–7 were attached to chapter 105; they are, however, separated from it by a blank space of one and a half lines.[35] Consequently, it is possible that the date of the EE itself is not that of chapters 106–7. At the very least we may say that the Enochic version of the birth story was available in written form in the latter part of the first century B.C.E. (the date of the script in which 4QEnoch[c] is written) and that it is probably older. The birth story appears to be a more integral part of the unified narrative in the *Genesis Apocryphon* than in *1 Enoch* 106–7, in which it seems to dangle at the end of the book. The Qumran

---

33. The study of the story about Noah's birth that follows is closely related to VanderKam, "The Birth of Noah," in *Studies Offered to J. T. Milik to Celebrate Forty Years of His Scholarly Work on Texts from the Wilderness of Judaea*, vol. 1: *Intertestamental Essays in Honour of Józef Tadeusz Milik*, edited by Z. J. Kapera (Krakow: Enigma Press, 1992), 213–31.

34. See, for example, Charles, *Book of Enoch*, xlvi–xlvii, 264 (he considered it part of a Noah Apocalypse); Black, *Book of Enoch*, 8–9, 23 (he stresses that these chapters are not foreign to the teachings of the book); Milik, *Books of Enoch*, 55–57 (he considers it an appendix to the entire Enochic corpus); and G. W. E. Nickelsburg, *Jewish Literature between the Bible and the Mishnah* (Philadelphia: Fortress, 1987), 151.

35. Milik, *Books of Enoch*, 55–57.

scroll can be dated to the late first century B.C.E. or early first century C.E.[36] The story occupied several columns on the scroll, but, apart from column 2, it has survived in extremely fragmentary condition. It is clear, though, from what is legible, that the account followed the same general lines as the version in *1 Enoch* 106–7.

The story about Noah's birth in *1 Enoch* is packaged as a first-person report by Enoch, Noah's great-grandfather, who resides with the angels at the ends of the earth.[37] Despite his great distance from Noah's birth-place, Enoch is a central character in the drama because he alone has access to indispensable information about the main issues in the tale: who was the child's father and what did the birth of this remarkable infant portend. Enoch credits his superior knowledge to data he had received from the angels and the heavenly tablets (106:19). In the story we first read a short genealogical statement and then of Noah's birth, after which comes a brief description of the amazing child who radiates light and praises God as soon as he is born:

And his body was white like snow and red like the flower of a rose, and the hair of his head (was) white like wool[38.] . . . and his eyes were beautiful; and when he opened his eyes, he made the whole house bright like the sun so that the whole house was exceptionally bright. And when he was taken [Greek: arose] from the hand of the midwife, he opened his mouth and spoke to the Lord of righteousness.[39]

When Lamech, who according to the Gen. 5 genealogy was Noah's father, saw the miraculous appearance and ability of the baby, he immediately suspected that a supernatural being was actually the child's father. Because he desperately wanted the question answered, he dispatched his own father, Methuselah, to visit his father, Enoch, at the

---

36. J. Fitzmyer, *The Genesis Apocryphon of Qumran Cave 1: A Commentary*, BibOr 18A (Rome: Biblical Institute, 1971), 14–15.

37. If the chronology of the *Book of Jubilees* underlies the story, then this episode occurred within his 365-year life span mentioned in Gen 5:23. For the details, see VanderKam, *Enoch and the Growth of an Apocalyptic Tradition*, 176–77.

38. Although Knibb omits it from his translation, the Ethiopic also mentions "his long locks"(Charles's trans. in *Book of Enoch*). The Greek, too, has this expression.

39. A few letters from these verses are preserved on 4QEnoch[c].

ends of the earth and to learn from him the truth about the matter. Methuselah complied and journeyed to Enoch, who informed him about two major points: while the child was indeed Lamech's son, his birth did prefigure that unprecedented events would happen on the earth. He foretold the flood, how Noah and his sons would survive, the renewed growth of even greater iniquity after the deluge, and the rise of a righteous generation. Methuselah then returned with the mixed news and named the child Noah.

In the *Genesis Apocryphon* the form of the story is not a first-person narrative by Enoch but, instead, an autobiographical report by Lamech. The opening lines of column 2 are phrased in the first person, and the speaker identifies himself in line 3 as Lamech. As late as column 5:26–27, Lamech is still speaking. The first preserved lines indicate that the issue of paternity is paramount in the *Genesis Apocryphon* as well: "So then I thought in my mind that the conception was due to Watchers or that it w[a]s due to Holy Ones, or to Nephi[lim . . . ;] and my mind wavered because of this child. Then I, Lamech, became frightened and I went to Bitenosh, my wi[fe. . . .]"[40] The version in the *Genesis Apocryphon* also differs from the one in *1 Enoch* 106–7 in that a heated argument rages between Lamech and Bitenosh (or, better, Batenosh), his wife, about who the father of the child really was. Her name reminds one of the name Gen. 6:1 gives to the women who cohabited with the sons of the *'elohîm*—the "daughters of men"; thus, her very name may have given the already anxious Lamech an extra cause for concern. Batenosh tries to reassure him in emphatic language that "this seed is from you; from you is this conception, and from you the planting of [this] fruit [ ], and not from any stranger, nor from any of the Watchers, nor from any of the sons of hea[ven]" (2:15–16). Her assertions did not relieve Lamech of his concern, so he sent his father, Methuselah, to the far-distant Enoch in order to "learn everything from him with certainty, since he (Enoch) is a favorite and o[ne cherished . . .]" (2:20). Columns 3–5, which are largely illegible on the one surviving copy, preserve just enough words to verify that the story then unfolds as it does in *1 Enoch* (see 3:3; 5:3, 4, 9, 10, 24–27).

The story about Noah's birth is not only intriguing in itself; the author has also written it in a highly learned and artistic way. The Enochic version has survived in far more complete form and must therefore serve

---

40. Translations of passages in the *Genesis Apocryphon* come from J. Fitzmyer and D. Harrington, *A Manual of Palestinian Aramaic Texts*, BibOr 34 (Rome: Biblical Institute, 1978).

as the basis for analysis, but the extant evidence from the *Genesis Apocryphon* provides valuable supplementary and at times contrasting information.

One major point to be noticed about the stories is the central place that etymologies hold in them. The Ethiopic text of *1 Enoch* 106:1 begins with little more than the bare outline of a four-generation genealogy: "And after *some* days my son Methuselah took for his son Lamech a wife, and she became pregnant by him and bore a son." The Greek text is considerably longer at this point, and its extra words now find partial support in the third copy of Enoch from Qumran. The Greek has: "After (some) time I took a wife for my son Methuselah. She gave birth to a son and named him Lamech.[41] Righteousness was brought low until that day. When he reached maturity, he took a wife for him, and she gave birth to a son for him" (my trans.). These sentences place Lamech's birth at the very beginning of the story and furnish the writer an opportunity to fashion a pun on his name. The paronomasia involved words that share the consonants in Lamech's name and mean "brought low indeed."[42] This playful explanation for Lamech's name is more widely attested; Philo, for example, explains it as meaning "humiliation."[43]

The play on Lamech's name in *1 Enoch* 106:1 reveals a dominant trait in the story about Noah's birth. In this regard it merely expands upon a repeated practice in the biblical chapters about Noah. In a sense we may say that etymologies of the names for patriarchs 6–10 (Jared–Noah) in the Gen. 5 genealogy serve as the elements that underscore different features in the story about Noah's birth. The few lines remaining from the *Genesis Apocryphon* show that this element was not absent from it. The name of Noah himself is explained in Gen. 5:29 as meaning "comfort," while *Jared* was interpreted in the Book of Watchers *(1 Enoch* 6:6) with reference to the descent of the angels in his day. *1 Enoch* 106–7 continues the process begun in these earlier texts by appealing directly or indirectly to the meanings of these two names and to those of the other three patriarchal characters in the story. As previously noted, Lamech's name was related to a word for "lowliness" in order to underscore the fact that, with his generation, truth had sunk to its nadir. It appears that it was the angelic watchers and their gigantic offspring who had caused the truth to plummet. When Lamech saw how bright his child

41. For the Aramaic here, see Milik, *Books of Enoch*, 207–8.
42. Ibid.; see also Black, *Book of Enoch*, 320.
43. L. Grabbe, *Etymology in Early Jewish Interpretation*, 177–78, in which he provides other references to this etymology.

appeared and witnessed his precocious ability to praise God, he told Methuselah: "I have begotten a strange son; he is not like a man, but is like the children of the angels of heaven, of a different type, and not like us. And his eyes *are* like the rays of the sun, and his face glorious. And it seems to me that he is not sprung from me, but from the angels . . ." (106:5–6a). In his pessimistic musings about the paternity of the child, Lamech, as he does in the *Genesis Apocryphon*, brings Noah's birth into direct connection with the central Enochic myth: the descent of the angels to earth, their marriages with women, and their shocking off-spring. Noah's remarkable features made Lamech fear that a watcher was his father, not a mere man whose name meant "lowliness, humiliation."

Jared and his generation play no part at this juncture in the story, but Enoch does name him in his reply to Methuselah: "for in the days of my father Jared some from the height of heaven transgressed the word of the Lord" (106:13; cf. *Gen. Apoc.* 3:3). Mention of Jared's name and of the angels who left their celestial home recalls the wordplay that allowed ancient expositors to date the angels' descent: they journeyed down from heaven to earth in the days of Jared, as the original text of *1 Enoch* 6:6 reads. Since the angels had descended already in the days of Jared, who lived in the sixth generation from Adam, by the time Noah was born they had had four generations in which to spread wickedness and make their lascivious ways known far and wide. The author also has an etymological reason for assigning Methuselah the role of messenger between Lamech and Enoch. He gives him this task because the last part of his name *(-selah)* is related to the Hebrew verb *to send.* In this case, too, he was employing a more widely attested explanation for the end of Methuselah's name.[44] Here the *Genesis Apocryphon* goes one step farther: Lamech says of Methuselah, "And he went through the length of the land [*mat*] of Parvaim, and there he found [Enoch . . .]" (2:23). The word *mat*, which is a rare Aramaic word for "land,"[45] was selected by the author because it allowed him to pun on the first part of Methuselah's name *(Meth-).* So, in the *Genesis Apocryphon* his full name is analyzed as signifying "one who was sent through a land."

We would expect Enoch's part in the story to bear some etymological relationship to his name, but there is some uncertainty regarding what

---

44. Grabbe, *Etymology in Early Jewish Interpretation*, 181–82. Several writers, including Philo and Origen, interpreted the entire name to mean "sending out of death," while others mention only the notion of sending (as in *1 Enoch* 106–7).

45. See Fitzmyer, *Genesis Apocryphon*, 94–95, for a defense of this reading.

ancient scholars took his name to mean. Philo and Origen, for example, parsed it as a noun with the second-person suffix meaning "your grace/ favor," but others took it in the sense of "renewal," "dedication."[46] Perhaps the writer of *1 Enoch* 106–7 expresses the idea of "grace/favor" by means of the privileged position that he gives to him in the company of the holy angels.[47] But another possibility is more plausible. The name Enoch is related to the Hebrew verb *ḥnk* one of whose meanings is "to train [a child]."[48] It may be that this educational nuance lies behind the heavily pedagogical role that Enoch plays in this story and elsewhere in *1 Enoch*, in which he constantly instructs his son Methuselah or all of his children, just as the meaning of his name suggests he should.

As a result, the etymologies of the names Jared, Enoch, Methuselah, and Lamech have a relationship of sorts with the roles that each of them plays in the infancy tale of Noah. In the cases of Jared, Enoch, and Methuselah, the paronomasiae must be inferred from the account, while the etymological significance of the name Lamech is explicit in *1 Enoch* 106:1. The writer of chapters 106–7 reserves his richest etymological labors for the name Noah, however, and in this respect he was anticipated by the authors of Gen. 5–9 who played with the connotations of his name to an unusual degree. Gen. 5:28–29 explains the significance of his name: "When Lamech had lived one hundred eighty-two years, he became the father of a son; he named him Noah, saying, 'Out of the ground that the Lord has cursed this one shall bring us relief from our work and from the toil of our hands.' " As expositors noticed long ago, the etymology does not fit the name. Or, in the words of *Gen. Rab.* 25.2: "Rabbi Judah said: The interpretation is not the name, and the name is not the interpretation" (my trans.). The same rabbinic scholar is also quoted as saying that the text should have said either, "Noah, this one will give us rest" or "Nahman, this one will comfort us." The LXX offers a more strictly accurate explanation of the name: "he will give us rest."[49]

In Gen. 6–9 we meet a variety of reminiscences of the name Noah and of other words that are used regarding his future work in Gen. 5:28–

---

46. See Grabbe, *Etymology in Early Jewish Interpretation*, 156–57.

47. The *Genesis Apocryphon* 2:20 calls him "a favorite and o[ne cherished."

48. M. Jastrow, *A Dictionary of the Targumim, the Talmud Babli and Yerushalmi, and the Midrashic Literature* (1886–90; reprint, New York: Jastrow, 1967), 483.

49. Philo used the word *rest* as an etymology—an obvious derivation that is, of course, attested in other writers as well (Grabbe, *Etymology in Early Jewish Interpretation*, 192–93).

29 (see Gen. 6:6–9; 8:4, 9; 9:24). It should also be recalled that the writer of these sections in Genesis connects Enoch and Noah by repeating that each of them (and only these two) "walked with the *ʾelōhîm*" (Gen. 6:9) and by hiding the letters of the name Enoch (spelled backwards) in this verse about Noah.[50] In this way he brings Enoch and Noah into association with one another, as the authors of *1 Enoch* 106–7 and *Gen. Apoc.* 2–5 do.

The writer of *1 Enoch* 106–7 also exploited the range of meanings that the name Noah suggested to him. Most of the etymologies are concentrated in 106:16 and 18. In 106:16 the clairvoyant Enoch predicts: "But this child who has been born to you will be left on the earth, and his three sons will be saved with him; when all the men who *are* on the earth die, he and his sons will be saved." And in verse 18 he orders his son Methuselah: "And now make known to your son Lamech that the one who has been born is truly his son. And call his name Noah, for he will be a remnant for you, and he and his sons will be saved from the destruction which is coming on the earth because of all the sin and all the iniquity which will be committed on the earth in his days." The expressions "will be left on the earth" (v. 16) and "for he will be a remnant for you" (v. 18) build on one possible meaning for the name; the Greek text of 106:18 expresses the notion of "rest"—a literal interpretation of the name Noah; and possibly the references to "save" in verses 16 and 18 also derive from an association with his name.[51] And, finally, the verb *comfort* in 107:3 clearly derives from Gen. 5:29.[52]

The writers of *1 Enoch* 106–7 and *Gen. Apoc.* 2 have thus produced a series of etymologies for the prediluvian ancestors from Jared through Noah and have put them to work to emphasize the principal topics in their story about the birth of Noah. In the time of Jared the angels *descended*, married women, and had children with the daughters of men. Enoch was sojourning with the angels, and from the information that they imparted to him he *instructed* others—Methuselah and Lamech, in this case. Methuselah was *sent* by his son Lamech through the *land* of Parvaim to Enoch in order to receive from him an answer regarding his paternal concerns, while Lamech's generation marked the *nadir* of the human condition because of the savage deeds and lust of the angels and their gigantic offspring. But righteous Noah marked the great turning

50. See J. Sasson, "Word-Play in Gen 6:8–9," *CBQ* 37 (1975): 165–66, for the reverse spelling of Enoch's name in this passage.
51. Milik, *Books of Enoch*, 214.
52. Grabbe, *Etymology in Early Jewish Interpretation*, 193.

point: he provided *comfort, salvation,* and the *continuation* of the human race.

Besides the artistry the writers of these versions of the infancy stories have put on display, they have also appealed to a tradition in which Enoch resembles the ancient Mesopotamian flood hero who, after surviving the deluge, was removed from human society to a place far distant. There he enjoys immortality as the gods do. This motif is most familiar from the eleventh tablet of the *Epic of Gilgamesh,* in which Utnapishtim is the distant hero. Gilgamesh journeys to his remote home in order to learn from him how he attained unending life—information that only Utnapishtim would have. In our story the motif is transferred from the flood hero to Enoch, who does not live immortally—at least not yet—with the gods but, rather, stays with the angels and supplies information *about* the flood hero. It may be that these Jewish writers wished to downplay traditional associations with the one who survived the flood and yet wanted to retain the theme of a distant primeval sage to whom, under extreme duress, one could turn when there was no other authoritative source of information. To do so, they transferred the notion of his far-off dwelling place to Enoch and made Enoch relay a message that the future flood hero Noah was in fact not divine or supernatural (like Utnapishtim); he merely had an extraordinary role to play in God's plan. That plan God made known to Enoch through his angelic confidants and, in turn, relayed it to Methuselah and Lamech.

CHAPTER 4

OTHER EARLY SOURCES

The Enochic booklets studied thus far are the major surviving witnesses to the ways in which traditions about the patriarch evolved in the third and second centuries B.C.E. In them we see Enoch as a frequent companion of the angels, recipient of otherwise inaccessible information about the universe and the course and culmination of human history, and as a preacher of righteousness who consoles an oppressed community and excoriates their wealthy, more powerful foes. The motif of companionship with the angels is an exegetical inference from Gen. 5:22 and 24 (his walk with the ʾelohîm); the other two motifs seem to be the results of drawing further conclusions concerning what he might have learned while he was with the angels of God and how he might have brought that information to bear on the lives of his family and wider audience. At some point, probably due to the play on the meaning of his father Jared's name (descend) and his chronological location near the time of the flood, Enoch became associated with the watcher story, a counteraccount or supplement to the biblical explanation for how evil became so powerful on the earth. Enoch's connection with that story begins in *1 Enoch* 12–16, continues in the latter chapters of the BW, and plays a key role in the historical apocalypses revealed to him. The hortatory sections of the EE do not appeal to this tale, although it is found in the Apocalypse of Weeks and the story of Noah's birth. Enoch's name was tied to all these roles and themes by the 160s B.C.E.

Outside the explicitly Enochic booklets there are a number of shorter references to him and his roles. In these other works his part is far more limited than it is in the AB, BW, EE, or BD, yet their treatments of his life and work prove that Enochic themes had wider appeal than just in the circles represented by the authors of the four Enochic works already studied. These other early texts that deal with Enoch should now be considered. The sections about them are arranged in chronological order insofar as that is possible.

A. *ARAMAIC LEVI*

The pseudepigraphic collection named the *Testaments of the 12 Patriarchs* contains the final words, will, and testament of each of Jacob's twelve sons. Levi is the third son in order of birth but clearly the first in importance throughout the work as well as in his own lengthy testament. Among the many fragmentary texts found in cave 4 at Qumran are two manuscripts—4Q213 and 214—whose texts resemble the *Testament of Levi* but are witnesses of an independent document that seems to have been a source, whether directly or indirectly, for the *Testament of Levi*. This *Aramaic Levi* text may be as old as the most ancient Enochic booklets, although the date cannot be determined with certainty. Whatever its precise place in time, it is likely that it was written at some point in the third century B.C.E.[1]

The only allusion to Enoch in *Aramaic Levi* occurs in a lengthy speech by the patriarch to his children. Much of this extended address survives in a series of textual witnesses, including 4Q213. The setting naturally is testamentary. Levi assembles his sons and grandsons in the 118th year of his life (l. 82; since he lives to be 137, he was 19 years too eager). He admonishes his children to pursue truth, justice, and wisdom: "And now, my sons, teach reading and writing and the teaching of wisdom to your children and may wisdom be with you for eternal glory" (88).[2] The accent on wisdom here is noteworthy when one considers how central the concept is in the Enochic tradition. Praise of the wise man occupies a prominent place in the speech; the teaching function of Levi's descendants also receives attention.

The reference to Enoch comes after these words and after a gap in the extant text. The broken remains include mention of the moon and stars, favorite topics in the Enochic literature. Milik reads and translates the difficult line in this way: "Did not Enoch accuse [. . ." (4QTestLevi[a] 8 iii 6).[3] In the next two lines Levi talks of blame that will fall on him and on his sons, whom he addresses directly. Concepts such as knowledge, abandoning the way of truth and the paths of righteousness, and walking in the darkness of Satan figure in the context.

Milik understands Enoch's accusation as an allusion to his speech to the watchers in *1 Enoch* 12–16. Kugler is more cautious:

A third detail that catches the reader's attention is Levi's claim that Enoch had already made a complaint related to his own accusations

---

1. So Milik, *Books of Enoch*, 24, who thinks this is the latest possible date for it.
2. Translation of R. Kugler, "The Levi–Priestly Tradition: From Malachi to *Testament of Levi*" (Ph.D. diss., University of Notre Dame, 1994), 177. Kugler sets out the Aramaic textual evidence for this section on pp. 176–77.
3. *Books of Enoch*, 23.

against his children regarding their future misbehavior. From the context one can guess that it has something to do with failure to exercise good judgment and wisdom. Unfortunately we lack the continuation of the thought in *AL* [*Aramaic Levi*] and have no clear idea regarding Enoch's accusation; therefore it is impossible to associate the reference to Enoch's sayings with any particular passage in the literature bearing his name.[4]

As we shall see, the *Book of Jubilees* also preserves a tradition about Enoch's admonitions and accusations.

B. THE WISDOM OF JESUS BEN SIRA

The Jerusalemite Jesus son of Sira composed his wisdom book in the first third of the second century B.C.E. (between 200 and 167). Two generations later his grandson, whose name is lost, translated Jesus son of Sira's Hebrew work into Greek. The information that the grandson includes in his prologue indicates that he produced his Greek version not far from 116 B.C.E. Today the book is considered biblical by Catholics and apocryphal by Protestants. For a long time the text was known only in Greek and derivative versions, but over the last century large portions of Sirach in Hebrew have been found. The oldest substantial Hebrew copy is the one found at Masada. It preserves parts of Sir. 39:27–44:17 and dates from the first half of the first century B.C.E.[5] A few other scraps have been discovered at Qumran, while larger portions of the text in Hebrew are available in medieval copies. The complete text is to be found in the Greek translation (which also contains the grandson's marvelous prologue) and in dependent versions such as the Latin.

One of the most famous sections in Sirach is the Praise of the Ancestors, found in chapters 44–50. In it the writer praises the deeds of Israel's heroes of the past and thus strengthens the memory that his contemporaries should have of them. After general comments in the introduction to the section, he surveys the great individuals of the biblical past and concludes with a postbiblical high priest named Simon. These chapters offer a fascinating look at the traditions known to the author and to the books in which he found them. In fact, he employed almost all of the books found in the Hebrew Bible today and used them largely in their

4. "Levi–Priestly Tradition," 182.
5. See P. Skehan and A. Di Lella, *The Wisdom of Ben Sira*, AB 39 (Garden City, N.Y.: Doubleday, 1987), 53.

current order. His witness to the traditions about Enoch is important because he comes from a different group than the Enochic authors. His is a nonapocalyptic, priestly viewpoint, and he thus serves as a measure of how widespread these traditions were in Jewish society at the time.

In the complete Greek version of the book the historical part of the Praise of the Ancestors, which is heavily weighted toward the priests and their concerns, begins and nearly ends with Enoch. That is, Enoch himself brackets Ben Sira's version of sacred history. The first reference to him comes in 44:16, but the verse is absent from some of the textual witness, including the Masada scroll. It is interesting to compare the evidence as it appears in the different versions.

Masada	Manuscript B[6]	Greek
	Enoch [was fo]und perfect and he walked with the Lord and [he was] taken, a sign of knowledge for generation after generation.	Enoch was pleasing to the Lord and he was removed, a sign of repentance for the generations.

The Masada manuscript is the oldest witness, and it lacks the verse entirely. This fact has led commentators to conclude that it did not belong in the original text. "His [Enoch's] popularity in the last centuries B.C. as the custodian of ancient lore would seem to have prompted this expansion on Ben Sira's text, putting Enoch at the head of the list of ancient ancestors."[7] This is not the only possibility, however. It may be that the Masada manuscript is haplographic at this point: the copyist may have accidentally skipped over verse 16 because it begins with words that resemble the first ones in the Hebrew text of verse 17:

Manuscript B: Enoch was found perfect
Masada: Noah a righteous man was found perfect.

If such a scribal blunder occurred, chapter 44, verse 16, with its words about Enoch, would have been a part of the original Hebrew text of Ben Sira. The Greek version represents an adaptation of the Hebrew for this verse to the Septuagint's wording of Gen. 5:24. Even if chapter 44, verse

---

6. Manuscript B is one of the medieval Hebrew copies.
7. Skehan and Di Lella, *Wisdom of Ben Sira*, 499.

16, were not in the Hebrew original, the fact that the verse exists in the Greek version implies that it was present in some copy of the Hebrew already in the late second century, when the grandson translated his grandfather's book.

The differing formulations of Sir. 44:16 raise the question of what the verse means. Both manuscript B and the Greek text model their contents on the wording of Gen. 5:22 and 24 as it appears in the Hebrew and Greek texts of these biblical verses. To the scriptural base, manuscript B adds the word *perfect*—a term used for Noah in Gen. 6:9. Both versions of Sir. 44:16 make it abundantly clear that the persons responsible for them understood Genesis's *ha-ʾelohîm* as referring to God, since they replace the ambiguous Hebrew term with the entirely unambiguous name "the Lord." For them this word did not mean "the angels," as it did in the Enochic tradition.

If we allow that the Hebrew and Greek of chapter 44, verse 16, differ in part because of the variant wording of Gen. 5:22 and 24 in the Hebrew and Greek versions of the Bible, then we may say that the two are very close to one another until the last few words. The medieval Hebrew manuscript B makes Enoch "a sign of knowledge for generation after generation"—an apt description for the protagonist of the early Enochic booklets. The Greek translation describes him as "a sign of repentance for the generations." The problematic pair of words is *knowledge/repentance*. The close similarity between the two versions in the remainder of the verse and their stark difference for this word would naturally make us suspect that a translator or scribe confused two words that look much alike. The Hebrew uses a word for "knowledge," and the Greek word for *repentance* has the element of "mind" or "understanding" in it. Possibly, a confusion of words from the roots *katanoeo* (to understand) and *metanoeo* (to repent) took place at some point in the tradition of copying, and thus the strange disagreement between the Hebrew and Greek texts of Sir. 44:16 resulted. If the Greek term *repentance* did not arise in this way but is an intentional modification of the Hebrew text in a negative direction, then we have in Sir. 44:16 (Greek) the earliest evidence for an assessment of Enoch which is in part pejorative. Others of this kind will be treated later (see, e.g., the discussions of Philo and *Gen. Rab.*).

Several chapters later Enoch puts in a second appearance in the Praise of the Ancestors (49:14). Once Ben Sira has brought his long survey of biblical characters to a close with Nehemiah (the last datable person in the Hebrew Bible), he returns to Enoch. The Masada manuscript does not reach to this point (the last preserved part is 44:17), but manuscript B and the Greek version read this way:

Manuscript B	Greek
Few have been fashioned on the earth like *ḥnyk* and he also was taken within.	No one has been fashioned on the earth such as Enoch for he was also taken up from the earth.

The context and the Greek text show that the letters *ḥnyk* are a simple error of copying for the name Enoch (*ḥnwk*), who is obviously under discussion here. At the beginning the Greek is strange. It asserts that *no one* was fashioned like Enoch because he was taken up. Anyone familiar with the Bible would know, however, that Enoch was not the only one to be taken up; Elijah, too, experienced such a translation. The more accurate statement is present in the Hebrew text, which claims not that he was unique but, rather, that *few* were like Enoch. The last expression (within/from the earth) seems also to point to a textual corruption.

Sirach must have thought highly of Enoch because he put him at the beginning and end of his survey covering biblical heroes. He mentions his walk with the Lord/his being pleasing to the Lord and elsewhere indicates that he knows the material in Gen. 5:21–24. Nevertheless, he shows no awareness here of the extrabiblical traditions that had grown up around him. This is curious because elsewhere Sirach probably alludes to the watcher story. In Sir. 16:7, part of a list of ancient sinners who received their just punishment, he writes: "He [God] did not forgive the ancient giants who revolted in their might." The NRSV here follows the reading of the Greek text for the phrase "ancient giants," while the Hebrew refers to "the princes of old." It is safe to say that the Greek represents an interpretation of the potentially ambiguous Hebrew text. "The allusion to Gen. 6:1–4 seen by the Gr (*archaiōn gigantōn*) is certainly present; but the choice (MSS A, B) of *nesîkê qedem*, *princes of old*, by Ben Sira, instead of the familiar *nepîlîm*, is conscious avoidance of the mythological overtones to the Genesis narrative so familiar from the Enoch literature and (later) Jubilees."[8] Here and in the two references to Enoch in the Praise of the Ancestors, Ben Sira manifests a certain restraint about Enoch. He tips his hand only slightly to reveal his awareness of a wider, extra-Genesis tradition in characterizing him as "a sign of knowledge for generation after generation"—a description that would not follow from Gen. 5:21–24.

---

8. Ibid., 270.

C. PSEUDO-EUPOLEMUS

The name Pseudo-Eupolemus has been assigned by modern scholars to the unknown author who wrote two small sections of text which have been preserved among the excerpts of an author named Eupolemus. Deciding what Pseudo-Eupolemus himself, who was probably a Samaritan, may have written is no small challenge because of the fate suffered by his book(s). His own composition has not survived, but his words were quoted by one Alexander Polyhistor, whose book *On the Jews* (mid-first century B.C.E.) is also lost. Happily, the fourth-century C.E. church historian Eusebius, in his *Preparation for the Gospel*, extracted material from *On the Jews* before it passed into oblivion, and among the sections that he quoted were the two passages now assigned to Pseudo-Eupolemus. Alexander Polyhistor attributed the longer of the two extracts to Eupolemus, a Jewish writer of the mid-second century B.C.E., and the other to an anonymous source. The fragments of Pseudo-Eupolemus cannot be dated with any precision, but there is reason to believe that they come from the first half of the second century B.C.E., if not earlier.[9] If something went awry with the text through all of this copying and loss over several centuries in antiquity, it would not be a great surprise.

Pseudo-Eupolemus proves to be of considerable interest because he combines biblical and extrabiblical information about Enoch, and the extrabiblical data are not always the same as those we find in the Enochic booklets. He mentions Enoch in the course of describing Abraham and his career. Of Abraham he writes: "He excelled all men in nobility of birth and wisdom. In fact, he discovered both astrology and Chaldean science."[10] Abra(ha)m may have attracted astrological or astronomical traditions to himself because of Gen. 15:5, in which the Lord brings him outside and tells him to look toward heaven and count the stars, if possible. Later Pseudo-Eupolemus claims that Abraham taught "the Phoenicians the movements of the sun and moon, and everything else as well." This point is repeated in the second fragment.

Abraham's pedagogical labors did not end with the Phoenicians, whom he encountered upon entering the land. When famine (Gen. 12:10–20) drove him and his family to Egypt and after the Sarai-Pharaoh episode, he came into contact with Egyptian priests from Heliopolis.

---

9. For introductory information about Pseudo-Eupolemus, see C. A. Holladay, *Fragments from Hellenistic Jewish Authors*, vol. 1: *Historians*, SBLTT 20, Pseudepigrapha Series 10 (Chico, Calif.: Scholars Press, 1983), 157–60.
10. Translations of Pseudo-Eupolemus are from ibid., 171, 173, 175.

While Abraham was living in Heliopolis with the Egyptian priests, he taught them many new things. He introduced them to astrology and other such things, saying that he and the Babylonians had discovered these things. But the original discovery he traced back to Enoch, saying that this man Enoch, not the Egyptians, had discovered astrology first. For the Babylonians say that first there was Belus (who was Kronos), and that from him was born Belus and Canaan. This Belus fathered Canaan, the father of the Phoenicians. To him was born a son, Cush, whom the Greeks called Asbolus, the father of the Ethiopians, the brother of Mizraim, the father of the Egyptians. The Greeks say that Atlas discovered astrology. (Atlas and Enoch are the same.) To Enoch was born a son, Methuselah, who learned all things through the help of the angels of God, and thus we gained our knowledge.

A city with the name Heliopolis would be an appropriate residence for anyone interested in promoting a solar calendar. Not only does its name include the Greek word for "sun," but the city was famous for the solar cult conducted there.[11] The account of Pseudo-Eupolemus reveals a culture war of sorts concerning who was the person who had discovered astrology. The Egyptians made this claim for themselves, but Pseudo-Eupolemus counters by citing Abraham's and the Babylonians' earlier successes in this area and by assigning the ultimate origin of astrology to Enoch himself. Pseudo-Eupolemus documents his claims by citing genealogical information that may come from Gen. 10 but which departs from it in some particulars. He points out that several generations separate Belus, the first among the Babylonians, from Egypt. Thus, the Babylonians owned a priority of some magnitude. The Greeks he handles differently: their astrological pioneer, Atlas, was identical with Enoch, who, as a prediluvian hero, was earlier in time than any of the individuals in the genealogy.

Pseudo-Eupolemus, then, knew about Enoch as the first astrologer. That is, he was familiar with the sort of material we find in the AB and the BW, in which the secrets of the heavenly bodies are revealed to Enoch. The Enochic booklets do not say that he was the first to uncover this science, but they do not mention any earlier expert either.

A second tradition about Enoch that was known to Pseudo-Eupolemus was that he had a son named Methuselah. He could have taken this information from Gen. 5, or he could have derived it from the AB, in which

---

11. Ibid., 184 n. 25.

Enoch discloses to Methuselah the astronomical information that Uriel had shown to him. The combination of astronomical teaching and Methuselah as the recipient of it make the AB a more likely source of information. It is curious, nevertheless, that Pseudo-Eupolemus seems to be saying at the end of the extract that Methuselah was the one who had learned everything through the assistance of the angels. These words would be more appropriate for Enoch himself than for his son. Enoch was the one who instructed Methuselah on the basis of the material that Uriel had revealed. It is likely that a mistake entered the text at some point in the long history of copying the fragment. Originally, it probably indicated that Enoch had learned all this information from the angels and that he then passed it along to his son, through whom we have gained our knowledge.

Only these items—astrology and transmission of data revealed by angels to Enoch's son Methuselah—are common to the earliest two Enochic booklets and to Pseudo-Eupolemus. In his short statement he says nothing about the angels who descended from heaven or the illicit sex and teachings (including astronomical ones) attributed to them. He also writes nothing about Enoch as an apocalyptic seer or as a preacher of righteousness. This may be the case simply because works such as the Apocalypse of Weeks and the Animal Apocalypse did not yet exist when Pseudo-Eupolemus wrote about Enoch. His interests seem to have been more narrow: to stake a claim for the greatest antiquity of the Hebrew culture hero, an antiquity far greater than that enjoyed by what were supposed to be the two most ancient states in the Near East—Babylon and Egypt. They too had heroes from the distant past, but Enoch, Israel's hero, antedated and hence outranked them all. In identifying Enoch with the Greek god Atlas, Pseudo-Eupolemus shows no scruples or hesitation. Such blatant assimilation of a Greek mythological figure would have been unthinkable to some Jews in early Maccabean times but seems to have been acceptable for this possibly Samaritan writer, who penned his words not far from the year 200 B.C.E. Perhaps he lived in a time and place more open to external influence than did some later, more nationalistic writers.

D. THE *BOOK OF JUBILEES*

One of the ancient Jewish texts that drew heavily on the Enochic tradition and did so explicitly is the *Book of Jubilees*. It was written around the middle of the second century B.C.E. and retells the stories in Genesis and Exod. 1–20. In other words, it is quite literally an example of the so-called Rewritten Bible. Renewed interest has attached to the book since copies of the original Hebrew version were found at Qumran. In fact, some fifteen copies have been identified, making it one of the best attested books there, although all of the copies are very fragmentary.

There are several places in which *Jubilees* is indebted to the Enochic texts and traditions. First is the annual calendar. As is well known, the author was a staunch defender of a solar calendar that lasted 364 days (6:20–38). Thus, he adheres to the same solar arrangement that the AB teaches in chapter 72 and elsewhere. However, there is an important difference that shows the writer of *Jubilees* did not just copy material from the AB. The AB not only presents a 364-day solar calendar, but it also sets out the data for a lunar calendar of 354 days (chaps. 73–74, etc.). It simply juxtaposes the two without weighing their relative merits. The angel Uriel disclosed the details about both to Enoch; hence, both were revealed and, therefore, accurate and valid. In *Jubilees* the solar calendar is defended, but the lunar one is strongly opposed.

> There will be people who carefully observe the moon with lunar observations because it is corrupt (with respect to) the seasons and is early from year to year by ten days. Therefore years will come about for them when they will disturb (the year) and make a day of testimony something worthless and a profane day a festival. Everyone will join together both holy days with the profane and the profane day with the holy day, for they will err regarding the months, the sabbaths, the festivals, and the jubilee. (6:36–37) [12]

Both the AB and *Jubilees* point out the ten-day discrepancy between the two calendars, but for the latter it is not permissible to use both systems: one is the revealed calendar; the other causes people to err in calculating the year and to walk in the festivals of the gentiles (6:35). As we will see, the calendrical texts from Qumran side with the AB in this regard.

Second, the author pens a remarkable portrait of Enoch[13] as he reproduces and augments the information found in the genealogy of Gen. 5. He clearly bases himself on the brief biblical givens for Enoch (Gen.

---

12. Translations of *Jubilees* passages are taken from VanderKam, *Book of Jubilees*, 2 vols., CSCO 510–11, Scriptores Aethiopici 87–88 (Leuven: Peeters, 1989), vol. 2.
13. The following section draws on the more detailed treatment found in VanderKam, "Enoch Traditions in Jubilees and Other Second-Century Sources," SBLSP, edited by P. Achtemeier (1978): 1.229–51.

5:21–24), but he goes beyond them and makes explicit references to writings of Enoch. He follows Genesis in identifying Enoch as the son of Jared (adding the pun on his name, during his time the watchers descended), and he names his mother Barakah (4:16). The entire statement about Jared is interesting: "He [Mahalalel] named him Jared because during his lifetime the angels of the Lord who were called Watchers descended to earth to teach mankind to do what is just and upright upon the earth." From these words we could conclude that *Jubilees* is merely alluding to the familiar Enochic theme of the watchers' descent, but the motive that it ascribes to their departure from heaven should catch our eye: initially, they came for a moral reason ("to teach mankind to do what is just and upright upon the earth"), not to satisfy their lust. This short notice is important, not only for introducing a new idea into the tradition but also for demonstrating that *Jubilees* draws on more Enochic lore than we have in our possession today. None of the earlier Enochic booklets has anything positive to say about the descent of the angels. The BW is overwhelmingly negative in its portrayals, while the apocalyptic visions are either silent about the motive or vocal about the negative results. Hence, while the play on Jared's name may come from *1 Enoch* 6:6, the righteous purpose of the departure from heaven must have come from a very different source.

After reporting the birth of Enoch, the writer begins to supplement the biblical text:

> He was the first of mankind who were born on the earth who learned (the art of) writing, instruction, and wisdom and who wrote down in a book the signs of the sky in accord with the fixed pattern of their months so that mankind would know the seasons of the years according to the fixed patterns of each of their months. He was the first to write a testimony. He testified to mankind in the generations of the earth: The weeks of the jubilees he related, and made known the days of the years; the months he arranged, and related the sabbaths of the years, as we had told him. While he slept he saw in a vision what has happened and what will occur — how things will happen for mankind during their history until the day of judgment. He saw everything and understood. He wrote a testimony for himself and placed it upon the earth against all mankind and for their history. (4:17–19)

In his expansion of the biblical text the writer of *Jubilees* is impressed with Enoch's being first in various categories, just as Pseudo-Eupolemus found him to be the first astrologer/astronomer. He was the first human to learn how to write. The source for this motif is not supplied, but the older Enochic booklets mention his ability to write, and they would not have existed if he had been unable to use a pen. For example, in the AB Enoch writes down the information that Uriel gives to him regarding the fixed times of the months and the degree to which the moon is illumined at these points (*1 Enoch* 74:2 — a verse that may underlie the reference in *Jub.* to fixed patterns of months). In chapter 81, verse 6, Uriel instructs Enoch to teach his children and write down another law, a warning for them. *1 Enoch* 82:1 has Enoch address Methuselah and tell him, among other things, that he has written a book for him. The next verse may identify that book with wisdom, a subject that *Jubilees* adduces in the same phrase as Enoch's skill at writing. The BW presents Enoch as a scribe of righteousness (12:4, 15:1) who records the petition of the watchers and the divine reply to it (see 14:4, 7). The journey sections of the BW (chaps. 17–19, 20–36) also note his writing (33:3), and the same is the case for the EE (92:1 [also characterized as containing wisdom]; cf. 108:1) and the BD, in which Enoch dates his first dream vision to the time when he was beginning to learn how to write (83:2; see 83:10). In his notice about Enoch as the pioneer author, then, the writer of *Jubilees* was not drawing on Genesis, which never mentions this about him, but probably on the information contained in the Enochic booklets.

Enoch's instruction and wisdom, also firsts, are pervasive in the literature that antedates *Jubilees*. On the basis of the revelations made to him, Enoch instructs his son Methuselah according to the testamentary setting for the AB, the BD, and the EE, while the BW pictures him as instructing the chosen, who are to live in a far-distant generation. The Enochic passages that most nearly resemble the formulation in *Jubilees* are *1 Enoch* 82:2–3, in which the wisdom of his teaching is stressed, and 92:1, in which he is called the wisest person (in the Aramaic) or the writer of wisdom for future generations (Ethiopic).

The references to astronomical topics — "who wrote down in a book the signs of the sky in accord with the fixed pattern of their months so that mankind would know the seasons of the years according to the fixed pattern of each of their months" — clearly point primarily to the AB. The sources for some of the phrases in *Jub.* 4:17 can be identified more precisely: "the signs of the sky" is borrowed from Gen. 1:14, in which the heavenly luminaries are called "signs," and "the fixed patterns" recall passages such as *1 Enoch* 74:2 and could come from a variety of places in this booklet. Enoch's astronomical teachings were to serve a practical purpose: so that mankind would known the seasons or times of the years (cf. 82:4).

The author of *Jubilees* betrays himself often in his book as strongly opposed to the gentiles and as an advocate of strict separation from them. In this section about Enoch, however, he displays his awareness of the wider world, in which the various literate nations made similar claims for their ancient heroes. The short passage quoted earlier from Pseudo-Eupolemus shows that this was the case in the area of astronomy/astrology: the Egyptians thought they were first, but Abraham and the Babylonians had preceded them, while Enoch (Atlas) was earlier than all. According to the third-century Babylonian writer Berossus, the primeval *apkallu* Oannes introduced letters, sciences, and crafts; he is also credited with imparting astronomical information.[14] Elsewhere the same sorts of claims were made for Egyptian Thoth, Phoenician Taautos, and Greek Hermes. Enoch, then, for the author of *Jubilees*, is the antediluvian patriarch who is worthy to stand in such supreme company or, rather, to stand over the other culture heroes, as the first to introduce the fundamental arts of civilization.

Jub. 4:18 speaks of a testimony that Enoch wrote. Although the latter part of the verse returns to the astronomical theme, it may be that the testimony of the first part is not being defined as having to do with the sun, moon, and stars. One reason for saying this is that chapter 4, verse 18, ends with "as we had told him." The pronoun *we* refers to the angels who revealed so much to Enoch in large parts of *1 Enoch*, but in the AB the angel Uriel is the only one who discloses information about the celestial bodies and thus about the calendar. It is likely that the astronomical notes given in verse 18 echo a wider cycle of Enochic sources than the AB alone.[15] The EE seems the most likely candidate among the Enochic booklets to be called a testimony. In particular, chapter 93, verses 1–2, speaks about Enoch's disclosing data from his books to his children; he had received the information from the angels. These verses are an introduction to the Apocalypse of Weeks, which, of course, surveys all of history. The writer also gives Enoch credit for relating the sabbaths of years. Such seven-year units remind us of the Animal Apocalypse, in which the shepherds and their seventy periods of rule offer an interpretation of Daniel's seventy weeks of years (drawn from Jeremiah's seventy years of desolation for Jerusalem). The notion of weeks is also the structuring principle for the Apocalypse of Weeks. Perhaps one or both of these booklets lie behind the author's statement.

---

14. For a discussion of this Oannes, see VanderKam, *Enoch and the Growth of an Apocalyptic Tradition*, 181.

15. Cf. Milik, *Books of Enoch*, 11, 61–69.

Jub. 4:19 mentions a vision that Enoch saw while he slept—a dream vision in which he viewed all of history until the judgment day. He recorded it and deposited the writing on the earth to serve as a testimony. Naturally, these words make one think of the BD, with its two visions, or of the EE, which contains the Apocalypse of Weeks. There are some small problems with identifying the source as the BD, since it contains two visions, and the second (the Animal Apocalypse) goes beyond the judgment. It may be the case again that the material in the EE in the vicinity of and in the Apocalypse of Weeks itself is what is meant. *1 Enoch* 92:1 alludes to an Enochic composition whose contents are intended for future generations; 91:1 says that he showed to his children everything that would happen to them forever; and 93:2 indicates that the Apocalypse of Weeks came to Enoch in a heavenly vision. The ten weeks of the Apocalypse of Weeks cover all of history and the judgment but have only a vague statement about the time beyond the judgment. Hence, it would fit the limit of "until the day of judgment" more precisely than the Animal Apocalypse. Moreover, the EE itself seems to be Enoch's testimony, as already noted.

Jub. 4:20 returns to the biblical framework when it speaks of Enoch's marriage and the birth of his first son. The text dates these events to the very year and also names his wife and gives her family connections. The precise dating corresponds with a characteristic trait of the book, and explaining the wife's identity demonstrates the writer's concern for purity in the chosen line. The name of Enoch's wife, Edni, reminds one of *1 Enoch* 85:3 (in the BD), in which her name is given as Edna. This latter spelling is also found in some of the manuscripts of *Jub.* 4:20.

At *Jub.* 4:21 the author again expands greatly on the bare scriptural skeleton:

He was, moreover, with God's angels for six jubilees of years. They showed him everything on earth and in the heavens—the dominion of the sun—and he wrote down everything. He testified to the Watchers who had sinned with the daughters of men because they had begun to mix with earthly women so that they became defiled. Enoch testified against all of them. (4:21–22)

In *Jubilees* a jubilee period lasts 49 years (7 weeks of years). So, in saying that Enoch spent 6 jubilees of years with the angels, the writer is stating that he was with them for 294 years. From this sentence it is clear that the writer understood "walked with the ʾelohîm" in Gen. 5:22 and 24 as meaning his sojourn with the angels. Gen. 5:22 says that he was with the ʾelohîm for 300 years after becoming the father of Methuselah, and *Jubi-*

Iees interprets this notice as referring to an approximately 300-year stay with the angels following Methuselah's birth. It is not immediately apparent why the writer does not make his stay last a full 300 years. The AB gives some indication that writers in the Enochic tradition shortened the sojourn with the angels so that Enoch would have time to return to the earth and pass along to his children what he had learned. In *1 Enoch* 81:5–7 seven angels bring him to his house and allow him one year to instruct Methuselah and his children and to testify to them; in the second year they would take him away for his second stay with the angels (after his earthly life ended). *Jubilees* grants Enoch a longer reprieve, perhaps to give him more time to instruct those around him in the incredible wisdom he had received.

The description of what the angels showed him fits the cosmological sections of the BW (*1 Enoch* 17–36) best. There the angels lead him on a tour of earthly and heavenly places, and the booklet concludes with a section (33–36) that summarizes astronomical material. Enoch is also said to have written all of this in a book (33:3). The phrase "the dominion of the sun" would point more directly, however, to parts of the AB, especially chapter 72.

Enoch's testimony against the watchers also leads us to the BW, in which, in chapters 12–16, he delivers God's words of judgment to the angels, who were unable to speak with the deity after their sin. The language used in *Jub.* 4:22 for the sin of the watchers is particularly close to *1 Enoch* 7:1 and 10:11.

The last verses in the Enoch paragraph of *Jubilees* relate to the time beginning when the angels removed him from the earth.

He was taken from human society, and we led him into the Garden of Eden for (his) greatness and honor. Now he is there writing down the judgment and condemnation of the world and all the wickedness of mankind. Because of him the flood water did not come on any of the land of Eden because he was placed there as a sign and to testify against all people in order to tell all the deeds of history until the day of judgment. He burned the evening incense of the sanctuary which is acceptable before the Lord on the mountain *of incense.* (4:23–25)

The paragraph builds upon and supplements Gen. 5:24: "Enoch walked with the *'elohîm;* then he was no more, because God took him." The verse is interpreted as referring to his second, permanent stay with the angels. This distinction is indicated in *1 Enoch* 81, in which he is returned to the earth for one year, following which he is to be removed a second time. It may be, too, that the Animal Apocalypse places Enoch in this part of his career. There (87:3–4) three angels take Enoch from the earth and raise him to a high place, a high tower, where he is told to stay until he sees everything that will happen to the giants, watchers, and their spouses. Nothing is ever said about his returning to the earth again until the time of judgment, when he is present (90:31). The place from which Enoch can view all of human history is called a "high tower"; this is the term in the Animal Apocalypse for a temple (see 89:50, 73). As a result, Enoch is in a heavenly sanctuary for most of the Apocalypse. In its supplement to the scriptural account *Jubilees* names the place to which Enoch was brought as the Garden of Eden. The garden is described in chapter 4, verse 25, as a sanctuary, and Enoch performs the rites of a priest in that temple. His priestly duties are a new element for Enoch's expanding portfolio. Moreover, his presence in Eden protected the garden sanctuary from the destructive waters of the flood. There are other indications in *Jubilees* that Eden was regarded as a sanctuary; for example, chapter 3, verses 9–14, derive the law of Lev. 11 regarding when a woman who has given birth may enter the sanctuary from the two times when Adam and Eve, respectively, went into the garden. Thus, here, as in the Animal Apocalypse, Enoch finds himself in a heavenly temple.

While Enoch is in Eden, he functions as a scribal recorder of the judgment that is destined to befall mankind (see *1 Enoch* 92:1, 104:7). Enoch himself is said to be a "sign" in Eden—the very term used for him in Sir. 44:16. In this case, however, he is not a sign of knowledge or repentance; rather, he continues to carry out his well-attested work of testifying against all people and relating all their actions until the end of time.

The Enoch paragraph in *Jub.* 4:16–25 demonstrates that the writer knows and uses Gen. 5:21–24 but also that he augments the scriptural data with information from all of the Enochic booklets studied to this point.[16] This is important not only for showing how the Enochic tradition kept being used and expanded but also for the date of *Jubilees*, which would have been composed after the BD was written in 164 or 163 B.C.E.

Before we leave *Jubilees* there are a few other references to Enoch that we should examine. The first is in chapter 7, verses 38–39. There Noah is concluding his instructions to his sons about various halakhic points, including the practice of allowing fruit trees to grow for three years before their fruit is picked in the fourth and presented as a first-fruits offering to the Lord: "For this is how Enoch, your father's father, com-

---

16. For detailed documentation of this claim, see VanderKam, "Enoch Traditions."

manded his son Methuselah; then Methuselah his son Lamech; and Lamech commanded me everything that his father had commanded him. Now I am commanding you, my children, as Enoch commanded his son in the first jubilees. While he was living in its seventh generation, he commanded and testified to his children and grandchildren until the day of his death." The words of Noah may be based in part on sections of *1 Enoch* 81–82. There, while he is back at home with his son Methuselah for one year before his permanent departure, he speaks about various, especially calendrical subjects, but does not deal with the season of the year when the trees ripen and produce their fruit (82:18–19). To this point in the tradition Enoch has not been associated with very many legal issues apart from the calendar. Here a more specific law is credited to him. *Jub.* 21:10 finds Abraham citing the words of Enoch and Noah as the authorities for the sundry sacrificial laws that occupy chapter 21, verses 6–10. It is worth noting that in both of these halakhic passages Enoch and Noah appear together: in the first the law is stated by Noah, and in the second both are the authorities for legislation. It may be that the author of *Aramaic Levi* has traditions such as these in mind when he talks about Enoch's accusations. The last words in *Jub.* 7:39 are peculiar in the extreme for someone so well versed in the biblical and Enochic tradition as the author of *Jubilees*. He writes of the patriarch's death — something that is found in no source before this time and which stands in direct contradiction to *Jub.* 4:23–25.

Finally, Enoch appears in *Jub.* 10:17, in which once more he and Noah are paired. Just before this we read that Noah died at age 950: he "lived longer on the earth than (other) people except Enoch because of his righteousness in which he was perfect ([i.e.,] in his righteousness); because Enoch's work was something created as a testimony for the generations of eternity so that he should report all deeds throughout generation after generation on the day of judgment." Noah lived far longer than the 120-year limitation imposed on humanity in Gen. 6:3. The writer explains here that he lived for such a long time because of his righteousness. He outlived all others except Enoch. Enoch, though he is credited with a mere 365 years in Gen. 5, did not die at that point but, as the sequel notes, continues to live and to report human activity until the end. Here, too, we meet the familiar association of Enoch and testifying in *Jubilees*.

Another unmistakable way in which the Enoch tradition influenced *Jubilees* is through the watcher story, in which angels married women and produced giants as children. It was noted that *Jub.* 4:15 ascribes to the watchers a positive reason for descending ("to teach mankind and to do what is just and upright upon the earth") and that *Jub.* 4:22 speaks of

118

his testifying against the watchers, but the major treatments of the story come later in the book (just as Gen. 6:1–4 follows Gen. 5:21–24). The passages in question are *Jub.* 5:1–10, 7:20–25, and 10:1–11. It will be useful to set out the principal elements in parallel columns with the two most extended versions of the story in *1 Enoch* chapters 6–16 and 86:1–89:6:[17]

1 Enoch 6–16	*1 Enoch* 86–89	*Jubilees*
A. Angels lust in heaven (6:2)	A.	A.
B. The oath (6:2–6)	B.	B.
C. Descent in the days of Jared (6:6)	C. A star (Asael) falls (86:1)	C. Descent in the days of Jared to teach and do what is right (4:15)
D. Marriages with women and illicit teachings (7:1; 8:1, 3)	D. Fall of many stars and marriages (86:3)	D. Marriages with women (5:1; 4:22)
E. The women give birth to giants (7:2)	E. Birth of elephants, camels, and asses (86:4)	E. The women give birth to giants (5:1; 7:22)
F. Violence, sexual sins, and various other kinds of evil result (7:3–6; 8:2, 4; 9:6–10, etc.)	E. Violence, sexual sins, and various other kinds of evil result (86:5–87:1)	F. Violence, sexual sins, and various other kinds of evil result (5:2–3; 7:21, 23–24)
G. The heavenly angels see all of this and tell God (9:1–11)	G.	G. God himself sees (5:3 = Gen. 6:12)
H. Punishments are announced by God (10) and carried out by angels	H. Punishments by angels (88:1–3)	H. God punishes (5:4, 6, 7–10), as do the angels (5:6)
1. Binding of Asael in nether places (10:4–6)	1. Binding of the first star and throwing him into an abyss (88:1)	1. Binding of the angels in nether places (5:6)
2. The giants kill one another as their	2. Elephants, camels, and asses kill one	2. The giants kill one another as their

| fathers watch (10:9; 14:6) | another (88:2) | fathers watch (5:7, 9, 10; cf. 7:22) |

There are several minor differences between the three accounts, but some major distinctions should be underscored. First, *1 Enoch* 6 locates the initial sin of lust in heaven; chapter 86, verse 1, refers only to the falling star without naming a reason for the fall; and *Jub.* 4:15 and 5:6 relate that God sent the watchers to the earth for positive reasons. Second, *1 Enoch* 6–16 combine the motifs of violence and illicit teachings, which take place after the angels have sinned with the women. The versions presented in columns 2 and 3 lack the instructional theme: violence and sexual immorality are the consequences of the marriages. *Jubilees* mentions righteous teaching as part of the original purpose, but it does not figure in the story once the angels have descended. Oddly enough, the author does refer to it but at a different point: in *Jub.* 8:1–4 Kainan (a postdiluvian patriarch) discovers an inscription that contains the watchers' teachings about the sun, moon, and stars. The context imposes a negative evaluation on these teachings. Therefore, the author knows the theme of the watchers' teaching but chose not to treat it within the story. Third, *1 Enoch* 12–16 and *Jubilees* know of a third generation, as it were: the evil spirits that emanate from the giants' corpses (*1 Enoch*) or were fathered by the watchers (*Jub.* 10:5). In *1 Enoch* the entire group of these evil spirits exercises its nefarious influence on humanity, whereas in *Jubilees* they do this only at the beginning. After Noah prays, however, nine-tenths of them are restrained and only one-tenth are allowed to mislead people. The version in the Animal Apocalypse lacks this element altogether. Fourth, the versions in the Animal Apocalypse and in *Jubilees* name different types of giants: they are elephants, camels, and asses in the Apocalypse; *Jubilees* names giant, *naphil*, and *elyo*. The texts of *1 Enoch* 6–16 lack these classes, although Syncellus, the Byzantine historian, includes the names found in *Jubilees* in his version of *1 Enoch* 7:1–2.

The author of *Jubilees*, then, knows and borrows much from the earlier Enochic works but nuances their themes to a certain extent so that they conform more nearly to the concerns expressed in his book. *Jubilees* is, unlike *1 Enoch*, tied directly to the full text of Genesis. This means that the writer could not downplay the importance of the Fall in Gen. 3 as drastically as the Enochic writers did. It may also have been difficult for him to imagine that the angels could have lusted after women from their heavenly home. Possibly, too, some of the blame is removed from the angels and switched to the women: it was when the angels, who were already on the earth, saw how beautiful they were that they married the daughters of men.[18] This shift of blame from the angels to the women will be met in other writings such as *Testament of Reuben* 5 and in Tertullian.

E. ENOCH AT QUMRAN

1. INTRODUCTION

The literary remains of the Qumran community have greatly enriched our knowledge of the Enoch literature and also of at least one setting in which that literature was known, valued, and copied. The earliest members of that exiled group may have established themselves at Qumran on the northwest shore of the Dead Sea in approximately 150 B.C.E. By that time all the Enochic booklets that have been studied in earlier sections — the AB, BW, EE, and the BD — had been composed. Copies of all these works have been found in cave 4 at Qumran, and in some cases there is evidence that more than one booklet was copied on a single scroll: Milik maintains that 4QEnoch^c included the BW, the Book of Giants, the BD, and the EE. Presumably, copies of these older works were brought to Qumran, where additional copies were made.

4QEnastr^a	end of third/beginning of second century B.C.E.
4QEnastr^b	early years C.E.
4QEnastr^c	mid-first century B.C.E.
4QEnastr^d	second half of first century B.C.E.
4QEnoch^a	first half of second century B.C.E.
4QEnoch^b	mid-second century B.C.E.
4QEnoch^c	last third of first century B.C.E.
4QEnoch^d	last third of first century B.C.E.
4QEnoch^e	first half of first century B.C.E.
4QEnoch^f	third quarter of second century B.C.E.
4QEnoch^g	mid-first century B.C.E.[19]

---

18. See Dimant, " 'Fallen Angels,' " 171.
19. The dates are from Milik, *Books of Enoch*, 7 (for the AB copies; see also 273–74), 140 (for copy a), 164 (for copy b), 178 (for copy c), 217 (for copy d), 225 (for copy e), 224 (for copy f), and 246 (for copy g).

There is good reason for thinking that the central Enochic theme of the angelic sin found ready acceptance at Qumran because it is mentioned in several of the texts that were left in the caves. The *Book of Jubilees*, represented on fifteen or sixteen copies at Qumran, has already been treated. It devotes a lengthy section to the watcher story and offers a positive explanation for the original descent of the angels.

2. THE *DAMASCUS DOCUMENT*

The *Damascus Document*, which preaches to and legislates for the Essene communities in towns of Judea and which is also found in multiple copies in the Qumran caves, appeals to the angel story in its hortatory sections. In speaking about the fact that people have fallen into error through lust, the author cites the myth:

> Hear now, my sons, and I will uncover your eyes that you may see and understand the works of God, that you may choose that which pleases Him and reject that which He hates, that you may walk perfectly in all His ways and not follow after thoughts of the guilty inclination and after eyes of lust. For through them, great men have gone astray and mighty heroes have stumbled from former times till now. Because they walked in the stubbornness of their heart the Heavenly Watchers fell; they were caught because they did not keep the commandments of God. And their sons also fell who were tall as cedar trees and whose bodies were like mountains. All flesh on dry land perished; they were as though they had never been because they did their own will and did not keep the commandment of their Maker so that His wrath was kindled against them. Through it, the children of Noah went astray, together with their kin, and were cut off. (2:14–3:1)[20]

It is interesting that the story, including the angels and their enormous children ("tall as cedar trees and whose bodies were like mountains") becomes an element of moral persuasion. Presumably, that was the purpose for the versions of this story in the earlier Enochic booklets, but the point is not explicit. Here, moreover, the sexual transgressions of the angels (which stems from their stubbornness of heart) have been commit-

---

20. Translation of G. Vermes, *The Dead Sea Scrolls in English*, 3d ed. (Sheffield: JSOT Press, 1987), 84.

ted against the "commandments of God." The same was true in *1 Enoch* of those who lived before the flood, in that they violated the Noachic laws.

3. 4Q180–4Q181

A second text that deals with the watcher theme is 4Q180, while another related one—4Q181—may also make mention of it. The first of these texts begins with "Pesher concerning the periods made by God."[21] It goes on to maintain that God arranged the actions of each period before creation and that such information is now engraved on the tablets of heaven (ll. 2–4). After an apparent reference to the ten generations from Noah's son Shem to Abraham's son Isaac, there is a blank space. When the text resumes it says:

7 [And] Pesher concerning ʿAzazʾel and the Angels "wh[o went in to the daughters of men]
8 [and] they [gave] birth to giants for them." And concerning ʿAzazʾel [who led them astray to deceit]
9 [to love] iniquity and to cause to inherit wickedness, all their Pe[riod for destruction]
10 [with jealou]sy of judgements and the judgement of the council [ ].[22]

The preceding section had indicated that the period in question involved the sons of Noah (see the earlier passage from the *Damascus Document*), and the watchers' influence, according to *1 Enoch* 12–16, continued into their time (see also *Jub.* 7:20–39, 10:1–14). But it should be recalled that Noah's sons were born one hundred years before the flood, so that the activity of Azazel and the angels probably begins then, according to this text.[23] Azazel (Asael), the spelling of whose name probably shows influence from Lev. 16, and the angels are the ones who are singled out for treatment; the preserved parts of the text do not mention Shemihazah. If so, this would be another indication that the situation in *1 Enoch* 12–16 is under consideration, since there only Asael and the angels associ-

21. Translation of Dimant, "The 'Pesher on the Periods' (4Q180) and 181," *Israel Oriental Studies* 9 (1979): 78.
22. Ibid., 79, with slight changes.
23. Ibid., 94–95.

ated with him are involved (see also the Animal Apocalypse). The language in line 8 is a near quotation from Gen. 6:4. Here the verse is interpreted, as in *1 Enoch* 6–16, to refer to the marriages between angels and women which produced gigantic children. The term *gibbôrîm* in Gen. 6:4 is made the object of the verb in line 8, not part of a phrase explaining who the children were, as in Genesis. As Dimant understands the sequel, Azazel alone is charged with misleading humanity into wicked ways throughout the period in question. The gap in the line prevents us from knowing whether his angelic colleagues were also charged with this crime. The tenth line makes it sufficiently clear that punishment is in store for the guilty ones. The general presentation in the fragment resembles what the Apocalypse of Weeks says about the second week: it mentions the great evil that will then arise, deceit, the first end, salvation of a man, and ensuing evil of still greater magnitude. After this a law is made for the sinners (*1 Enoch* 93:4).

4Q181 alludes to the same Genesis text as 4Q180, but its relation to the watcher story is less clear. It begins thus:

1 [To Abraha]m [until he bego]t Isaac, [the Ten Generations 'Aza-
z'el and the Angels who came to]
2 [the daughters of] men and [they] gave birth to giant[s] for
them [   ]
3 Israel. In the seventy weeks [   ].[24]

It is a pity, in light of the importance that attaches to the number 70 in the BW, the Apocalypse of Weeks, and the Animal Apocalypse, that the connection between the seventy weeks in line 3 and the preceding is not evident. The phrasing of line 2 shows that Gen. 6:4 is being quoted nearly verbatim, just as in 4Q180. What more the text may have said about this episode is lost.

Another fragment of the same document contains a few hints that the watcher story may be in the author's mind, but here also the text is too broken to understand the train of thought.

1 . . . for guilt in a community with a counc[il] of shamef[ulness]
to wal[l]ow in the sin of mankind and for great judgement and
grave diseases
2 of the flesh. Corresponding to God's great deeds, and in accordance with their wickedness, corresponding to the council of their

---

24. Ibid., 86, with slight changes.

impurity, he takes the sons of he[aven] and earth to a community of wickedness until
3 its end.[25]

If, in fact, "the sons of he[aven]" is to be read (there is virtually nothing left of the word *heaven*), these would probably be angels, since "sons of heaven" is one of the titles used in *1 Enoch* for the angels. Mention of them in a context in which impurity and sin are also present is suggestive of the Enochic watcher story.[26]

4. THE *BOOK OF GIANTS*

In presenting the information (see sec. 1) about copies of the booklets of Enoch found in Qumran cave 4, the title the *Book of Giants* appeared. This is another of the important contributions that the Qumran texts have made to our knowledge of the Enochic literary tradition. The *Book of Giants* was known before the Qumran texts were discovered through much later, fragmentary versions in a stunning variety of Asiatic languages. A book by this name was one of the authoritative texts in the Manichaean religion, a syncretistic blend of elements found in various other faiths such as Judaism, Christianity, and Zoroastrianism. The Manichaean *Book of Giants* is now known to be based closely on the Jewish work that has surfaced in cave 4. The founder of Manichaeism, Mani (216–77 C.E.), spent time as a young man living among the Elchasaites, a Jewish-Christian group that used extrabiblical Jewish texts. It may be that, while he was a part of this group, Mani came into contact with the Jewish version of the *Book of Giants* and revised it for his own edification and that of his followers.

Milik has identified a surprisingly large number of fragmentary copies of the *Book of Giants* in the Qumran corpus. There are two from cave 1 (1Q23–24), one from cave 2 (2Q26), and five from cave 4 (4Q203, 530–33). Milik thinks that 4Q203 (4QEnochGiants[a]) was part of one of the Enoch manuscripts (4QEnoch[c]), a text from the second half of the first century B.C.E.).[27] If we combine the evidence of these fragmentary remains, something of a story line emerges, one that can be supplemented

---

25. Ibid., 87, with changes.
26. Ibid., 101.
27. *Books of Enoch*, 58.

from other sources for the *Book of Giants*.[28] The reconstruction of the existing material given here is based on the recent work of J. Reeves.[29]

What appears to be the first part begins with language strongly reminiscent of *1 Enoch* 6–16.

1. . . . they became defiled . . .
2. . . . Giants and Nephilim . . .
3. . . . they begat, and behold, all . . .
4. . . . its blood (?) and by means of tu[rmoil (?) . . .
5. . . . for it was not enough for them . . .
6. . . . and they sought to consume much . . .
7. . . . [empty]
8. . . . the Nephilim smote it . . .
9. . . . and they knew . . . much . . . upon earth . . . and they killed many . . . Giants . . . which [30]

It appears that the writer is detailing the results of the angels' descent: impurity, children of unusual character, perhaps bloodshed, the rapacious appetites of the giants, and a battle between the giants.

The order of the following fragments is uncertain, but, as Reeves arranges them, the next section mentions Enoch: the text may be saying that information about the calamities on earth were revealed to Enoch. A flood is mentioned, and, later, reference is made to a cry against the killers.[31] There follow, it seems, parts of a prayer for God's intervention, as in *1 Enoch* 9. A major section then introduces an important theme that is new relative to *1 Enoch*. Two of the giants, the children of the watchers, have a dream, and they tell their dreams to the other giants. The dream of at least one has to do with a garden that was tended and which produced plants. Water and fire are also mentioned. The dreams puzzle the other giants. They apparently decide that Enoch, the distinguished scribe, should be consulted regarding the dreams' meanings. 'Ohyah, he brother of the first dreamer, then relates that he saw the ruler of heaven descend to earth in his dream. When he finished, the giants were afraid.

---

28. See ibid., 58–59, 310–17.
29. *Jewish Lore in Manichaean Cosmogony: Studies in the* Book of Giants *Traditions*, Monographs of the Hebrew Union College 14 (Cincinnati: HUC Press, 1992).
30. Ibid., 62.
31. Ibid.

21. . . . and] they [sum]moned Mahaway, and he came to . . .
Giants, and they sent him to Enoch
22. . . . and they said to him, Go . . . to you that
23. . . . you have heard his voice, and say to him . . . the
dreams.[32]

The situation reminds one of *1 Enoch* 106–7, in which Lamech sends
Methuselah to the distant Enoch to ascertain the paternity of his remarkable son Noah.

The messenger Mahaway carries out his mission. He flies (riding on a
bird?) to Enoch and presents to him some sort of proof or authorized
message from the giants. He asks Enoch for the interpretation of the
dreams that he relates to him. We learn later that Mahaway the messenger is the son of Baraq'el, one of the watchers who descended with
Shemihazah (*1 Enoch* 6:7). There is some unclear talk about a first and
second tablet and another mention of Enoch as a scribe. It seems that
the message or interpretation of the dreams which Enoch gives is stated
in a series of partially preserved lines. He condemns Shemihazah and, it
seems, his associates; he also mentions their wives and sons, their fornication, and complaints concerning the actions of the sons. This has reached
Raphael, one of the angels who executes the punishment in *1 Enoch* 10.
There is also a command that prisoners be freed and prayers be offered.[33]

Later 'Ohyah again seems to be describing a dream in which he is
unable to defeat some heavenly forces. The text becomes too fragmentary to follow, but it does appear that the giants weep. Mention is made
of Azazel and of imprisoning someone.

The *Book of Giants*, then, insofar as it is now known, builds upon the
watcher story in *1 Enoch* 6–16 (it names the leading characters and at
least mentions the principal events) but shifts the focus from the first
generation of angelic sinners to their enormous children. The leading
angel, Shemihazah, is the father of 'Ohyah and Hahyah, while Baraq'el,
another of the prominent watchers, is the father of Mahaway.[34] The
story of the dreams that the giant brothers had and the mission by Mahaway to Enoch combine motifs found in *1 Enoch* 12–16 and 106–7 (see
Gen. Apoc. 2). Like the watchers who sent a petition through Enoch but
received a divine message of doom from him, the giants here send to

---

32. Ibid., 63.
33. Ibid., 64–65.
34. See ibid., 86.

him for the interpretation of dreams and receive a message of destruction in return. The book elaborates an earlier tradition and shows that the doom of the giants to mutual slaughter—a theme treated only briefly in *1 Enoch*—also was announced beforehand through Enoch, just as the punishment of their fathers was. In this way the writer ties Enoch even more closely to the story line than the author of *1 Enoch* 12–16 did.

5. 4Q227 FRAGMENT 2 *(PSEUDO-JUBILEES)*

When he published most of the Aramaic fragments of Enoch from Qumran cave 4, Milik situated them by adducing and studying references to Enoch in other Qumran texts and elsewhere. Among the Qumran texts that he presented was a small fragment that has some obvious similarities with *Jubilees'* section about Enoch. Because it is not an actual text of *Jubilees* but is definitely related to it, Milik designated this text (and two others, 4Q225–26) as *Pseudo-Jubilees*. The second fragment of 4Q227 reads as follows:

1. [E]noch after we taught him
2. [   ] six jubilees of years
3. [the ea]rth among the sons of mankind. And he testified against all of them.
4. [   ] and also against the watchers. And he wrote all the
5. [   ] sky and the paths of their host and the [mon]ths
6. [   ] s]o that the ri[ghteous] should not err.[35]

The script dates the fragment to the last third of the first century B.C.E. The first line preserves three of the four letters in the Hebrew spelling of the name Enoch and a verb that should be translated "they taught him." However, another scribe has added a letter above the line that makes it read "we taught him." The change brings the line into harmony with the setting in *Jubilees*, in which an angel of the presence reveals the contents of the book to Moses but at various times refers, in the first-person plural, to himself and his colleagues. One of those passages is in *Jub.* 4:18 ("as we told him"), in which Enoch's astronomical

---

35. *Books of Enoch*, 12; See now Milik and VanderKam's offical edition in J. VanderKam, consulting ed., *Qumran Cave 4, VIII: Parabiblical Texts, Part I*, DJD XIII (Oxford: Clarendon, 1994), 171–75.

teachings are rehearsed (see ll. 4–5 in this fragment). *Jub.* 4:23 is similar: "we led him." The impression that the corrected version reflects the setting of *Jubilees* is strengthened by the next line, of which only the words *six jubilees of years* have survived. This is the very expression used in *Jub.* 4:21 to indicate the amount of time that Enoch spent with the angels after the birth of Methuselah: "He was, moreover, with God's angels for six jubilees of years." The third line, as *Jubilees* often does, turns to the testifying work of Enoch. The line finds close parallels in *Jub.* 4:18 ("He testified to mankind in the generations of the earth"); 4:19 ("He wrote a testimony for himself and placed it upon the earth against all mankind and for their history"); and 4:22 ("Enoch testified against all of them"). This last passage relates to the watchers. The watchers appear in line 4, in which the context implies that Enoch is testifying against these angels. It also draws attention to the fact that he wrote something completely. Line 5 may be read as telling us what he wrote: information about something in the sky, the courses of the stars, and the months. These subjects come under consideration in *Jub.* 4:17–18 and 21. The final preserved line gives a reason, apparently, for having correct calendrical data: so that the righteous should not err. *Jub.* 4:17 states that Enoch "wrote down in a book the signs of the sky in accord with the fixed pattern of their months so that mankind would know the seasons of the years according to the fixed patterns of each of their months." These topics are, of course, treated in greater detail in the AB, in which, for example, chapter 82, verse 4, says: "Blessed are all the righteous, blessed are all those who walk in the way of righteousness, and do not sin like the sinners in the numbering of all their days in which the sun journeys in heaven."

6. OTHER TEXTS

We have already noted that a number of the calendrical texts found at Qumran juxtapose and harmonize a solar calendar of 364 days and a lunar calendar of 354 days. The documents follow the procedure found in the AB, in which Uriel reveals to Enoch first the solar then the lunar year.[36] We have also seen that, by having both systems, the AB and Qumran calendars disagree with *Jubilees*, which sets forth the solar calendar of 364 days as something revealed to Enoch and condemns those

---

36. *Books of Enoch*, 62–64, gives a quick summary of the data from some of the calendrical texts.

who employ lunar calculations that inevitably result in mixing sacred and secular days.[37]

F. THE WISDOM OF SOLOMON

The witness about Enoch supplied by Sirach and Pseudo-Eupolemus is more modest, more subdued, than the picture that emerges from the Enochic booklets and from other Qumran texts. Though they go beyond the meager biblical givens, they stop well short of presenting the full Enochic image that is found in the AB and the BW. In the first century B.C.E. (or C.E.) the writer of the Wisdom of Solomon did the same. In this learned composition Enoch puts in an appearance, but it is brief, and he is never named. This last point loses much of its force when we remember that Wisdom fails to name any of its characters (including Solomon), but the brevity and allusive character of the Enoch section show that he was not at the heart of the author's concerns.

The pertinent section belongs within Wisdom 1:1–6:21, the first major unit in the book. There the fundamental issues of justice and immortality receive creative treatment. In this profound section the writer underscores several major points by contrasting a righteous person and a group of wicked opponents (1:16–5:23). The righteous individual suffers, while the evil triumph. Yet their victory soon proves illusory when the righteous one who suffered and died is vindicated by God, and the seemingly successful wicked people are stunned when they realize that they have thoroughly misread the situation.

One theme that the writer underscores repeatedly throughout the righteous-wicked conflict is the misleading character of appearances (as Enoch does in the EE). He maintains that an undefiled but barren woman and a virtuous eunuch are more blessed than adulterers surrounded by children. Childlessness with virtue outranks illicit fertility. The results, in the author's estimation, prove the point (3:13–4:6). This note of reversal or false appearances continues in the next pericope, in which Enoch plays his indirect role. In it the problem of a short life engages the writer. He argues that the righteous who die early are at rest and that old age is actually a qualitative, not a quantitative, phenomenon:

---

37. The name Enoch appears in three other Qumran texts: 5Q13 2; 3Q14 7:1 (Milik's reading; see *Books of Enoch*, 61); and 4Q243 fragment 9. In none of these texts is there enough context to understand why he is named.

"but understanding is gray hair for anyone, and a blameless life is ripe old age" (4:9).

There were some who pleased God and were loved by him,
and while living among sinners were taken up.
They were caught up so that evil might not change their understanding
or guile deceive their souls.
For the fascination of wickedness obscures what is good,
and roving desire perverts the innocent mind.
Being perfected in a short time.
    they fulfilled long years;
for their souls were pleasing to the Lord,
therefore he took them quickly from the midst of wickedness.
Yet the peoples saw and did not understand,
or take such a thing to heart,
that God's grace and mercy are with his elect,
and that he watches over his holy ones.
(4:10–15)

There can be little doubt that Enoch is in the writer's mind in these verses.[38] He would have known the Greek translation of Genesis, in which Enoch pleased God (rather than walked with the 'elohîm, as in the Hebrew). Enoch was unique among the patriarchs in Gen. 5 in that he lived only 365 years, whereas every other one lived centuries longer (the shortest-lived, Lamech, lived 777 years, 412 years longer than Enoch). He thus becomes an example of a righteous person, one pleasing to God, who dies before his time. Though the wicked may construe a relatively brief life as God's punishment on such people, the truth is far different. God removed them to protect them from the corrosive effects of wick-edness. People such as Enoch were perfected in a short time and therefore taken quickly. It is interesting that, while Enoch is a model, the possibility is entertained that a righteous person of his caliber would be misled. This is an idea that will resurface in Philo and rabbinic litera-ture. It is also intriguing that Enoch is one member of a larger group— some who pleased God. Whatever may be the meaning of the various allusions in these verses, it is clear that the author of Wisdom needed no

---

38. See D. Winston, *The Wisdom of Solomon*, AB 43 (Garden City, N.Y.: Double-day, 1979), 139–40.

more information than what the Greek translation of Genesis supplied in order to make of Enoch an example of mistaken appearances. He was the quintessential model of a person whose virtue could not be impugned but whose life was nevertheless surprisingly short. A personal trait of Enoch here becomes an eloquent example in a moral discourse.

G. THE SIMILITUDES (PARABLES) OF ENOCH
(1 ENOCH 37–71)

While Sirach, Pseudo-Eupolemus, and Wisdom belong to the modest consumers of Enochic traditions, the Similitudes of Enoch are remarkably different. They are the longest part of the present collection of booklets that go under the name *1 Enoch*. They have exercised a certain fascination for students of the New Testament Gospels because in them a major character is called "Son of man," a title or epithet used by Jesus in the Gospels.[39] Some New Testament scholars have maintained that the use of this term in the Gospels, especially Matthew,[40] is indebted in some way to the Enochic usage of "Son of man" for a superhuman judge of the end time, while others, for various reasons, have held that the two—*1 Enoch* 37–71 and the Gospels—are independent of each other in their employment of the peculiar phrase. According to some scholars, the Similitudes were written later than the New Testament Gospels. Milik has been the most extreme proponent of this approach. He has argued that the Similitudes are a Christian composition that displaced the *Book of Giants* from the second position in *1 Enoch* and that they were written not far from 270 C.E.[41] His view has not carried the day. Rather, the contemporary debate has turned around two options: the Similitudes were composed in the first century B.C.E. or the first (possibly the beginning of the second) century C.E.[42]

In recent decades the Similitudes have attracted renewed interest because of the Qumran evidence. The present composite book *1 Enoch* has

---

39. For a survey of the material and reactions to it, see G. W. E. Nickelsburg, "Son of Man," in *ABD* 6.137–50; cf. also J. Donahue, "Recent Studies on the Origin of 'Son of Man' in the Gospels," *CBQ* 48 (1986): 584–607.
40. For the title "son of man" in Matthew, see 10:23; 13:37, 41; 16:13, 27–28; 19:28; 24:30–44; 25:31; 26:2, 24, 45, 64.
41. *Books of Enoch*, 89–107.
42. See VanderKam, "Some Major Issues in the Contemporary Study of 1 Enoch: Reflections on J. T. Milik's *The Books of Enoch: Aramaic Fragments of Qumrân Cave 4*," *Maarav* 3 (1982): 85–97.

five parts, and fragments of all of these parts have surfaced in Qumran cave 4, except the Similitudes. We could attribute this fact to chance were it not the case that the Similitudes are the longest part of the collection and therefore statistically more likely to be represented than any other part. What is the explanation for this absence from the caves of Qumran? We do not know the answer. Some scholars have spotted what they take to be differences of opinion between parts of the Similitudes and the teachings of the scrolls. Whether this is an accurate reading of the situation is open to question. It is possible that the Similitudes were composed in another kind of Jewish community that also valued the writings and person of Enoch.

For the present purposes the subject of most interest is the presentation of Enoch himself in the Similitudes. The text introduces him at the beginning and sets him at center stage throughout, right to the end of chapter 71. Here we find the traditional association of Enoch with the end of time, but now his role during the last days and the judgment is greatly expanded and new titles or epithets are attributed to him. It is extremely difficult to imagine that a Christian could have written this book, which credits Enoch with a major role assigned to Jesus in Christian eschatology.

1 Enoch 37 is an introductory chapter that refers to what follows as a "second vision which he saw, the vision of wisdom which Enoch, the son of Jared, the son of Malalel, the son of Cainan, the son of Enosh, the son of Seth, the son of Adam, saw." Milik thinks that this "second vision" is meant to contrast the book with the earlier revelations in the Aramaic and Greek versions of Enoch's writings—the AB, BW, *Book of Giants*, BD, and the EE.[43] Presumably, the book is being distinguished from older visions, but there is nothing in the text to inform us what those first visions were. If we take seriously the position the book now occupies in *1 Enoch*, a logical suggestion is that it differentiates this book from *1 Enoch* 1–36, which is called a vision in chapter 1, verse 2. It should be added that both the BW and the Similitudes introduce Enoch's address as his parable (1:2 [in one Greek version and in Aramaic]; 37:5). The writer immediately comments that Enoch's vision is characterized by wisdom, and wisdom becomes a prominent motif here (see vv. 2–4), as it is in the EE. The reverse genealogy reproduces the one found in Gen. 5. By citing it, no question (if there was one) about which Enoch was intended or about his antiquity would remain unanswered. *1 Enoch* 1 had neglected to spell out who Enoch was, and even the reference to Jared

---

43. *Books of Enoch*, 89.

and Noah in chapters 6 and 10 did not bring these patriarchs into direct connection with him. Now his identity is clearly established.[44] Enoch addresses his wise words to a broad audience: "I raised (my voice) to speak *and say* to those who dwell on the dry ground. *Hear,* you men of old, and see, you who come after, the words of the Holy One which I will speak before the Lord of Spirits" (37:2). Enoch claims to be speaking God's words and calls the deity by two titles. "The Holy One" had been used already in *1 Enoch* 1:3, and "the Lord of Spirits" becomes a frequent designation in the Similitudes. It is very likely that the writer employs it as a replacement for or rephrasing of the scriptural "the Lord of hosts." Evidence for this comes from a passage such as *1 Enoch* 39:12: "Those who do not sleep bless you, and they stand before your glory and bless and praise and exalt, saying: 'Holy, holy, holy, Lord of Spirits; he fills the earth with spirits.' " Whereas Isa. 6:3 has the Seraphim say "Holy, holy, holy is the Lord of hosts; the whole earth is full of his glory," the author of the Similitudes, whose universe is densely populated with spiritual beings, introduces *spirits* at two places in the verse: "the Lord of hosts," that is, the Lord of the heavenly armies, becomes "Lord of Spirits," and "his glory" becomes "spirits."[45]

Enoch himself announces to the reader that the revelation to him was divided into three "parables," and in fact the book does fall into three such units: Parable 1 is found in chapters 38–44, parable 2 in 45–57, and parable 3 in 58–69. These divisions are not left to the reader's discretion; they are explicit in the book. The three are meant for all people, for all who dwell on the earth.

A principal theme that runs throughout the Similitudes of Enoch, as it does in the EE and Wisdom, is the notion of reversal. At the present time the righteous are the oppressed, while the sinners, the kings, and the mighty are the ones who afflict them and seem to have far the better share. Enoch exhorts those righteous people to hold fast and gives them a revealed glimpse behind the scenes of the universe so that they can see what the situation actually is. The final judgment will be the time when all wrongs are made right, when the virtuous are rewarded and the evil are punished in just measure.

When the community of the righteous appears, and the sinners are judged for their sins and are driven from the face of the dry ground, and when the Righteous One appears before the chosen

---

44. See Black, *Book of Enoch*, 194.
45. Ibid., 189–92.

righteous whose works are weighed by the Lord of Spirits, and (when) light appears to the righteous and chosen who dwell on the dry ground, where (will be) the dwelling of the sinners, and where the resting-place of those who have denied the Lord of Spirits? It would have been better for them if they had not been born. And when the secrets of the righteous are revealed, the sinners will be judged and the impious driven from the presence of the righteous and the chosen. And from then on those who possess the earth will not be mighty and exalted, nor will they be able to look at the face of the holy ones for the light of the Lord of Spirits will have appeared on the face of the holy, the righteous, and the chosen. And the mighty kings will at that time be destroyed and given into the hand of the righteous and the holy. And from then on no one will (be able to) seek mercy from the Lord of Spirits, for their life will be at an end. (chap. 38)

This citation from the beginning of the first parable already introduces many of the cast of characters in the book. It should be noticed that the righteous ones, who are mentioned frequently and who probably form the writer's community, are related in some way to a corresponding righteous one[46] who is to appear before them. This is one of four titles used in the Similitudes of Enoch for an extraordinary figure who is finally identified as Enoch himself. The apotheosis that he experiences in this text is truly remarkable, one that will be difficult to match in the ensuing tradition.

The four titles that are applied to a leader (or leaders) at the end of time are: righteous one, anointed one (messiah), chosen one, and Son of man.[47] This last expression is formulated in three different ways in the Ethiopic text—the only extant form of Enoch's Similitudes. The first two of these four epithets occur infrequently, while the latter two are very prominent in large stretches of the work.

There is one passage in which the first of these, "righteous one," is the correct reading of the text, and the reference is to an eschatological leader. In *1 Enoch* 53 Enoch sees sinners devouring the produce of the

---

46. At least this is true in Knibb's translation. The word *righteousness* has better manuscript support in 38:2 than the term *righteous one*, which he reads.

47. For more detailed analysis of the material for the four titles, see VanderKam, "Righteous One, Messiah, Chosen One, and Son of Man in 1 Enoch 37–71," in *The Messiah: Developments in Earliest Judaism and Christianity*, edited by J. H. Charlesworth (Minneapolis: Fortress Press, 1992), 169–91.

righteous but also notices some angels who were preparing instruments of punishment. Upon asking, he learns that the instruments are for the destruction of the kings and powerful. "And after this the Righteous and Chosen One will cause the house of his congregation to appear; from then on, in the name of the Lord of Spirits, they will not be hindered. And before him these mountains will not be (firm) like the earth, and the hills will be like a spring of water; and the righteous will have rest from the ill-treatment of the sinners" (53:6–7). The context is definitely eschatological: after the punishment of the wicked, the righteous one, who is intimately associated with his community—the righteous ones—makes the house of his congregation appear. The reaction of the earth resembles the biblical descriptions of natural convulsions (mountains writhe and melt, etc.; see Exod. 19:16–18; Mic. 1:3–4) when God descends to earth. In this single certain occurrence of "righteous one" as a title for an end-time leader he is also called the "chosen one." The two are apparently interchangeable titles for the same unnamed individual. It may be that the designation "righteous one" was taken from Isa. 53:11, which says: "The righteous one, my servant, shall make many righteous, and he shall bear their iniquities." The Enochic passage does not say all of this about the righteous one, but the title is the same. This is only one of many borrowings by the author of the Similitudes from 2 Isaiah (Isa. 40–66). The facts that the virtuous people are often termed "the righteous" and that *righteousness* is a very frequent term in the Similitudes probably inclined the writer to chose this title for his eschatological leader of the just community.

The author applies the familiar title "anointed one [Messiah]" to the leader in two passages, *1 Enoch* 48:10 and 52:4, both of which fall within the second parable. The first instance figures in a context in which the blessed fate of the righteous and the dreadful destiny of the wicked are under discussion. The distress of the wicked, who are here identified as the kings and mighty ones, is increased by their punishment at the hands of the righteous. For them there will be no hope: "And on the day of their trouble there will be rest on the earth, and they will fall down before him and will not rise; and there will be no one who will take them with his hands and raise them, for they denied the Lord of Spirits and his Messiah" (48:10). The author here echoes the words of Ps. 2:2: "The kings of the earth set themselves, and the rulers take counsel together, against the Lord and his anointed." Since in the context he is talking about the kings and mighty ones, it may be that those terms suggested the scriptural verse to him.

The only other occurrence of the title is in *1 Enoch* 52:4. There Enoch sees secrets of heaven and earth and a mountain consisting of different metals. When he asks his angelic companion about these phenomena, the latter explains: "All these (things) which you have seen serve the authority of his Messiah, that he may be strong and powerful on the earth." As *1 Enoch* 48:10 and 52:4 are the only passages in the Similitudes in which the anointed one makes an appearance, the title was probably not of great importance to the author, just as *righteous one* plays only a modest role.

The situation is quite different for the title "chosen one." In fifteen or sixteen cases the author resorts to it to describe the eschatological leader of his book. As with *the righteous one* and *the righteous*, the title is at times correlated with its cognate, *the chosen*, who are obviously the community around the chosen one. There is no need to adduce all of the references to him; a few examples should illustrate the functions he performs.

In *1 Enoch* 45:3 the chosen one is introduced into a context in which the ones who deny the Lord of Spirits are under discussion. The writer mentions the punishment that will come to them on "the day of affliction and distress. On that day the Chosen One will sit on the throne of glory, and will choose their works, and their resting-places will be without number." The chosen one does something important on this day of judgment, and his work strengthens the members of his community. In fact, according to *1 Enoch* 45:4, on that day the chosen one will live with them when the Lord transforms the earth to make it a blessing for them. A similar message emerges from *1 Enoch* 51:3. The context talks of earth and Sheol giving up what they had and salvation for the righteous ones: "And in those days the Chosen One will sit on his throne, and all the secrets of wisdom will flow out from the counsel of his mouth, for the Lord of Spirits has appointed him and glorified him." *1 Enoch* 51:5 uses the expression that at this time "the Chosen One will have risen; and the earth will rejoice, and the righteous will dwell upon it, and the chosen will go and walk upon it." These sorts of expressions, some of which are used with respect to God in the Bible (e.g., the throne at the judgment, as in Dan. 7), demonstrate that the chosen one possesses extraordinary status in the scheme of things. In this vein *1 Enoch* 52:6 is eloquent: the extraordinary mountains that Enoch has seen "before the Chosen One will be like wax before the fire." As Black notes,[48] the verse recalls *1 Enoch* 1:6, in which melting mountains accompany God's appearance, and borrows from biblical texts such as Ps. 97:5; Nah. 1:5; and Mic. 1:4. In each of these passages the imagery is used in connection with God's appearance on earth; here it is transferred to the chosen one's arrival.

---

48. *Book of Enoch*, 216.

This chosen one is identified with the righteous one in *1 Enoch* 53:6. The chosen one is even to judge Azazel and his companions (55:4); hence, he comes into contact with the central Enochic myth. References to the chosen one, frequently seated on a throne, are found in all three parables but end with *1 Enoch* 62:1. As with the title "righteous one," "chosen one" is a designation given to the servant of the Lord in the prophecies of 2 Isaiah (41:8, 9; 42:1; 43:10, etc.).

The remarkable uses of the fourth title, "son of man," in the Similitudes have peaked the interest of New Testament scholars, some of whom, as noted, find the Similitudes to be important background information or even a direct source for the Gospels' attribution of this title to Jesus. The title appears sixteen times in the Similitudes (i.e., about the same frequency as "chosen one") and is phrased in three slightly different ways in the Ethiopic text.

Some of the occurrences show clearly the source from which the writer derived the designation. One of the formulations *(walda sab²)* figures in a compact section of the second parable (46:2, 3, 4; 48:2) and is heavily influenced by Dan. 7, in which "one like a son of man" comes with the clouds of heaven to the place of judgment.

And there I saw one who had a head of days, and his head (was) white like wool; and with him (there was) another, whose face had the appearance of a man, and his face (was) full of grace, like one of the holy angels. And I asked one of the holy angels who went with me, and showed me all the secrets, about that Son of Man, who he was, and whence he was, (and) why he went with the Head of Days. And he answered me and said to me: "This is the Son of Man who has righteousness, and with whom righteousness dwells; he will reveal all the treasures of that which is secret, for the Lord of Spirits has chosen him, and through uprightness his lot has surpassed all before the Lord of Spirits forever. And this Son of Man whom you have seen will rouse the kings and the powerful from their resting-places, and the strong from their thrones, and will loose the reins of the strong, and will break the teeth of the sinners. And he will cast down the kings from their thrones and from their kingdoms, for they do not exalt him, and do not praise him, and do not humbly acknowledge whence (their) kingdom was given to them. And he will cast down the faces of the strong, and shame will fill them, and darkness will be their dwelling, and worms will be their resting-place; and they will have no hope of rising from their resting-places, for they do not exalt the name of the Lord of Spirits. (46:1–6)

Readers familiar with Dan. 7 will recognize in the head of days Daniel's *ancient of days*, in the son of man Daniel's *one like a son of man* (thus interpreting the phrase as referring to an individual, not a group), and in the kings and kingdoms parallels to the four kingdoms in Daniel's animal vision. That passage served our author as a fitting source for his description of the last day or day of judgment. So, he borrowed its imagery and shaped it to his own purposes.

The other mention of the son of man in this general context comes in *1 Enoch* 48:2, in which intriguing language is again employed for this eschatological character.

> And at that hour that Son of Man was named in the presence of the Lord of Spirits, and his name (was named) before the Head of Days. Even before the sun and its constellations were created, before the stars of heaven were made, his name was named before the Lord of Spirits. He will be a staff to the righteous and the holy, that they may lean on him and not fall, and he (will be) the light of the nations, and he will be the hope of those who grieve in their hearts. All those who dwell upon the dry ground will fall down and worship before him, and they will bless, and praise, and celebrate with psalms the name of the Lord of Spirits. And because of this he was chosen and hidden before him before the world was created, and for ever. But the wisdom of the Lord of Spirits has revealed him to the holy and the righteous, for he has kept safe the lot of the righteous. (48:2–7a)

The passage indicates that the son of man was in the mind of God before the creation,[49] but he has been revealed to the holy and righteous only much more recently. His eternal naming in the presence of God reminds one somewhat indirectly of Jeremiah's call by God before he was formed in his mother's womb (Jer. 1:5) or of the servant of the Lord who says: "The Lord called me before I was born, while I was in my mother's womb he named me" (Isa. 49:1; cf. also Eph. 1:4–5).[50] This predestined individual is not only the staff and support of the righteous but also the light of the nations. There is no mistaking the author's appeal to the servant of the Lord in 2 Isaiah, in which he is to be a light to the nations (42:6; 49:6). The grieving place their hope in the son of man; indeed,

---

49. Although the case is somewhat different, Prov. 8 speaks of Wisdom as existing at the time of creation and apparently as helping in the process.
50. See *Book of Enoch*, 210.

people will even worship him. In these verses from chapters 46 and 48, therefore, the son of man is depicted in terms drawn primarily from Dan. 7 and the servant passages of 2 Isaiah.

Elsewhere the title *son of man* is applied to one who, like the chosen one, sits on a throne (62:5, 9), while 62:7 talks of his present hiddenness and future unveiling to the chosen. The righteous and chosen will live with that son of man forever (62:14); the sinners, however, are judged and condemned by him (63:11; 69:26–27). The term is used for a figure of the end time who strengthens and supports the righteous and damns the wicked, the kings, and the powerful.

While it would be possible for these four titles in the Similitudes to designate four different eschatological characters, there is evidence in the booklet that requires us to understand all four as referring to a single individual, who turns out to be Enoch himself. In some places two of the terms are applied to the same person. *1 Enoch* 48:6 relates that the son of man was chosen, and chapter 62, in describing the one character, calls him both the chosen one and the son of man (see vv. 1, 3, 5, 7, 9, 14). Also, in this chapter two of the three designations for *son of man* are applied to the individual who is termed the chosen one (the third was used in chap. 48 for the one who is chosen). Then in 52:4 the anointed one is mentioned, while in 52:6 he is said to be the chosen one. And, as noted, the one passage in which *righteous one* occurs names him the chosen one as well (53:6). The various instances of *chosen one* and *son of man* also demonstrate that the eschatological work they do is the same. Both titles are given to the judge at the last trial (e.g., 45:3; 62:5), and the ones who suffer from his verdicts are the kings and powerful people of the earth (53:5–6; 46:4–6; 63:1–11). It is interesting, too, that a description that we might expect with, say, *chosen one* (an epithet for the servant of the Lord in 2 Isaiah) is used for the *son of man: 1 Enoch* 48:4, an example previously adduced, labels the son of man "the light of the nations." It turns out that the two most frequent titles for the eschatological figure in the Similitudes—the chosen one and the son of man—are used in separate blocks of text:

in chapters 38–45 the chosen one
in chapters 46–48 the son of man
in chapters 49–62:1 the chosen one
and in chapters 62:2–71 the son of man.

All of this would perhaps be of some significance in itself, but it becomes important for the present study because Enoch is eventually identified as the son of man in the Similitudes and, therefore, as the righteous one, the chosen one, and the anointed one, since all four titles refer to the same person. The crucial section in this regard is *1 Enoch* 70–71. A number of scholars have argued that these two chapters have been tacked on to the original form of the Similitudes that ended at chapter 69. Two of the key elements in their argument have been that the preexistence of the son of man is difficult to reconcile with the assertion that Enoch is that son of man and that, throughout the Similitudes, Enoch is distinguished from the son of man (whom he sees), only to be identified with him in chapter 71. These points are, however, not convincing; the last two chapters do, in fact, form the natural conclusion of the work. The details of that dispute need not be rehearsed here.[51] For the present purposes it is enough to say that, as the book now stands, chapters 70–71 depict the all-important climactic moments.

In *1 Enoch* 70–71 Enoch first enters paradise (70:2–4); here the verb that is used for his elevation is a form of the one found in Isa. 52:13 for the servant's exaltation from his former lowly status. In the next section Enoch proceeds to the lower heavens (71:1–4) and then moves into the heaven of heavens (71:5–16). For these latter two parts of the ascent the verb is the very one employed in Gen. 5:24 for God's taking of Enoch at the end of his 365 years. In other words, these sections present a sequence regarding the stages through which Enoch achieves his ultimate ascent, his final approach to God at the end of his earthly career. There is some evidence that the Similitudes follow a chronological progression through Enoch's life, beginning with the genealogy in chapter 37. *1 Enoch* 39:3 says that he was carried off by a whirlwind (much like Elijah) to the end of the heavens. This is not his final removal but, rather, the first one (his initial 300-year stay with the angels). All of *1 Enoch* 37–69 seems to be set within those 300 years because Enoch has the time to report about those visions before the final ascent (37:2).

Chapter 71 forms a fitting if mind-boggling conclusion to Enoch's quest for information about who the son of man was (see 46:2). As the spirit carries him to the highest heaven, the divine throne room, he sees innumerable angels and other astounding sights (cf. *1 Enoch* 14–16). But he also sees the head of days, the title used in *1 Enoch* 46 for Daniel's ancient of days. This is a hint that something about the son of man, the title employed in the same chapter in Daniel, is to be disclosed. In the divine presence "that angel came to me, and greeted me with his voice, and said to me: 'You are the Son of Man who was born to righteousness, and righteousness remains over you, and the righteousness of the Head

---

51. For the particulars, cf. VanderKam, "Righteous One, Messiah," 177–85.

of Days will not leave you' " (71:14). The surprise implied by the passage matches the surprise felt by the reader who had not been led to make this identification. With this happy state of affairs, the great problem addressed by the Similitudes finds its reassuring answer. The oppressed righteous have this son of man on their side. "And so there will be length of days with that Son of Man, and the righteous will have peace, and the righteous *will have an upright way*, in the name of the Lord of Spirits for ever and ever" (71:17).

The skillful author of the Similitudes has drawn a portrait of Enoch which derives principally from Dan. 7 (the son of man language) and Isa. 40–55 (the servant of the Lord material). As we should expect, he did not simply copy his sources; he molded them to serve his purposes. One way in which he did this is to understand Daniel's son of man, who will be present at the judgment, as an individual who will do the judging, and another is to interpret 2 Isaiah's suffering servant as God's chosen one, who himself does not suffer but, instead, aids those who belong to him. The Similitudes exhibit less interest in such traditional Enochic themes as the watcher myth. They are far more concerned with the person of Enoch and his value for the righteous, the chosen, who are suffering at present. With this exalted judge of the end time on their side, they will be the ultimate victors.

CHAPTER 5

LATER JEWISH SOURCES

Enoch continued to be a factor in Jewish literature for centuries after the flowering of Enochic booklets and after the books already considered were written. His influence can be tested in different ways. The most obvious one would be to find occurrences of his name apart from simple reproductions of the material in Gen. 5:21–24, and there is an appreciable number of these. A second would be to search for allusions to books that are attributed to Enoch's authorship and that are cited as authorities. These raise interesting questions about which texts constituted an authoritative corpus for various Jewish groups in antiquity—the books that would later be called canonical by Christians. A third and less direct means would be to track a theme having impeccable connections with the ancient Enochic traditions and to see how it was used and modified by later writers. It would be especially helpful if we could isolate a group or several of them who treasured, preserved, and augmented the Enochic traditions. We know that the Qumran Essenes copied, studied, and valued the writings and teachings ascribed to Enoch, and they may have written their own works about Enoch (e.g., 4Q227). Other than this group, however, we do not know of an organized Jewish sect or party that prized the Enochic tradition. In early Christianity some writers clearly ranked the writings and teachings of Enoch at a high level and appealed to them in their compositions.

In the next sections the reader will find a survey of Jewish texts (some with Christian admixtures) in which Enochic influence in one of the senses already described may be documented. The texts are treated in chronological order, insofar as that is possible. As will soon become apparent, however, some of these works are datable only within very wide limits.

A. THE *TESTAMENTS OF THE 12 PATRIARCHS*

The work bearing this title contains twelve sections, each of which reproduces within a narrative framework the last words and testament of one of Jacob's twelve sons. There has been a long and unproductive scholarly debate about whether the Testaments are Jewish works with

143

Christian additions or Christian works that use Jewish traditions. Some date them to the second century B.C.E. (subtracting the obvious Christian glosses), while others see in them a second-century C.E. Christian work. The Dead Sea Scrolls have added some new data to the debate, since the *Aramaic Levi* text, which seems to be a source for the Testament of Levi, and a Testament of Naphtali in Hebrew have been found among them. These fragmentary works at least indicate that such texts existed in the last centuries B.C.E. The *Testaments of the 12 Patriarchs* is, nevertheless, a much larger and more complicated pseudepigraphon than just these two components that have been found at Qumran. None of the other testaments has as yet surfaced in pre-Christian forms. The text is placed here in our survey because it seems more likely that it is a Jewish than a Christian book; at the very least some of its traditions are very old.

There are six references in five testaments to writings of Enoch. Oddly enough, all of the references to Enochic compositions claim that they contained information found in none of our booklets of Enoch.

1. *T. Simeon* 5:4: The dying patriarch says to his children: "For I have seen in a copy of the book of Enoch that your sons will be ruined by promiscuity, and they shall injure with a sword the sons of Levi."[1] Jacob's second oldest son appeals to the book of Enoch just after he has talked about Joseph, who was a model of sexual restraint, and the need to avoid promiscuity. There is, of course, no extant book of Enoch that predicts sexual disaster for Simeon's grandsons. The Animal Apocalypse would be the most likely candidate, but it speaks of Israel's descendants (and thus Simeon's as well) as sheep who are torn apart by wild animals, not as sexually licentious beasts. Various parts of *1 Enoch* do deal with the subject of sexual sins, but not with regard to Simeon's children, nor do they mention injuring Levi's sons (the priests and Levites) with a sword. Yet it should be said that a writer, translator, or copyist found it helpful to make Simeon base his claim on a writing of Enoch. This is the case, regardless whether he invented such a book or whether there is a textual problem here so that a name other than Enoch stood in the original.

2. *T. Levi* 10:5: "For the house which the Lord shall choose shall be called Jerusalem, as the book of Enoch the Righteous maintains."

---

1. All citations of the *Testaments of the 12 Patriarchs* are from H. C. Kee, "Testaments of the Twelve Patriarchs," in *OTP* 1.

Again one might think first of the Animal Apocalypse as the source
for this prediction, but it never mentions the word *Jerusalem*, nor
does any other passage in *1 Enoch*. There are only indirect references to it. This is telling because the point of Levi's remark is the
name itself. The appeal to Enoch occurs in a chapter in which there
is some Christian language (e.g., the phrase "against Christ, the
Savior of the world," in v. 2). Noteworthy here is the epithet "the
Righteous" attached to the name Enoch. The concept of righteousness is often associated with him in the BW, *Jubilees*, and the
Similitudes, as we have seen.

3. *T. Levi* 14:1: "And now, my children, I know from the writings of
   Enoch that in the endtime you will act impiously against the Lord,
   setting your hands to every evil; because of you, your brothers will
   be humiliated and among all the nations you shall become the occasion for scorn." Again there is no clear passage in the extant
   Enochic works to which Levi might be referring. There certainly
   are instances in which a scattering among the nations plays a role,
   but this is never attributed to priestly malfeasance as it is here.

4. *T. Dan* 5:6: "For I read in the Book of Enoch the Righteous that
   your prince is Satan and that all the spirits of sexual promiscuity
   and of arrogance devote attention to the sons of Levi in the attempt
   to observe them closely and cause them to commit sin before the
   Lord." Here, too, we may grant that various sections of *1 Enoch*
   document and warn against such vices, but they do not say that
   Dan's descendants will have Satan as their prince (however interesting this verse may be for the book's evaluation of the tribe of Dan).
   For the second time in the Testaments Enoch is called "the Righteous."

5. *T. Naph.* 4:1: "I say these things, my children, because I have read
   in the writing of holy Enoch that you also will stray from the Lord,
   living in accord with every wickedness of the gentiles and commit-
   ting every lawlessness of Sodom." Unless Naphtali is mingling his
   descendants with all the other children of Jacob who will stray according to the Animal Apocalypse, this is another unattested
   writing. The extant books of Enoch do not deal with Sodom.

6. *T. Ben.* 9:1: "From the words of Enoch the Righteous I tell you
   that you will be sexually promiscuous like the promiscuity of the
   Sodomites and will perish, with few exceptions." Benjamin seems to
   have in mind the same book as Naphtali, although the terms for
   the source (*writing* of holy Enoch in Naphtali, *words* of Enoch the
   Righteous in Benjamin) are not the same.

Besides the allusions to one or several Enochic compositions that may or may not have existed, the Testaments indicate in several other passages an acquaintance with Enochic themes. The watcher theme surfaces in two places. *T. Reub.* 5 makes use of the angel story when the patriarch, who had sinned with Bilhah, his father's concubine, exhorts his sons to great care with regard to women, since "women are evil" (5:1). He warns them about their wiles, and, as he does so, he adduces the watcher story:

> For a woman is not able to coerce a man overtly, but by a harlot's manner she accomplishes her villainy. Accordingly, my children, flee from sexual promiscuity, and order your wives and your daughters not to adorn their heads and their appearances so as to deceive men's sound minds. For every woman who schemes in these ways is destined for eternal punishment. For it was thus that they charmed the Watchers, who were before the Flood. As they continued looking at the women, they were filled with desire for them and perpetrated the act in their minds. Then they were transformed into human males, and while the women were cohabiting with their husbands they appeared to them. Since the women's minds were filled with lust for these apparitions, they gave birth to giants. For the Watchers were disclosed to them as being as high as the heavens. (5:4–6)

Reuben offers a remarkable new perspective on the story: for him the ones at fault are the women whose beauty enticed the angels and who lusted after these extraordinary specimens. Here the giants' size is attributed to the influence of the height in which the angels-become-men appeared to the women. For Reuben the clear implication was that men should be insistent that their wives and daughters not adorn themselves as those prediluvian women did. *1 Enoch* 8:1 reports that Asael taught women about various kinds of adornment, but it does not lay the blame on them. The example is a foretaste of the use to which some early Christian writers will put the watcher myth (see, e.g., Tertullian).

T. Naph. 3 also employs the angel tale. Naphtali orders his children not to alter God's law, just as the sun, moon, and stars do not change their order—a theme met in *1 Enoch* 2–5. The gentiles have idolatrously gone astray from the way prescribed for them, but Naphtali's offspring are to discern the Lord behind created things, "so that you do not become like Sodom, which departed from the order of nature. Likewise the Watchers departed from nature's order; the Lord pronounced a curse on them at the Flood. On their account he ordered that the earth be without dweller or produce" (5:4–5). The point made here reminds one of the emphasis on crossing ordained boundaries in *1 Enoch* 12–16: angels are heavenly and should pray for people, not people—not even Enoch, who could ascend to heaven—for angels, who had left their proper home. Note that here, as in some of the references previously quoted, an Enochic theme is mentioned in the same context as Sodom.

Finally, *T. Ben.* 10:6, at a point at which the dying patriarch speaks about the time when the Lord will reveal his salvation to the nations, mentions Enoch and several other scriptural worthies: "And then you will see Enoch and Seth and Abraham and Isaac and Jacob being raised up at the right hand in great joy." After their resurrection Benjamin and his sons, too, will be raised. As he often is in the Enochic literature, the seventh from Adam is again associated with the end of time.

B. THE *SIBYLLINE ORACLES*

The lengthy collection of Jewish oracles that were modeled on the Greek Sibyllines grew over several centuries. Collins favors the turn of the eras as a date for the Jewish material in the first *Sibylline Oracle*.[2] The initial oracle includes a review of earliest biblical history, and when it reaches the second generation the watchers make a brief but unusual appearance. According to it, God fashioned the second generation "from the most righteous men who were left":

These were concerned with fair deeds, noble pursuits, proud honor, and shrewd wisdom. They practiced skills of all kinds, discovering inventions by their needs. One discovered how to till the earth with plows, another, carpentry, another was concerned with sailing, another, astronomy and divination by birds, another, medicine, again another, magic. Different ones devised that with which they were each concerned, enterprising Watchers, who received this appellation because they had a sleepless mind in their hearts and an insatiable personality. They were mighty, of great form, but nevertheless they went under the dread house of Tartarus guarded by unbreakable bonds to make retribution, to Gehenna of terrible, raging, undying fire. (1.88–103)

The Sibyl's watchers are people, a second generation of humanity which proved to be supremely enterprising and curious. The first advances in

---

2. J. Collins, "Sibylline Oracles," in *OTP* 1.331.

civilization credited to them are positive, yet, as the list moves along, some negative arts—divination and magic—appear. The name *watchers* is explained in an unexpected way: they are unceasingly curious and do not sleep to get rest from their pursuits. They are now imprisoned in the netherworld. As Collins notes, the word *Giants* in 1.123 refers to these watchers whose large size is mentioned ("of great form" [1.100]).[3]

C. PHILO

Philo (ca. 20 B.C.E.–50 C.E.), a Jewish scholar from Alexandria in Egypt, wrote much about the early chapters of Genesis and the characters in them. He consistently found lessons in the stories and individuals as he read the first biblical chapters through the lenses of his own philosophical system. His method of interpretation is usually called *allegory;* the method and the results demonstrate that Philo did not read the text of Genesis in the same way that the authors in the Enochic tradition did.

1. *On the Posterity of Cain and his Exile:* In this treatise Philo discusses, among other topics, how three names figure in both the Cainite and Sethite genealogies in Gen. 4 and 5: Enoch, Methuselah, and Lamech. He observes that these names can have different meanings if they are attached to members of Cain's line or if they are connected with their counterparts in Seth's genealogy. As he deals with the biblical material about the Cainite Enoch, he explains that the name means "your gift/ grace" (35)[4]—a folk etymology achieved by analyzing the consonants of Enoch's Hebrew name as if they were from *ḥen* (grace) with a suffix added. When he comes to our Enoch he writes:

Thy gift is, on some people's lips, an address to the mind within us; on the lips of the better kind of men it is addressed to the universal Mind. Those who assert that everything that is involved in thought or perception or speech is a free gift of their own soul, seeing that they introduce an impious and atheistic opinion, must be assigned to the race of Cain, who, while incapable even of ruling himself, made bold to say that he had full possession of all other

---

3. Ibid., 337 n. i.
4. Translations of *On the Posterity of Cain and His Exile* are taken from F. H. Colson and G. H. Whitaker, *Philo* II, LCL (1927; reprint, Cambridge: Harvard University Press/London: Heinemann, 1979). This etymology was mentioned earlier, in our study of *1 Enoch* 106–7.

things as well. But those who do not claim as their own all that is fair in creation, but acknowledge all as due to the gift of God, being men of real nobility, sprung not from a long line of rich ancestors but from lovers of virtue, must remain enrolled under Seth as the head of their race. This sort is very hard to find, since they make their escape from a life beset with passions and vices, with its treachery and unscrupulousness, its villainy and dissoluteness. For those who have been well-pleasing to God, and whom God has translated and removed from perishable to immortal races, are no more found among the multitude. (42–43)

Philo is working with the Greek text of Genesis and deriving from it moral lessons to edify his audience. Building on his contrived etymology of *Enoch*, he considers him a model of those who properly acknowledge what has been received from God and do not claim it as their own. God has removed people who have this virtue from corrupt forms of life to an imperishable one. This is the meaning of "and he was not found, for God took him," in Gen. 5:24 (LXX). Philo gives no hint here that he knows about the angelic interpretation of the Enoch pericope.

The Alexandrian scholar does, of course, speak at length about the giants in connection with Gen. 6:1–4 because his Greek text of Gen. 6:4 read the word *giants* twice. Nevertheless, in his treatise *On the Giants* he does not understand the word in the sense that they were the offspring of unnatural unions between angels and women. For him the angels of God in this passage are evil souls that woo the daughters of men who represent sensual pleasures. He considers the giants in verse 4 to be one of the classes of souls—those that are earthborn.[5]

2. *On the Change of Names:* Philo expounds parts of the Enoch passage in a similar way in *On the Change of Names*. He is again making the point that certain types of people are rare or difficult to find. Philo maintains that "God is the maker of the wise and good only" (32),[6] and by such people he means those who "have voluntarily stripped themselves of the external goods that are so abundantly supplied to us, and further have despised what is dear to the flesh" (32). These disciplined people are

---

5. For this summary, see Colson's "Analytical Introduction" to *On the Giants*, in *Philo* II, 443–45. Philo derives this meaning through a play on the Greek words for *giants* and *earthborn*.
6. Translations are from F. H. Colson and G. H. Whitaker, *Philo* V, LCL (1934; reprint, Cambridge: Harvard University Press/London: Heinemann, 1988).

"pale, wasted and withered, so to speak" (33), compared to the lusty athletic types who "use the body as a menace to the soul."

They have made over the bodily muscles to serve the powers of the soul, and in fact are resolved into a single form, that of soul, and become unbodied minds. Naturally then the earthly element is destroyed and dissolved when the mind in all its powers has a fixed purpose to be well pleasing to God. But that kind is rare and hardly to be found, though that such should be is not impossible. This is shown by the oracle vouchsafed about Enoch. "Enoch was well pleasing to God and was not found." (33–34)

A few lines later Philo expounds the words *was translated* (Gen. 5:24, in Greek) to mean that Enoch, the wise and good person, "changed his abode and journeyed as an emigrant from the mortal life to the immortal" (38).

3. *On Abraham:* Here Philo expatiates on two trios of early biblical heroes—Enos/Enoch/Noah and Abraham/Isaac/Jacob—each of whom represents a certain virtue, or, as he says, "in these men we have laws endowed with life and reason" (5).[7] His treatment of Enoch is particularly interesting because he shows how one could read parts of Gen. 5:21–24 in a negative way. After he examines Enos as a symbol of hope, he turns to Enoch:

The second place after hope is given to repentance for sins and to improvement, and, therefore, Moses mentions next in order him who changed from the worse life to the better, called by the Hebrew Enoch but in our language "recipient of grace." We are told of him that he proved "to be pleasing to God and was not found because God transferred him," for transference implies turning and changing, and the change is to the better because it is brought about by the forethought of God. For all that is done with God's help is excellent and truly profitable, as also all that has not His directing care is unprofitable.

And the expression used of the transferred person, that he was not found, is well said, either because the old reprehensible life is blotted out and disappears and is no more found, as though it had never been at all, or because he who is thus transferred and takes

---

7. Translations are from Colson, *Philo* VI, LCL (1939; reprint, Cambridge: Harvard University Press/London: Heinemann, 1984).

his place in the better class is naturally hard to find. For evil is widely spread and therefore known to many, while virtue is rare, so that even the few cannot comprehend it. (17–19)

The person of worth secludes himself for nobler pursuits and is thus not easy to find. His transference is "from impiety to piety, and again from voluptuousness to self-control, from vaingloriousness to simplicity" (24). Philo then proceeds to Noah, with whom he associates perfection (cf. Gen. 6:9). The tradition represented in his reading of the Enoch passage inferred from the fact that he is said to have pleased God only after the birth of Methuselah, whereas nothing of this is mentioned for the first 65 (in Hebrew) or 165 (in Greek) years of his life, that there was a change in Enoch's character—from a life not pleasing to God to one that was. Philo also seized on the verb used in the Greek of Gen. 5:24 for Enoch's removal and found in it the notion of transfer, which he then related to his change in life (for the negative reading of parts of the Enoch pericope, see also Sir. 44:16 [Greek] and Pseudo-Philo's *Bib. Ant.* 1:16). Philo confirms this analysis in the conclusion to his section about the first triad. He finds a gradation in them: Noah was perfect; Enoch was in the middle, "since he devoted the earlier part of his life to vice but the latter to virtue to which he passed over and migrated" (47); and Enos, the one who hopes, is defective because he has not yet obtained the object of his hope.

4. *On Rewards and Punishments:* Philo makes the same points about Enos, Enoch, and Noah in his treatise *On Rewards and Punishments* 10–27. Once more he starts with Enos (hope) and moves second to Enoch, who is the embodiment of repentance:

Repentance also has two rewards assigned to its double achievement in abandoning the base and choosing the excellent. These rewards are a home and a life of solitude; for he says of him who fled from the insurgency of the body to join the forces of the soul "he was not found because God transferred him." By "transference" he clearly signifies the new home and by "not found" the life of solitude. (16–17)[8]

5. *Questions and Answers on Genesis:* Paragraphs 82–86 contain Philo's expository comments on Gen. 5:21–24. Enoch, as we now expect, exem-

---

8. Translation of Colson, *Philo* VIII, LCL (1953; reprint, Cambridge: Harvard University Press/London: Heinemann, 1989).

plifies repentance. This new way of life began with the birth of Methuselah. He adds that it was not long after Cain was forgiven that Enoch repented, since "forgiveness is wont to produce repentance" (82).[9] He engages in some number speculation to explain why Enoch lived 165 years before he repented and 200 years afterward. Philo has three reasons for Enoch's total of 365 years: there are 365 days in a solar year, and Genesis symbolizes the life of the repentant patriarch by the sun's revolution; the life of the penitent consists of light and dark, when, alternately, virtue or the passions influence him; and the full number includes and overlooks the time before he repented (84). Enoch is said to have pleased God after his end because the soul is immortal and again pleases God once the body is gone. His translation is interpreted as removal from a sensible, visible place to one that is incorporeal and intelligent (86). He concludes by noting the similarity between Enoch's experience and that of Moses and Elijah.

For Philo, then, Enoch represents a certain type of person who repents and is thus transferred to a different kind of life. Enoch never conjures up for him the elaborate stories of angels who descended from heaven and mated with women or of apocalyptic visions that covered all of history. Philo works with the text of the Bible, reads it through the filter of his philosophical system, and in this way demonstrates that he is far removed in his views from the authors who wrote the Enochic booklets.

D. JOSEPHUS

The Jewish historian Josephus (37 C.E.–ca. 100) has left behind two lengthy books and other shorter writings. The *Antiquities of the Jews*, his twenty-volume history of his people—from Adam to his own time—surveys the biblical period in the first eleven volumes. In the early part of his retelling he presents the material in Gen. 5. Josephus knows about a range of interpretations that were offered for the earliest scriptural stories. For example, he reports that for seven generations (i.e., through Enoch's time) people believed in the Lord but they later abandoned their pious ways and adopted sundry vices. In this setting he adduces the angel story: "For many angels of God now consorted with women and begat sons who were overbearing and disdainful of every virtue, such confi-

---

9. Translation of R. Marcus, *Philo Supplement I: Questions and Answers on Genesis*, LCL (1930; reprint, Cambridge: Harvard University Press/London: Heinemann, 1979).

dence had they in their strength; in fact the deeds that tradition ascribes to them resemble the audacious exploits told by the Greeks of the giants" (1:73).[10] But Josephus does not bring this Enochic-sounding angel story into connection with the seventh patriarch; rather, he makes Noah preach to them—unsuccessfully, as it turns out. It is not impossible that Josephus took his information from a source such as *1 Enoch* 6–11, which mentions Noah but not Enoch, although in those chapters Noah does not try to improve the overbearing giants.

Just before this (1:68–71) Josephus had reproduced a story about the discovery of astronomical learning. He attributes the achievement not to Enoch but, instead, to the descendants of Seth, all of whom were virtuous. They inscribed their discoveries on a brick and on a stone pillar so that the contents would survive a destruction by fire or water (see *Life of Adam and Eve*, app.).

His specific references to Enoch are brief and suggest that he associated with him none of the stories found in the Enoch tradition. In *Ant.* 1:85, in which he is giving the genealogy of Gen. 5, Josephus writes: "Jared lived 969 years and was succeeded by his son Anoch, born when his father was in his 162nd year; Anoch lived 365 years and then returned to the divinity, whence it comes that there is no record in the chronicles of his death." His chronology for Enoch is the familiar one, and Josephus has little to add, other than to gloss the words "and he was not, for God took him." In his only other reference to Enoch, Josephus names him when writing about Elijah's removal: "However, concerning Elijah and Enoch, who lived before the Flood, it is written in the sacred books that they became invisible, and no one knows of their death" (9:28).[11]

E. PSEUDO-PHILO'S *BIBLICAL ANTIQUITIES*

Pseudo-Philo's *Biblical Antiquities* was written perhaps at some point in the first century C.E., although the arguments in support of this dating are quite general.[12] It retells biblical history from Adam to the time of

10. Translations are from H. St. J. Thackeray, *Josephus IV: Jewish Antiquities Books I–IV*, LCL (Cambridge: Harvard University Press/London: Heinemann, 1967).
11. Translation of Marcus, *Josephus VI: Jewish Antiquities Books IX–XI*, LCL (1937; reprint, Cambridge: Harvard University Press/London: Heinemann, 1966).
12. See D. Harrington, "Pseudo-Philo," in *OTP* 2.299. The following translation is from this source.

King David. This means that the author had to deal in some way with the genealogy in Gen. 5, in which Enoch is the seventh in line from Adam. Much of chapter 1 reproduces that genealogy but with significant additions, prominent among which are the names of the patriarchs' sons and daughters. The section about Enoch reads this way: "*And Enoch lived 165 years and became the father of Methuselah. And after he became the father of Methuselah, Enoch lived 200 years and became the father of five sons and three daughters. Now Enoch pleased God in that time and he was not to be found, for God took him away.* Now the names of his sons: Anaz, Zeum, Achaun, Feledi, Elith; and of his daughters: Theiz, Lefith, Leath" (1:15–17). The chronology for Enoch's age when he becomes the father of Methuselah, and thus for the period after his birth as well, is the one known from the Greek translation of Genesis; the expression "Now Enoch pleased God" points toward the same source. The writer says nothing here about angels who sinned or Enoch's sojourn with other angels; he merely supplements the biblical lines with a few extra words and with numbers and names for the children. The extra prepositional phrase "in that time" could be noteworthy in that it may be distinguishing this time in Enoch's life from some other, less God-pleasing time in his earthly career. If so, then Pseudo-Philo and Philo would agree on the point. How distant Pseudo-Philo is from the Enochic tradition may be seen from his treatment of Gen. 6:1–4 (3:1–2). He simply quotes the scriptural text of 6:1–3 and ignores verse 4, which, in the Enoch tradition, was understood to designate the various sorts of giants who were born of the angel-human unions.

F. 2 BARUCH

This lengthy treatise about God's plan, where the destruction of Zion and the temple fits in it, and what is destined to happen was written after the destruction of Jerusalem and the temple in 70 C.E. It is often dated, again for rather general reasons, to a time shortly after 100 C.E.[13] The concern of this book with evil and God's response to it could have inclined the writer to turn to the watcher story in order to explain the magnitude of wickedness, but this did not happen. Rather, the story of the angels who sinned makes only a brief appearance in chapter 56, a chapter that contains the first part of the angel Ramael's explanation of

---

13. See A. F. J. Klijn, "2 (Syriac Apocalypse of) Baruch," in *OTP* 1.616–17. The following translation is from this source.

a vision that Baruch had seen (in chap. 53). Baruch had seen a cloud that dropped first black then bright water, a pattern that repeated itself twelve times. The angel explains that the first black water symbolized Adam's sin:

> And from these black waters again black were born, and very dark darkness originated. For he who was a danger to himself was also a danger to the angels. For they possessed freedom in that time in which they were created. And some of them came down and mingled themselves with women. At that time they who acted like this were tormented in chains. But the rest of the multitude of angels, who have no number, restrained themselves. And those living on earth perished together through the waters of the flood. Those are the first black waters. (56:9–16)

It may be significant that the only mention of the watcher story comes in connection with an apocalyptic vision—a common medium in the Enochic tradition. But the story is not fundamental to the thought of the book. These angels appear briefly and play no further role. The few words about them show that the author knew elements of the story: angels descended, commingled with women, and were punished. However, he alludes to a new feature: the freedom of the angels. That is, they made the choice by their own volition, while their more worthy colleagues restrained themselves. This may be an echo of the oath scene in *1 Enoch* 6, in which the text emphasizes that the angels knew what they were doing, understood it was wrong, and did it nevertheless.

G. *LIFE OF ADAM AND EVE*

The title *Life of Adam and Eve* is given to two texts: a Greek text that is called the *Apocalypse of Moses* and a Latin one named the *Life of Adam and Eve*. It is another one of those works that is difficult to date, but it is often assigned to approximately 100 C.E.[14] As the book focuses on the experiences of Adam and Eve, it is understandable that it lacks any references to Enoch or the descent of the angels. But in a transparently Christian appendix to the Latin *Life*, Enoch does put in an appearance. Eve, when on her deathbed, had instructed her children to make "tablets

---

14. See M. D. Johnson, "Life of Adam and Eve," in *OTP* 2.252. Quotations are from Johnson's translation.

of stone and other tablets of clay and write in them all my life and your father's which you have heard and seen from us. If he should judge our race by water, the tablets of earth will dissolve and the tablets of stone will remain; but if he should judge our race by fire, the tablets of stone will break up and those of clay will be thoroughly baked" (50:1–2; see the first *Sibylline Oracle*). Seth did as his mother had ordered (51:3). This note apparently inspired the addition to the text. It explains in more detail how Seth went about fulfilling his dying mother's request by saying that he put the tablets in the place where his father used to pray; it also records that the tablets survived the flood. Many saw them after the flood, but no one read them until Solomon, who asked the Lord about them. An angel explained to him what they were and related their connection with Adam's oratory to Solomon's building the temple, the house of prayer. Only then do we learn specifically what was on these (?) tablets:

And on the stones themselves was found what Enoch, the seventh from Adam, prophesied before the Flood, speaking of the coming of Christ, "Behold, the Lord will come in his holiness *to pronounce judgment on all* and to convict the impious of all their works which they spoke of him, sinners and impious, murmurers and irreligious, who walked according to their lust and whose mouth has spoken pride." (51:9)

It is curious that the words of Enoch were incised on stones that supposedly contained the lives and sayings of Adam and Eve. There may be some problem with the text.[15] However that may be, the Enoch material here is taken nearly verbatim from Jude 14–15, which in turn quotes from *1 Enoch* 1:9.

H. THE *TESTAMENT OF ABRAHAM*

The standard uncertainties surround the *Testament of Abraham:* it is difficult to situate in time and place. Textually, it also presents major problems, since it exists in two different but related recensions. E. Sanders thinks it dates from ca. 100 C.E. and that it was written in Egypt.[16] It is a Jewish work that was copied by Christians, and in the process it

---

15. See ibid., 2.294 n. d.
16. "Testament of Abraham," in *OTP* 1.874–75.

acquired some Christian features. Of the two recensions A may be closer to the hypothetical original, although B seems at times to preserve the more pristine wording of individual passages.[17] The reference to Enoch occurs only in Recension B, and therefore doubts about its place in the original text arise.

The context for the Enochic reference is Abraham's journeys in the company of Michael. Michael had been sent to take Abraham at the time scheduled for his death, but Abraham wanted a tour of the inhabited world first. As they traveled, Abraham asked to see the place of judgment (10:1), and Michael transported him there. He views the scene at the appropriate place and becomes interested in the judge who hears the cases that come before him and metes out the sentences. When he asks Michael who the judge and the prosecuting attorney are, he learns that the judge is Abel and the prosecuting attorney is Enoch. The description of Enoch contains a theme not met before:

> "And the one who produces (the evidence) is the teacher of heaven and earth and the scribe of righteousness, Enoch. For the Lord sent them here in order that they[18] might record the sins and righteous deeds of each person." And Abraham said, "How can Enoch bear the weight of the souls, since he has not seen death? Or how can he give the sentence of all the souls?" And Michael said, "If he were to give sentence concerning them, it would not be accepted. But it is not Enoch's business to give sentence; rather, the Lord is the one who gives sentence, and it is this one's (Enoch's) task only to write. For Enoch prayed to the Lord saying, 'Lord, I do not want to give the sentence of the souls, lest I become oppressive to someone.' And the Lord said to Enoch, 'I shall command you to write the sins of a soul that makes atonement, and it will enter into life. And if the soul has not made atonement and repented, you will find its sins (already) written, and it will be cast into punishment.' " (B 11:3–10)

From the earlier Enoch texts, especially the Similitudes, we would expect Enoch to be present at a scene of ultimate judgment. Yet his role is diminished in this excerpt: the writer states explicitly that Enoch does

---

17. Ibid., 1.871–73.
18. Some manuscripts read singular pronouns instead of *them* and *they* in this sentence. They do so because Enoch alone is said to do the recording of sins and righteous deeds (see ibid., 1.900 n. c).

not do the actual judging. Abel performs that role, while God is the one who gives sentences. The scene may be directed against those devotees of Enoch who saw him as the son of man, the judge of the last days.

I. 2 ENOCH

A curious book has received the name *2 Enoch*. It has survived only in a Slavonic version but may have been composed in Hebrew and translated from a Greek rendition of the original. There are no strong clues for dating the book. We may be able to grasp some of the uncertainty surrounding it, if we see that scholars are not agreed whether it is Christian or Jewish. The words of F. I. Andersen, who has prepared the most recent translation and study of the book, should be cited:

> In every respect 2 Enoch remains an enigma. So long as the date and location remain unknown, no use can be made of it for historical purposes. The present writer is inclined to place the book—or at least its original nucleus—early rather than late; and in a Jewish rather than a Christian community. But by the very marginal if not deviant character of their beliefs, its users could have been gentile converts to moral monotheism based on belief in the antediluvian God of the Bible as Creator, but not as the God of Abraham or Moses.[19]

With these uncertainties the book is included here only to show that another book of Enoch was written after a hiatus of perhaps two centuries, possibly many more. It shows the large-scale influence and some modification of earlier Enochic lore and may serve as a convenient end point for the study of such material in Jewish (?) texts outside the Rabbinic corpus.

2 Enoch is set in Enoch's 365th year, when two angels come to take him. After he speaks to his children the angels guide him through the several heavens. In the first he sees the sorts of astronomical phenomena that fill the AB. In the second heaven he sees darkness and sad angels. The angels there were imprisoned and remained under guard and in constant torment. Enoch's guides explain to him that the angels "are those who turned away from the Lord, who did not obey the Lord's

---

19. "2 (Slavonic Apocalypse of) Enoch," in *OTP* 1.97; for the problem of date, see pp. 94–97.

commandments, but of their own will plotted together and turned away with their prince and with those who are under restraint in the fifth heaven" (7:3). The angels ask him to pray for them, but Enoch declines on the grounds that he is just a man. These angels remind us of the watchers and their mutual oath to commit the deed that led to their imprisonment in *1 Enoch* 6–11. As we continue to read in *2 Enoch*, however, it becomes evident that there are problems in the way of making this identification.

The tour continues with the third heaven, in which Enoch sees Paradise prepared for the righteous and a northern place of torment. The fourth heaven, like the first, contains astronomical items such as six gates on each side. Here we read about a year of 364 days (chap. 13) but also of 365 1/4 or 1/2 days. The fifth heaven, which was mentioned in the description of the second heaven, as the place in which angelic colleagues of those in the second heaven belonged, contains *Grigori*—a transcription of the Greek word for *watchers*. They are said to be larger than giants. There are two hundred myriads of them (note the two hundred who descended in *1 Enoch* 6), and they are similar to the ones in the second heaven. Here one reads that three of them had descended to earth, broke their promise on Ermon (Mount Hermon), and gave birth to giants and other monsters. The angels who remain in the fifth heaven now mourn for their brothers who were sentenced under the earth (18:7). This note indicates that the angels in the second heaven are not the ones who were condemned for descending to earth and fathering giants. A group of those in the fifth heaven formed the guilty cohort. Enoch makes these fifth-heaven angels, who had become silent, resume the liturgy.

The sixth heaven contains seven groups of glorious angels who are over every phenomenon and who harmonize all things. After this the textual situation becomes somewhat confused or at least difficult to follow.[20] Enoch comes to the seventh heaven, where he sees many glorious angels who show him God himself enthroned in the tenth heaven. The angelic guides leave Enoch at the edge of the seventh heaven, and Gabriel comes to bring him into God's presence. Heavens 8 and 9 are not described, although 21:6 mentions that Enoch saw them. In chapter 22 he sees the face of God as he comes before him in the tenth heaven. At this point an important ceremony occurs: Enoch's earthly clothing is removed by Michael; he is anointed with oil and dons heavenly apparel (22:8–9). The text says that he thus became like one of the glorious angels (v. 10); in fact, Enoch joins the heavenly company.

---

20. See Andersen's note a, ibid., 134–35.

Once he is in the divine presence, Enoch receives a stupendous writing assignment. An angel with a name that appears to be the Slavonic version of Uriel (Vrevoil) gives Enoch a pen for swift writing. Books were then read to him. Enoch writes 366 books at the dictation of Vrevoil, who speaks for thirty days and thirty nights. What Enoch records includes the deeds of everyone. Moreover, great secrets were revealed to Enoch. God himself, while Enoch was seated to his left alongside Gabriel, explains the process of creation to Enoch (chaps. 24–32). The book is far more interested in this subject than in the course of history and its events. Enoch was to give the books he wrote to his children so that they would acknowledge God as the only God. The books would not disappear in the flood because two angels were charged to preserve them. God relates to Enoch everything that has happened and will occur and assures Enoch that someone will reveal his books to the people after the flood.

Even though he is already in his 365th year, Enoch is allowed to return to earth for thirty days to admonish his sons. He is sent to tell them what has been, is, and will be (39:5). His message is presented as coming from the Lord himself and delivered by the one who had seen his face. Unlike some apocalyptic texts, his books were not to be concealed. Methuselah wanted to prepare some food for his father, but Enoch refused it, explaining that since his heavenly anointing (i.e., when he became an angel) he had not desired food. Methuselah then summoned the family and the elders, and Enoch instructed them. Once it was known that the Lord would soon take him, about two hundred people proceeded to Akhuzan, where Enoch was staying, in order to kiss him. Their words to him are extraordinary:

> O our father, Enoch! May you be blessed by the Lord, the eternal king! And now, bless your ⟨sons⟩, and all the people, so that we may be glorified in front of your face today.
> For you will be glorified in front of the face ⟨of the Lord for eternity⟩, because you are the one whom the Lord chose in preference to all the people upon the earth; and he appointed you to be the one who makes a written record of all his creation, visible and invisible, and the one who carried away the sin of mankind and the helper of your own household. (64:4–5)

Enoch's role as the chosen one who carries away the sins of mankind is derived from the picture of the servant in Isa. 53.[21] Hence, *2 Enoch*, like

---

21. See ibid., 190 n. c, for the textual problems here.

the Similitudes, draws upon the traits of this prophetic character in order to describe the glorious status of Enoch.

Enoch addressed his sons once more, but then the Lord sent down darkness. While the people were unable to see because of the darkness, angels took Enoch so that he was found no more. We learn that his first ascent occurred on the first of Nisan (the first month), and the second took place on the sixth of Tsivan (Sivan). An altar was built at Akhuzan where Methuselah served as priest (69). The text continues for two more chapters, which tell about the appointment of Nir as next high priest, the decay that began in his time, and the remarkable birth of Melchizedek.

Whenever and by whom *2 Enoch* was written, it is in some respects closely related to many familiar Enochic themes but in others is strange to the tradition. The same cosmological interest that stamps several of the Enochic texts (esp. the AB and the BW but also the Similitudes) is pronounced here in the section about creation. Enoch has certainly been no stranger to the varied parts of heaven (see *1 Enoch* 14 and 70–71). We also meet the well-known Enochic calendar of 364 days (and one of more than 365 days). Enoch as scribe and recorder of human deeds is also familiar. Moreover, the text builds upon the chronological framework of Gen. 5:21–24. Yet *2 Enoch* provides far more detail about the days of creation than we are accustomed to find in the texts named after the patriarch, and it is the first Enochic document to number the heavens. The story of the watchers is present in *2 Enoch*, but it is a minor theme and one told with some variations from the versions in *1 Enoch* (e.g., the three angels who descended from the fifth heaven). Finally, *2 Enoch* crowds all of its activity, including the two removals, into the 365th and last year of Enoch's life. The older texts also knew of two sojourns with the angels, but they were tied to the two notices in Genesis that "Enoch walked with the *'elohîm*" from age sixty-five onward and again after his removal. That connection is substantially modified in *2 Enoch*.

J. ENOCH IN RABBINIC SOURCES

As time passed, Enoch may have become in the minds of some Jewish thinkers not so much an unusual character in the Hebrew Bible as a symbol for a kind of apocalyptic thought. For a number of early Christian writers he proved to be fairly important, but the same cannot be said for those Jewish scholars whose reflections are preserved in the vast Rabbinic corpus. There he appears rarely. The few references to him in the more ancient Rabbinic literature do allow us to see, however, that there were differences of opinion about him and his significance. If this survey were to continue into later Rabbinic sources, it would be possible to find more influences especially of the angel story.

In a survey of the Rabbinic references to Enoch, M. Himmelfarb was able to find only one reference to him that may be Tannaitic. In the talmudic period, by which she meant circa 70–600, Enoch is almost never mentioned.[22] His name does not appear in the text of the Mishnah nor in that of the Jerusalem and Babylonian talmuds. This may be surprising, but possibly it is conditioned in part by the nature of the material found in these compositions. The Enoch literature devotes little attention to legal topics and is, as we have seen, surprisingly reticent even about the law revealed on Mount Sinai. These subjects are, of course, at the heart of the Mishnah and talmuds. Nevertheless, if Enoch and the traditions that were associated with him had been important within the different Jewish communities during the first four or five centuries of the common era, we would have expected him to be more prominent in these lengthy documents.

The only possibly Tannaitic reference to Enoch which Himmelfarb could find is in a section of *Midrash Ha-Gadol*. The midrash itself is a much later composition—it was compiled in the thirteenth or even the fourteenth century[23]—but its treatment of Gen. 5:24 shows signs of coming from an earlier source. In its two comments on the verse the text first notes that all sevenths are loved. This theme of the "Beloved Sevenths" is explained to mean that the one who lived in the seventh generation is beloved. The phrase "he walked with God" is quoted to document the point. Another beloved seventh is Moses, who is the seventh among the fathers (counting from Abraham). In connection with the words "and he was no more, because God took him" the commentator names three biblical heroes who ascended and now serve above: Enoch, Moses, and Elijah. This is a simple inference from biblical givens (Gen. 5:24; Deut. 34:1–6; 2 Kings 2:11), although in the case of Moses a little help from extra-scriptural traditions might be needed. The fact that Enoch is included among those who are beloved displays a positive attitude toward him, and his place among those who serve on high reiter-

22. "A Report on Enoch in Rabbinic Literature," SBLSP, edited by P. J. Achtemeier (1978): 1.259–69.
23. See H. L. Strack and G. Stemberger, *Introduction to the Talmud and Midrash* (Edinburgh: T. & T. Clark, 1991), 386–87.

ates a tradition that is attested already in the Animal Apocalypse and in *Jubilees*.[24]

Another source of information about earlier Rabbinic attitudes toward Enoch appears in *Genesis Rabbah*. This great compilation achieved its present form in the first half of the fifth century.[25] As it reaches Gen. 5:24, it offers some different readings of the text—readings that reflect disagreement about Enoch and his fate.

"Enoch walked with God, and he was not for God took him" (Gen. 5:24):

Said R. Hama bar Hoshaia, "['And he was not' indicates that] he was inscribed not in the scroll of the righteous but in the scroll of the wicked."

R. Aibu: "Enoch was a dissembler. Sometimes he was righteous, sometimes wicked. Said the Holy One, blessed be he, 'While he is in his righteous phase, I shall take him away.' "

Said R. Aibu: "On the New Year he judged him, when he judges the entire world."

Heretics asked R. Abbahu, saying to him, "We do not find that death is stated with regard to Enoch."

He said to them, "Why?"

They said to him, "The word 'taking' is used both here and with respect to Elijah. [Just as Elijah did not die, but was taken bodily into heaven, so the same thing happened to Enoch.]"[26]

He said to them, "If use of the word 'taking' is what you propose to interpret, then take note that in this case, the word 'taking' is used, and also with respect to Ezekiel: 'Behold, I take away from you the desire of your eyes' (Ez. 24:16) [which refers only to the death of Ezekiel's wife, and hence the word signifies a quite ordinary death, not translation into heaven]."

Said R. Tanhuma, "He answered them very nicely."

A noble lady asked R. Yose, "You do not find that Enoch died."

He said to her, "If the text had said, 'And Enoch walked with God' (Gen. 5:24) and had then fallen silent, I should state matters as you do. But when it says, 'And he was not, because God took

---

24. For the text, see M. Margulies, *Midrash Haggadol on the Pentateuch: Genesis* (Jerusalem: Mosad Harav Kook Publishing, 1967), 132.

25. Strack and Stemberger, *Introduction to the Talmud and Midrash*, 303–4.

26. 2 Kings 2:2 is quoted here in some copies.

him,' it means, 'he is not in the world,' 'because God took him.' "[27] (25.1)

The text begins with a strongly negative reading of the verse. In a manner not clarified here, Rabbi Hama bar Hoshaia inferred from Gen. 5:24 that Enoch was enrolled among the wicked. However he arrived at this position, it shows that there were scholars who read the text to Enoch's disadvantage. The second opinion is more moderate and agrees with the interpretation found in Philo (and the Greek of Sir. 44:16): Enoch had his good and bad moments. The process of reasoning that lies behind Rabbi Aibu's interpretation is also not given, but it does indicate that Enoch was righteous in the last part of his life because God was kind enough to take him away during a good phase, lest he suffer another relapse. More detail is available for the discussion of what the verb *take* means in Gen. 5:24. The heretics *(mînîm)* understood it in the sense familiar from the Enochic tradition: he bypassed death. Rabbi Abbahu, however, was able to show, by citing the example from Ezekiel, that *take* does not necessarily entail this conclusion. The lady who conversed with Rabbi Yose about the matter learned that *take*, considered in the fuller context, does mean avoidance of death. The sentence "and he was no more, because God took him" leads to that conclusion.

The section is of interest, therefore, because it shows a variety of views regarding how to read Gen. 5:24. Yet even the commentators who interpreted it to mean that Enoch did not die are not credited with accepting any other part of the vast Enochic lore, such as the watcher story or his role in the last judgment. The discussion here is straightforward and restrained, limited to debating the meaning of the text. Moreover, the treatment of Gen. 6:1–4 in *Genesis Rabbah* reveals how those quoted in it assigned the passage a nonangelic meaning. The angelic interpretation of "the sons of the *'elohîm*" may be lurking somewhere in the background of Rabbi Simeon ben Yoshaia, but it is never articulated. In its treatment of Gen. 6:2 (the sons of the *'elohîm*), the text includes these comments: "R. Simeon b. Yohai referred to them as sons of the nobility." "R. Simeon b. Yohai cursed anyone who called them 'sons of God' " (26.5). A few lines later the question is posed:

---

27. The interpretive translation is from J. Neusner, *Genesis Rabbah: The Judaic Commentary to the Book of Genesis. A New American Translation*, 3 vols., BJS 104–6 (Atlanta: Scholars Press, 1985), 1.271. The extra numbers and letters with which Neusner identifies each line have been omitted.

Then why does Scripture refer to them as "sons of God"?

R. Hanina and R. Simeon b. Laqish say, "Because they lived a long time without suffering and without anguish."

R. Huna in the name of R. Yose: "It was in order that men might understand the astronomical cycles and calculations."[28]

Rabbis say, "It was so that they should take the punishment coming both to themselves and to the generations after them [having lived a long and easy life, they would merit the punishment that was to come, so they lived like gods]." (26.5)[29]

Understanding the sons of the *'elohîm* as *angels* seems not to be an option.

K. GEN. 5:21–24 IN THE TARGUMS

Another indication of the differing ways in which various Jewish experts explained the meaning of the curious Enoch pericope in Gen. 5:21–24 is the varied formulations of the passage in the targums. These Aramaic renderings of the Hebrew Bible were first made already in pre-Christian times, as the presence of two such translations at Qumran (Leviticus and Job) shows. But the more familiar ones were compiled in later centuries, and at times, when they depart from a word-for-word translation, they betray the exegetical moves that were made by at least some scholars.

The more official Targum of Onkelos shows the negative attitude that some held toward Enoch. It offers a literal rendering of Gen. 5:21 but turns some passages in the remaining verses in an unfavorable direction:

22: And Enoch walked *in reverence of the Lord* for 300 years after he begot Methuselah, and he begot sons and daughters.

23: Now all the days of Enoch were 365 years.

24: And Enoch walked *in reverence of the Lord*, then he was no more, for the Lord *had caused him to die*.[30]

---

28. Here Neusner adds Freedman's explanation that making the observations necessary for this demanded a long life.

29. Both translations are from Neusner, *Genesis Rabbah*, 1.282.

30. Translation of B. Grossfeld, *The Targum Onqelos to Genesis*, Aramaic Bible 6 (Wilmington, Del.: Michael Glazier, 1988), 51–52. Two copies insert a negative in the last clause so that it reads: "for the Lord did not cause him to die."

The targumist may be following the interpretation that Enoch waffled between good and bad periods, since he takes "he walked with the *ʾelohîm*" to mean that he was reverent to God at those times. But the blunt statement at the end—"for the Lord *had caused him to die*"—places him squarely in the camp of those who did not accept the extraordinary claims made for Enoch by those who wrote the Enochic tractates. The fact that he uses *Lord* as the divine name in verses 22 and 24 also proves that he did not think *ha-ʾelohîm* referred to the angels.

The other targums to Genesis reflect a range of views. Targum Neofiti presents a somewhat hesitant perspective. After verse 21, which it translates verbatim, we read:

> 22: And Enoch *served in truth before the Lord* after he had begotten Methuselah for three hundred years, and *during these years* he begot sons and daughters.
> 23: And all the days *of the life* of Enoch were three hundred and sixty-five years.
> 24: And Enoch *served in truth before the Lord* and *it is not known where he is*, because *he was withdrawn by a command from before the Lord*.[31]

The targum seems to agree with the views expressed in Onkelos through verse 23, but in verse 24 a more positive, or at least less negative, picture emerges. Enoch was not executed by the Lord; rather, the Lord withdrew him. Yet the targumist stops short of the reading found in the Enochic booklets by inferring from "and he was no more" that his whereabouts are unknown. With this we may compare *1 Enoch* 12:1: "And before everything Enoch had been hidden, and none of the sons of men knew where he was hidden, or where he was, or what had happened." The difference is, however, that in *1 Enoch* the author knows where Enoch was—with the angels. The targumist confesses ignorance.

The marginal notes in Targum Neofiti add to the evidence that there were disagreements about Enoch's fate. At the end of verse 23 there is a marginal gloss that says: "and he died and was gathered from the midst of the world." In verse 24, after the words "*and it is not known where he is*," another note (this one supported by other Palestinian witnesses) reads: "and behold he is not."

---

31. Translation of M. McNamara, *Targum Neofiti 1: Genesis*, Aramaic Bible 1A (Collegeville, Minn.: Liturgical Press, 1992), 70–71. The translations of the marginal glosses are from the same source.

Targum Pseudo-Jonathan moves in a different direction and echoes views that are in harmony with the Enochic traditions:

22: Enoch *worshiped*[32] in truth before the Lord after he had begotten Methuselah three hundred years, and he begot sons and daughters.
23: All the days of Enoch *with the inhabitants of the earth* were three hundred and sixty-five years.
24: Enoch *worshiped in truth before the Lord* and *behold* he was not *with the inhabitants of the earth* because he was taken away and *he ascended to the firmament at the command of the Lord, and he was called Metatron, the Great Scribe.*[33]

A reasonable inference from verse 23 is that Enoch spent all 365 years of his life on earth. Since in this targum, too, *ha-ʾelohîm* is rendered as *Lord*, nothing is implied about a stay with angels. The version of verse 24, however, shows that for the targumist Enoch's removal by the Lord was not the normal ending of a human life. The Lord himself commanded that he ascend to the firmament, and he attains the title "Metatron, the Great Scribe." We do not know exactly what the translator meant by this epithet, but in other Jewish texts it is used for an angel who is God's lieutenant or, in the later *3 Enoch*, for Enoch himself, who is also termed the "the lesser Yahweh" (*3 Enoch* 12:5, 48C:7, 48D:1 [90]). About this remarkable figure P. Alexander writes:

Metaṭron is, in a number of respects, similar to the archangel Michael: Both angels were known as "the Great Prince"; both were said to serve in the heavenly sanctuary; both were guardian angels of Israel; what is said in one text about Michael is said in another about Metaṭron. A possible explanation of these similarities would be that originally Metaṭron and Michael were one and the same angel: Michael was the angel's common name, Metaṭron one of his esoteric, magical names. At some point, however, the connection between Metaṭron and Michael was obscured, and a new, independent archangel with many of Michael's powers came into being. ....
Metaṭron was merged with two other heavenly figures, (1) the archangel Yahoʾel, and (2) translated Enoch ....

---

32. The verb here is the same as the one translated *served* in Targum Neofiti.
33. Translation of M. Maher, *Targum Pseudo-Jonathan: Genesis*, Aramaic Bible 1B (Collegeville, Minn.: Liturgical Press, 1992), 36–37.

Metatron's absorption of translated Enoch could only have taken place in circles acquainted with the Palestinian apocalyptic Enoch traditions. The apocalyptic texts do not seem to go so far as to say that Enoch was transformed into an archangel when he was translated into heaven, but some of them speak of his exaltation in language which could be taken to imply this (see esp. 2 En 22:8).[34]

This one targum, them, finds a place for the sorts of speculation known only from the special Enochic traditions.

---

34. "3 (Hebrew) Enoch," in *OTP* 1.243–44. See, too, Milik, *Books of Enoch*, 125–35, for a survey of the texts, including the magical ones, that mention Metatron. He also discusses the etymology of the term.

CHAPTER 6

THE NEW TESTAMENT
AND EARLY CHRISTIAN TEXTS

A. THE NEW TESTAMENT

If we were to read the introduction to R. H. Charles's standard English edition of *1 Enoch*, we would gain the impression that there are numerous allusions to and reflections of *1 Enoch* in the New Testament. Pages xcv–ciii in his book contain a section entitled "The Influence of *1 Enoch* on the New Testament." Charles found two kinds of evidence for the effect of the book on New Testament writers: passages that "in phraseology or idea directly depend on or are illustrative of passages in *1 Enoch*" and doctrines from *1 Enoch* which shaped the matching New Testament teachings. But his list is misleading because only a small number of his parallels amount to serious candidates for direct or even indirect influence. For example, he compares the words "Jesus Christ the righteous" in 1 John 2:1 with Enoch's title "the righteous one" in *1 Enoch* 53:6. The similarity is obvious, but it is a slim basis for positing any relationship between the two works. Charles may have been correct in claiming that some New Testament wording was influenced by *1 Enoch*, but only in a few cases may we say with confidence that something in the New Testament shows influence from an item or theme in *1 Enoch*. Enoch himself is mentioned rarely in the New Testament, and themes specifically associated with him are found in only a few passages. The evidence should now be presented.

1. HEBREWS 11

While his name appears in Jesus' reverse genealogy in Luke (3:38; the list follows Gen. 5 at this point), other passages deal with Enoch in more detail. He is one of the heroes of faith in Hebrews 11. After the writer devotes a verse to Abel (11:4), Enoch has his turn: "By faith Enoch was taken so that he did not experience death; and 'he was not found, because God had taken him.' For it was attested before he was taken away that 'he had pleased God.' And without faith it is impossible to please God, for whoever would approach him must believe that he exists and that he rewards those who seek him" (11:5–6). The writer is expounding Gen. 5:24, but he goes beyond Genesis when he asserts that Enoch "did not experience death." While that is a logical way of reading the text, Genesis does not say this in so many words. As we have seen, the same verse was taken to mean that he had died according to one opinion expressed in *Genesis Rabbah*. The author of Hebrews quotes from the Greek version of Genesis and thus has Enoch pleasing God. Since one must have faith to please God, Enoch must have been a model of that virtue.

2. THE EPISTLE OF JUDE

The short Epistle of Jude, which designates its author "a servant of Jesus Christ and brother of James" (v. 1), is usually regarded as one of the latest New Testament writings.[1] Early Christian lists of authoritative books betray some uncertainty in different parts of the church regarding its standing. Jude's use of traditions from documents not found in the more widely accepted forms of the Old Testament may well have had something to do with its dubious status.[2] Among these traditions are words that he not only quotes from *1 Enoch* but whose source he acknowledges explicitly.

Much of Jude consists of examples that illustrate how God had punished sinners like those against whom the author directs his message:

1. the generation of the exodus from Egypt were later destroyed when they failed to believe (v. 5);
2. the "angels who did not keep their own position, but left their proper dwelling, he has kept in eternal chains in deepest darkness

---

1. Cf. W. G. Kümmel, *Introduction to the New Testament* (London: SCM, 1966), 300–302; translated from the 14th (1965) German edition; but see R. J. Bauckham, *Jude, 2 Peter*, WBC 50 (Waco: Word Books, 1983), 13–14, who puts it in the second half of the first century C.E. The author himself, Bauckham thinks, may have been from Palestinian Apocalyptic circles (see most recently his study "Jude, Epistle of," in *ABD* 3.1100–1102).
2. See R. Beckwith, *The Old Testament Canon of the New Testament Church and Its Background in Early Judaism* (Grand Rapids, Mich.: Eerdmans, 1985), 400–401. He cites Didymus the Blind and Jerome in support of this point. Bauckham (*Jude, 2 Peter*, 17) mentions Origen, Eusebius, Didymus, and Jerome as attesting to doubts about the book because it used apocryphal material.

170

for the judgment of the great Day" (v. 6) (the wording reminds us of the emphases expressed especially in *1 Enoch* 12–16, in which the angels' sin of leaving their proper, created place is highlighted [see 12:4; 14:5; 15:2–10]; *1 Enoch* 6–11 speaks of how they were imprisoned until the final judgment [10:4–6, 12–14]);[3]

3. Sodom, Gomorrah, and surrounding cities (v. 7). Sodom is mentioned in connection with Enochic themes in *Damascus Document* 2; *T.Naph.* 4:1; *T. Ben.* 9:1.

Since the writer has drawn his examples from Exodus/Numbers, *1 Enoch*, and Genesis, he must have believed each of them was an appropriate source of information about the Lord's record in punishing sinners. Like Genesis and Exodus/Numbers, *1 Enoch* discloses facts about what God has done. The angel story—particularly the judgment that they experienced—serves as an example of how the Lord, in times past, had destroyed individuals whose behavior deteriorated.

A few verses later Jude quotes from *1 Enoch:*

It was also about these that Enoch, in the seventh generation from Adam, prophesied, saying, "See, the Lord is coming with ten thousands of his holy ones, to execute judgment on all, and to convict everyone of all the deeds of ungodliness that they have committed in such an ungodly way, and of all the harsh things that ungodly sinners have spoken against him." (vv. 14–15)

We should note that Enoch is credited with "prophesying," and, as the context shows, the sense of the verb here is that he predicted: the seventh from Adam had already spoken about the ungodly intruders who unsettled Jude.[4] In his forecast Enoch not only condemned Jude's impious foes but also spoke about the final judgment. So, we may conclude, Jude knew several parts of the BW (chaps. 1, 6–16, at least) and believed that the ancient patriarch had extraordinary predictive powers. In calling Enoch the seventh from Adam, Jude uses a phrase found in *1 Enoch* 60:8, although it may have been a simple inference from Gen. 5.[5]

---

3. Charles, *Book of Enoch*, xcv.
4. Note the repeated use of *ungodliness/godly* and *ungodly* for these opponents in verse 4.
5. Charles, *Book of Enoch*, xcvi.

3. 1 PETER

Although the date of the letter is disputed, it was probably written at some time between 60–100 C.E. It may have been composed in Rome — the Babylon of 5:13.[6] In chapter 3, after exhortations to wives[7] and husbands (vv. 1–7), the writer urges his readers to become unified and calls on them to be ready to suffer, if need be, just as Christ suffered for sins:

> He was put to death in the flesh, but made alive in the spirit, in which also he went and made a proclamation to the spirits in prison, who in former times did not obey, when God waited patiently in the days of Noah, during the building of the ark, in which a few, that is, eight persons, were saved through water. (3:18b–20)

Commentators have recognized that the spirits to whom Christ preached could not be those of deceased people. The reference to the time of the flood shows that they are the imprisoned spirits who, according to *1 Enoch*, sinned at the time of Noah. These spirits who had languished in prison for millennia now become the audience for Christ's post-passion proclamation.[8] If this is what the author had in mind, he is calling the angelic watchers of *1 Enoch* — the ones who were imprisoned in the earth — "spirits in prison." *1 Enoch* 15:4, 6, and 7 characterize the watchers as spiritual before lust overpowered their created nature. It is likely, however, that 1 Peter reflects a passage such as *1 Enoch* 19:1,[9] in which Uriel explains to Enoch a scene of judgment: "The spirits of the angels who were promiscuous with the women will stand here; and they, assuming many forms, made men unclean and will lead men astray so that they sacrifice to demons as gods———(that is,) *until the great judgement day* on which they will be judged so that an end will be made of them."

4. 2 PETER

This short epistle is often dated to the end of the first century (the opponents do not appear to be Gnostic; as a result, their character does

---

6. Cf. Kümmel, *Introduction to the New Testament*, 292–99; K. P. Donfried, "Peter," in *ABD* 5.262–63.

7. Note the reference to adornment, etc., in verses 3–4.

8. Cf. Josephus, *Ant.* 1:73, in which Noah preaches to the giants.

9. See Charles, *Book of Enoch*, xcvi.

not require a second-century date) and localized in Asia Minor, where the author would have had a good chance to become familiar with Jewish and Greek traditions.[10] The writer issues a warning about false teachers who will arise as deceptive prophets did in the past and declares that their punishment was determined long ago (2: 1–3). He documents his case by citing ancient instances of God's definitive judgments: "For if God did not spare the angels when they sinned, but cast them into hell[11] and committed them to chains of deepest darkness to be kept until the judgment; . . . then the Lord knows how to rescue the godly from trial, and to keep the unrighteous under punishment until the day of judgment . . ." (vv. 4, 9). The same Enochic sections that underlie Jude 6 also inspired this passage,[12] although, unlike Jude, the writer does not name Enoch as the authority on which his words rest.

B. EARLY CHRISTIAN TEXTS

A significant number of Christian authors quoted and/or alluded to a *Book of Enoch* in the first several centuries of church history. Study of the evidence shows that for some writers the book enjoyed an authoritative status, while many also appealed to the watcher myth in support of different sorts of arguments. Since we have moved beyond the biblical period here, no attempt will be made to provide an exhaustive examination of the evidence. A sampling will be cited under three headings: references to a book of Enoch, references to the watcher story, and references to Enoch himself as an eschatological figure.[13]

1. A *BOOK OF ENOCH*

Several authors from the first three centuries refer to Enoch's teachings or to his book. They tend to use terms such as *scripture* or *prophecy* in classifying what he wrote or said. We have already examined Jude's

---

10. Cf. J. Neyrey, *2 Peter, Jude*, AB 37C (Garden City, N.Y.: Doubleday, 1993), 111–41.
11. Cf. *1 Enoch* 20:2.
12. Charles, *Book of Enoch*, xcvi.
13. The material in the following sections is distilled from VanderKam, "1 Enoch and Enoch in Early Christianity," in *The Jewish Apocalyptic Heritage in Early Christianity*, edited by J. C. VanderKam and W. Adler, CRINT 3.4 (Assen/Maastricht: van Gorcum/Minneapolis: Fortress Press, 1995).

quotation of Enoch's prophecy. The *Epistle of Barnabas*, a late-first- or early-second-century composition, alludes to Enoch's words in connection with the final judgment, and Athenagoras, Irenaeus, Clement of Alexandria, Tertullian, and Origen employ the Enochic angel story to various ends.

Tertullian, who wrote his treatises just before and after the year 200, is a particularly interesting case because he is the only patristic author to formulate arguments defending the authenticity and status of a book of Enoch which, judging by his several allusions to it, had much in common with our *1 Enoch*. He exploits the angel story to support his belief that women's finery is to be traced back to the sinful teachings of the angels (*De cultu feminarum* 1.3). In order to buttress his case he fashions an apology for this book of Enoch.

> [1.] I am aware that the Scripture of Enoch *[scripturam Enoch]*, which has assigned this order (of action) to angels, is not received by some, because it is not admitted in the Jewish canon *[armarium Iudaicum]* either. I suppose they did not think that, having been published before the deluge, it could have safely survived that world-wide calamity, the abolisher of all things. If that is the reason (for rejecting it), let them recall to their memory that Noah, the survivor of the deluge, was the great-grandson of Enoch himself; and he, of course, had heard and remembered, from domestic renown and hereditary tradition, concerning his own great-grandfather's "grace in the sight of God," and concerning all his preachings; since Enoch had given no other charge to Methuselah than that he should hand on the knowledge of them to his posterity. Noah therefore, no doubt, might have succeeded in the trusteeship of (his) preaching; or, had the case been otherwise, he would not have been silent alike concerning the disposition (of things) made by God, his Preserver, and concerning the particular glory of his own house.
> [2.] If (Noah) had not had this (conservative power) by so short a route, there would (still) be this (consideration) to warrant our assertion of (the genuineness of) this Scripture *[scripturae]*: he could equally have *renewed* it, under the Spirit's inspiration, after it *had* been destroyed by the violence of the deluge, as, after the destruction of Jerusalem by the Babylonian storming of it, every document of the Jewish literature is generally agreed to have been restored through Ezra.
> [3.] But since Enoch in the same Scripture *[scriptura]* has preached likewise concerning the Lord, nothing at all must be rejected by us which pertains to us; and we read that "every Scripture *[scripturam]*

suitable for edification is divinely inspired." By the Jews it may now seem to have been rejected for that (very) reason, just like all the other (portions) nearly which tell of Christ. Nor, of course, is this fact wonderful, that they did not receive some Scriptures which spake of Him whom even in person, speaking in their presence, they were not to receive. To these considerations is added the fact that Enoch possesses a testimony in the Apostle Jude. (*De cultu feminarum* 3.1, 1–3)[14]

Here, then, for the first time in extant Christian literature we encounter arguments for the genuineness or scriptural status of what appears to be much of our *1 Enoch*, which, on Tertullian's view, speaks not only about the evil origins of feminine finery but about Christ himself. This latter claim may point to the Similitudes of Enoch, in which a judicial son of man figures. However, it may be that the theophany in *1 Enoch* 1:3–9 or similar passages are meant. It is certain that Tertullian knows the story in *1 Enoch* 6–11, while the allusion to the transmission of Enoch's words through his son Methuselah is probably drawn from passages such as *1 Enoch* 81–82.

Beginning some time around the year 300 C.E., such favorable references to the writings of Enoch were apparently no longer made by Christian writers. Presumably, a variety of causes contributed to this change, but Augustine of Hippo (354–430) has left us some indication of the objections he had to the writings of Enoch. The issue arises in connection with the interpretation of Gen. 6:1–4. Augustine argues against the view that the "sons of God" (as his Bible read) were angels. Once he has expatiated on the matter, he offers some more general comments on writings such as those of Enoch:

Let us omit, then, the fables of those scriptures which are called apocryphal, because their obscure origin was unknown to the fathers from whom the authority of the true Scriptures has been transmitted to us by a most certain and well-ascertained succession. For though there is some truth in these apocryphal writings, yet they contain so many false statements, that they have no canonical authority. We cannot deny that Enoch, the seventh from Adam, left some divine writings, for that is asserted by the Apostle Jude in his canonical epistle. But it is not without reason that these writings have no place in that canon of Scripture which was preserved in

_____

14. The translation is taken from ANF 4.15–16.

the temple of the Hebrew people by the diligence of successive priests; for their antiquity brought them under suspicion, and it was impossible to ascertain whether these were his genuine writings, and they were not brought forward as genuine by the persons who were found to have carefully preserved the canonical books by a successive transmission. So that the writings which are produced under his name, and which contain these fables about the giants, saying that their fathers were not men, are properly judged by prudent men to be not genuine; just as many writings are produced by heretics under the names both of other prophets, and, more recently, under the names of the apostles, all of which, after careful examination, have been set apart from canonical authority under the title of Apocrypha. There is therefore no doubt that, according to the Hebrew and Christian canonical Scriptures, there were many giants before the deluge, and that these were citizens of the earthly society of men, and that the sons of God, who were according to the flesh the sons of Seth, sank into this community when they forsook righteousness. (15.23)[15]

The Enoch literature continued to be read, copied, and translated, but it was only in the fairly isolated Christian Church of Ethiopia that the full text of *1 Enoch* was preserved and achieved the status of a biblical book.

2. THE ANGEL STORY

Early Christian appeal to the watcher story in its various permutations is more widespread than citation of or specific allusion to a book of Enoch. Examples may be found in all the major centers of Christianity. We have previously noted that the story is mentioned in the New Testament books 1–2 Peter and Jude. Christian authors of varied persuasions — mainstream writers, Gnostics, anti-Paulinists, Montanists — found the story helpful in one way or another.[16]

One group of authors found in the angel story an explanation for idolatry. The earliest among them may have been Justin Martyr, who died ca. 167. Justin argues that Greek religion is demon based, and in his second apology (ca. 161) he explains who those demons are. He notes

---

15. The translation is from M. Dods, trans., *The City of God by Saint Augustine*, Modern Library edition (New York: Random House, 1950).
16. We noted, in connection with the *Book of Giants*, that Mani may have first encountered such material among the syncretistic Elchasaites.

that God entrusted the care of humanity and all things under heaven to angels:

> But the angels transgressed this appointment, and were captivated by love of women, and begat children who are those that are called demons; and besides, they afterwards subdued the human race to themselves, partly by magical writings, and partly by fears and the punishments they occasioned, and partly by teaching them to offer sacrifices, and incense, and libations, of which things they stood in need after they were enslaved by lustful passions; among men they sowed murders, wars, adulteries, intemperate deeds, and all wickedness. Whence also the poets and the mythologists, not knowing that it was the angels and those demons who had been begotten by them that did these things to men and women, and cities, and nations, which they related, ascribed them to god himself, and to those who were accounted to be his very offspring, and to the offspring of those who were called his brothers, Neptune and Pluto, and to the children again of these their offspring. For whatever name each of the angels had given to himself and his children, by that name they called them.[17]

Justin covers several aspects of the angel story—their lust, fatherhood, and teachings—including their role in religion. However, for him the demons are the offspring of the angels and not emanations from the giants' dead bodies (as they are in *1 Enoch* 15–16). Here, as in 1 Pet. 3:19–20, the basis for Justin's claims is *1 Enoch* 19:1: "The spirits of the angels who were promiscuous with women . . . made men unclean and will lead them astray so that they sacrifice to demons as gods." Justin charges that the immoral gods of Greek mythology were the evil demons of the Enochic angel tale.

Tertullian, who defended the authority and authenticity of Enoch's writings, put the angel story to use in the context of urging that virgins wear veils. In a treatise written after he had become a Montanist—*On the Veiling of Virgins* (written in 208 or 209)—he explored the matter at some length and in the process demonstrated that he read the relevant part of Genesis in the light of *1 Enoch*. He begins his case with 1 Cor. 11:

> If "the woman ought to have power upon the head" [1 Cor. 11:10], all the more justly ought the *virgin* to whom pertains the essence

---

17. The translation is taken from ANF 1.190.

of the cause (assigned for this assertion). For if (it is) on account of the angels—those, to wit, whom we read of as having fallen down from God and heaven on account of concupiscence after females—who can presume that it was bodies already defiled, and relics of human lust, which such angels yearned after, so as not rather to have been inflamed for *virgins*, whose bloom pleads an excuse for human lust likewise? For thus does Scripture withal suggest: "And it came to pass," it says, "when men had begun to grow more numerous upon the earth, there were withal daughters born to them; but the sons of God, having descried the daughters of men, that they were fair, took to themselves wives of all whom they elected." [Gen. 6:1–2] For here the Greek name of *women* does seem to have the sense *"wives,"* inasmuch as mention is made of marriage. When, then, it says "the *daughters* of men," it manifestly purports *virgins*, who would be still reckoned as belonging to their *parents*—for *wedded women* are called their *husbands'*—whereas it *could* have said, "the *wives* of men": in like manner not naming the angels adulterers, but husbands, while they take *unwedded* "daughters of men," who it has above said were "born" thus also signifying their *virginity:* first "born;" but here, wedded to angels. Anything else I know not that they were except "born" and subseqently wedded. So perilous a face, then, ought to be shaded, which has cast stumbling-stones even so far as heaven: that when standing in the presence of God, at whose bar it stands accused of the driving of the angels from the (native) confines, it may blush before the other angels as well; and may repress that former evil liberty of its head,—a liberty now to be exhibited not even before human eyes. But even if they were females already contaminated whom those angels had desired, so much the more "on account of the angels" would it have been the duty of virgins to be veiled, as it would have been more possible for *virgins* to have been the cause of the angels' sinning. (*On the Veiling of Virgins* 7)[18]

He formulates his case by combining 1 Cor. 11 and Gen. 6. The scriptural text from which Tertullian quotes read "sons of God," not "angels of God," yet he interprets the phrase as if it did say "angels of God," and, in doing so, he moves beyond the literal text. Other elements, including the angels' act of abandoning heaven, which was motivated by sexual desire, also show that he does have the more elaborate Enochic

---

18. The translation is taken from ANF 4.31–32.

version in mind, since neither of these themes is mentioned in Genesis. Tertullian sides with those who placed a sizable share of the blame for the angels' sin on the lovely and fair daughters of men (e.g., *T. Reub.* 5). In order to guard against a recurrence of such a disaster, virgins should veil their enticing faces.

As noted earlier, Christians of different perspectives turned to the watcher story for sundry purposes. Here it will be instructive to examine the way in which the story appears in the Pseudo-Clementine literature. The *Recognitions* and the *Homilies* are the two units that constitute this anti-Pauline corpus, and it is believed that these two related works stem from an original that was composed in the third century. The passage from the *Homilies* (VIII.12–18) is too long to quote, but it offers an interesting version of the story. According to it, the angels in the lowest part of heaven asked God's permission to descend to the earth, to become human, and to convict and punish people for ingratitude toward God. Their wish was granted, and the angels chose to transform themselves into various objects. They also changed themselves into men in order to demonstrate that it was possible to live a holy life. Once they were human, however, they acquired full humanity, including sexual desire. They consorted with women, and, as they did, they lost the ability to restore themselves to their original form. The women wanted these males to exhibit in front of them their former angelic natures; when they were not able to do so, they instead showed them the precious metals and stones in the earth and taught them magic and astronomy. They also instructed them in the use of roots, in melting gold and silver, and in dyeing cloth. So, women's ornamentation and makeup can be traced to these fallen and now former angels. The children of the marriages between these creatures and women were giants. In order to satisfy their appetites God sent manna to them, but they preferred the taste of blood and flesh. The shedding of blood defiled the air and led to diseases. God finally sent a flood to destroy the giants. The souls of the giants lived on, and they were given a law that allowed them to rule and be worshiped only by those who accepted these conditions. This is the explanation for pagan worship.

The bizarre elaboration and transformation of the myth in the *Homilies* contains some familiar ideas, such as the positive reason for the angels' descent (cf. *Jubilees*) and the basic outline of the classical story. We have even met the changing shapes of the angels before this (see *1 Enoch* 19:1; *T. Reub.* 5:4–6), but their decision to reveal nature's secrets only after they were incapable of showing the women their former selves, the manna, and other features are new and memorable. Through it all the *Homilies* provide an account of pagan religions like that of Justin Martyr.

The *Recognitions*, which are otherwise much like the *Homilies*, advance a very different reading of Gen. 6:1–4 — a reading that will soon come to dominate Christian exegesis of the passage and put an end to the angelic interpretation. In I.29 we read that the sons of God lived in the eighth generation and were so designated because they were virtuous people who had lived like angels. They were enticed by the beauty of women, became promiscuous, and compelled others to sin against God. In the ninth generation giants were born, and in the tenth the flood was sent. Once this understanding of "sons of God" as virtuous humans (who were the offspring of Seth in most examples) gained the day, no room would remain for the Enochic elaboration of the story. Gen. 6:1–4 would relate only another episode in devolving human depravity, not a celestial injection of massive evil into the world.

It should be apparent from these examples that there were different versions of the watcher story and that not all of them seem to have come directly from *1 Enoch* (as we have it). They have been presented here to illustrate the partially direct and partially indirect influences of the Enochic booklets on early Christian authors.

3. ENOCH AS AN ESCHATOLOGICAL FIGURE

A widespread theme in the Enochic booklets is that Enoch would either be present at the final judgment (e.g., in the Animal Apocalypse) or would be involved in the judging himself (the Similitudes). Enoch continued to have a place in the great events of the end time as they were explained by some Christian authors, but his role could hardly be that of judge, since either God himself or Jesus, the eschatological son of man, exercised that function in Christian eschatological expectations. Nevertheless, a small group of writers believed that Rev. 11:1–13 referred to Enoch as an important actor in the final drama.

Rev. 11:1–13 talks about two witnesses who, after giving their testimony, will be killed by the beast from the abyss, who will leave their corpses exposed in Jerusalem for three and a half days. At that time a divine breath will revivify them. A voice then calls them into heaven, to which they ascend. These events are placed by the writer near the end of time, between the sixth and seventh trumpets (8:1–9:21; 11:15) and between woes 2 and 3 (7:13–8:12; 11:14). Rev. 11 opens with the Danielic prediction that the nations will trample the holy city for forty-two months. The two witnesses prophesy for a similar amount of time (1,260 days) in sackcloth.

John of Patmos seems to drop enough hints to identify the two witnesses. The one should be Elijah, who, like the first witness, consumed with fire the soldiers sent against him and shut the sky so that no rain would fall (Rev. 11:5–6; 2 Kings 1:10, 12; 1 Kings 17–18). The second witness appears to be Moses because he, like the leader of the exodus, turns water to blood and strikes the earth with many kinds of plagues (actually, both witnesses do this; see 11:6b).

The witnesses of Rev. 11 appear, then, to be Elijah and Moses, two Old Testament heroes, one of whom did not die, while the burial of the other is described in a way so intriguing ("no one knows his burial place to this day" [Deut. 34:6]) that it could give rise to questions about what actually happened to him.[19] The story of the transfiguration, when Elijah and Moses appear to Jesus (e.g., Mark 9:4–5), shows that the two were believed to be alive centuries after their earthly lives had ended. These two will still be living in the last days. A minor Christian exegetical tradition, however, saw in the second witness none other than Enoch himself, another biblical character who did not die. One of the most interesting of these exegetes is Hippolytus of Rome (ca. 170–236). He deals with the subject in his treatise on *Christ and the Antichrist* and in his commentary on Daniel. He follows the lead of the author of Rev. 11, who begins the chapter with material from Daniel, by reading the two-witness pericope within the framework offered by Daniel's prophecies, specifically his vision of the seventy weeks of years (Dan. 9). In chapter 9 Daniel is pondering the meaning of Jeremiah's prediction that Jerusalem would lie in ruins for seventy years. He is told that the seventy years were actually seventy weeks of years. Dan. 9:25 refers to units of seven and sixty-two-year weeks, leaving only one week that figures in verse 27 (half of it is also named). In *Christ and the Antichrist* Hippolytus offers an interpretation of the Daniel passage that incorporates his reading of Rev. 11. He does this in connection with his study of Rev. 17–18 and as part of his attempt to explain when the torments of the last days will occur.

But it becomes us further diligently to examine and set forth the period at which these things shall come to pass, and how the little horn [Dan. 7:8, 11, 20–21, 24–26] shall spring up in their midst. For when the legs of iron have issued in the feet and toes, according to the similitude of the image and that of the terrible beast

---

19. For a summary of some later traditions about Moses and his death, see D. M. Beegle, "Moses," in *ABD* 4.916–18.

[Dan. 2 and 7] . . . , (then shall be the time) when the iron and the clay shall be mingled together. Now Daniel will set forth this subject for us. For he says, "And one week will make a covenant with many, and it shall be that in the midst (half) of the week my sacrifice and oblation shall cease." [Dan. 9:27] By one week, therefore, he meant the last week which is to be at the end of the whole world; of which week the two prophets Enoch and Elias will take up the half. For they will preach 1,260 days clothed in sackcloth, proclaiming repentance to the people and to all the nations. (43) [20]

The tradition of seeing in Enoch one of the two witness continues for centuries longer than the Christian use of the watcher myth.

Here we may end our survey. In most areas populated by Christians the Enochic writings had, by the fourth century, fallen from favor and with them their famous story about the angels who descended and married women. For reasons that are not fully known, it no longer served as a convincing or believable way to explain the rise of pagan religion or even to account for the exponential growth of wickedness before the flood. A few writers continued to believe that Enoch would be one of the eschatological witnesses, but in general Enoch slipped back into his ancient niche in Gen. 5, remaining there as a mysterious but largely ignored descendant of Adam.

---

20. The translation is taken from ANF 5.

APPENDIX

ENOCH'S WRITINGS IN "CANONICAL" PERSPECTIVE

In the course of examining the Enochic booklets and allusions to Enochic writings and traditions, we saw that the authors of those booklets claim to be recording divine revelations, while those who refer to them often indicated that they considered them authoritative. These data raise questions about the status of Enoch's writings in Jewish and Christian circles. Were any of them considered biblical?

It is impossible to speak with any certainty about the status of the Enochic writings among most Jewish groups in the late-second-temple period for the simple reason that there is too little evidence. The Jewish texts that mention Enoch and traditions about him come from authors who held varied points of view — from apocalypticists at Qumran to anti- or nonapocalypticists such as Sirach and Philo. The books or traditions were familiar to writers of different persuasions, but most of the authors left no hint regarding the level of authority they ascribed to the compositions that bear Enoch's name. We should also recall that there probably was no fixed, closed list of authoritative books that all Jewish people accepted as the revelation of God to Israel. That development seems to have come later than the second-temple period.

The only exception to the dearth of information from Jewish sources about the status of Enochic writings is the Essene community, which wrote, copied, and read the manuscripts found in the Qumran caves. In their library numerous copies of the Enochic booklets were found, and there is evidence that Enoch's teachings were valued. The next paragraphs present a case for thinking that some Enochic writings were considered highly authoritative by the learned men of Qumran. Or, to be anachronistic, they regarded them as biblical/canonical.

1. The authors of all the Enochic booklets assert that the contents came to Enoch by divine revelation. The patriarch announces frequently that he had seen visions shown to him by angels (1:2; 14:1, 8; 19:3; 37:1; 39:4; 83:1–2; 88:3; 90:2, 42; 93:2; 106:13) or simply that he had seen dreams or visions (in a segment so short as *1 Enoch* 17–19 Enoch says he *saw* something seventeen times). The book opens with words that iden-

tify Enoch as "a righteous man whose eyes were opened by the Lord, and he saw a holy vision in the heavens which the angels showed to me. And I heard everything from them, and I understood what I saw . . ." (1:2). The texts at times name God himself as the source of the disclosures (10:1–11:2; 14:1, 24; 15:1–16:4; 37:4; 39:2; 45:3–6; 55; 62:1; 63:12; 67:1; 90:22; 105:1–2; 106:19). Another source is said to be the tablets of heaven (81:1–2; 93:1; 103:2; 106:19; 107:1). Consequently, the writers leave little doubt in the readers' minds that what they are reporting comes from above.

2. Not only do the Enochic booklets aver that they are God's revelations to the ancient sage; there is evidence that some people took the claim seriously. One kind of documentation is the fairly large number of copies found at Qumran: eleven manuscripts that contain one or several of the four Enochic booklets known there (the AB, BW, BD, and EE), more if we include the *Book of Giants*. These totals are higher than for most of the books that became parts of the Hebrew Bible or Old Testament. When we recall the cost and labor involved in producing a manuscript in antiquity, such numbers say much about the value accorded the Enochic writings.

3. Not only do the various Enochic compositions claim to be revelations and a relatively large number of copies have been identified in cave 4, but the contents of those books are cited as authoritative in other works. It has been shown that the watcher story is attested (not frequently) in the Qumran texts, and this theme seems to have originated in the BW. Moreover, the calendrical system of Qumran is clearly based on the sort of information found in the AB. The numerous calendars prove that the Essenes not only had a solar calendar of 364 days but also a schematic lunar arrangement of 354 days. Both of these are presented side by side in the AB, and the two are synchronized in some of the texts from cave 4. In this respect the Qumran community followed the practice of the AB and not the exclusively solar teachings of *Jubilees*.

Therefore, so the argument goes, if a book claims to be revealed by God, others accept that claim, and they act on it by citing the book to prove points, then it follows that the book was considered authoritative or, in later terms, canonical.

In early Christianity, too, at least some of the Enochic texts were assigned authoritative status. This follows from the way in which the writers refer to what Enoch said or wrote. Jude quotes *1 Enoch* 1:9 and introduces it with the words "Enoch, in the seventh generation from Adam, prophesied, saying . . ." (v. 14). The *Epistle of Barnabas* 16:5 alludes to something in the Animal Apocalypse with the formula "the Scripture says." The second-century apologist Athenagoras included Enoch's teachings about the angels among what he called the "prophecies" (*Embassy for the Christians*, para. 24). Clement of Alexandria, in *Selections from the Prophets* 2.1, seems to enroll Enoch among the prophets, and, as we have seen, Tertullian writes an entire section in defense of the book of Enoch (*de cultu feminarum* 3.1). In his earlier years Origen seems to have placed *Enoch* among the scriptures (e.g., *On First Principles* 1.3.3; 4.4.8 [in which he calls Enoch a prophet]). By the time he wrote *Against Celsus*, however, he no longer considered it sacred Scripture (5.54–55). While in most of the Christian communities the book(s) eventually were rejected, the Abyssinian Church in Ethiopia, which became isolated at a relatively early time and retained an earlier, more comprehensive set of sacred books than other churches did, included *1 Enoch* in its canon of Holy Scripture.[1]

The Qumran community did not assign the Similitudes to the category of the revealed books of Enoch, since no copy of it has been found there. It is not always possible to say, in dealing with the Christian sources, which Enochic booklets were considered authoritative and whether some might not have held such status. One reason for this is that we do not know when the present collection of five units was brought together to form what we call *1 Enoch*. It is clear, however, that some Jewish people (the Qumran group) and some Christians placed at least some of Enoch's writings among their collections of the sacred, authoritative books revealed by God himself.

---

1. For the evidence, see R. Cowley, "The Biblical Canon of the Ethiopian Orthodox Church Today," *Ostkirchliche Studien* 23 (1974): 318–23.

185

BIBLIOGRAPHY

Albright, W. F. "The Babylonian Matter in the Predeuteronomic Primeval History (JE) in Gen 1–11." *JBL* 58 (1939): 91–103.

Alexander, P. "3 (Hebrew) Enoch." In *OTP* 1.223–315.

Andersen, F. I. "2 (Slavonic Apocalypse of) Enoch." In *OTP* 1.91–221.

Bauckham, R. J. *Jude, 2 Peter.* WBC 50. Waco: Word Books, 1983.

———. "Jude, Epistle of." *ABD* 3.1098–1103.

Beckwith, R. *The Old Testament Canon of the New Testament Church and Its Background in Early Judaism.* Grand Rapids, Mich.: Eerdmans, 1985.

Beegle, D. M. "Moses." *ABD* 4.909–18.

Black, M. *The Book of Enoch or I Enoch: A New English Edition.* In consultation with James C. VanderKam, with an appendix on the "Astronomical" chapters (72–82) by Otto Neugebauer. SVTP 7. Leiden: Brill, 1985.

Charles, R. H. *The Book of Enoch or 1 Enoch.* Oxford: Clarendon Press, 1912.

Collins, J. "Introduction: Towards the Morphology of a Genre." In *Apocalypse: The Morphology of a Genre*, edited by J. Collins. *Semeia* 14 (1979): 1–20.

———. "Sibylline Oracles." In *OTP* 1.317–472.

———. "Genre, Ideology and Social Movements in Jewish Apocalypticism." In *Mysteries and Revelations: Apocalyptic Studies since the Uppsala Colloquium*, edited by J. J. Collins and J. H. Charlesworth, 11–32. JSP Supplement Series 9. Sheffield: Sheffield Academic Press, 1991.

Colson, F. H., and G. H. Whitaker. *Philo* II. LCL. 1927. Reprint. Cambridge: Harvard/London: Heinemann, 1979.

———. *Philo* V. LCL. 1934. Reprint. Cambridge: Harvard/ London: Heinemann, 1988.

Colson, F. H. *Philo* VI. LCL. 1935. Reprint. Cambridge: Harvard/London: Heinemann, 1984.

———. *Philo* VIII. LCL. 1939. Reprint. Cambridge: Harvard/London: Heinemann, 1989.

Cowley, R. "The Biblical Canon of the Ethiopian Orthodox Church Today." *Ostkirchliche Studien* 23 (1974): 318–23.

Crenshaw, J. "Impossible Questions, Sayings, and Tasks." In *Gnomic Wisdom*, edited by J. D. Crossan. *Semeia* 17 (1980): 19–34.

Di Lella, A. See Skehan, P.

Dimant, D. "The 'Fallen Angels' in the Dead Sea Scrolls and in the Apocryphal and Pseudepigraphic Books Related to Them." Ph.D. diss., Hebrew University of Jerusalem, 1974 (in Hebrew).

———. "The 'Pesher on the Periods' (4Q180) and 181." *Israel Oriental Studies* 9 (1979): 77–102.

———. "History According to the Vision of the Animals (Ethiopic Enoch 85–90)." *Jerusalem Studies in the Thought of Israel* 2 (1982): 18–37 (in Hebrew).

———. "Jerusalem and the Temple in the Animal Apocalypse (*Ethiopic Enoch* 85–90) in Light of the Views of the Sect of the Judean Wilderness." *Shenaton* 5–6 (1982): 177–93 (in Hebrew).

Dods, M. *The City of God by Saint Augustine*. Modern Library edition. New York: Random House, 1950.

Donahue, J. "Recent Studies on the Origin of 'Son of Man' in the Gospels." *CBQ* 48 (1986): 584–607.

Donfried, K. P. "Peter." *ABD* 5.251–63.

Fitzmyer, J. *The Genesis Apocryphon of Qumran Cave 1: A Commentary*. BibOr 18A. Rome: Biblical Institute, 1971.

Fitzmyer, J., and D. Harrington. *A Manual of Palestinian Aramaic Texts*. BibOr 34. Rome: Biblical Institute, 1978.

Grabbe, L. L. *Etymology in Early Jewish Interpretation: The Hebrew Names in Philo*. BJS 115. Atlanta: Scholars Press, 1988.

Grelot, P. "La légende d'Hénoch dans les apocryphes et dans la Bible: origine et signification." *RSR* 46 (1958): 5–26, 181–220.

Grossfeld, B. *The Targum Onqelos to Genesis*. Aramaic Bible 6. Wilmington: Michael Glazier, 1988.

Harrington, D. "Pseudo-Philo." In *OTP* 2.297–377. Also see Fitzmyer, J.

Helfmeyer, F. J. "*Halakh.*" In *TDOT* 3.388–403.

Himmelfarb, M. "A Report on Enoch in Rabbinic Literature." SBLSP, edited by P. J. Achtemeier (1978): 1.259–69.

Holladay, C. *Fragments from Hellenistic Jewish Authors*, vol. 1: *Historians*. SBLTT Pseudepigrapha Series 10. Chico, Calif.: Scholars Press, 1983.

Jastrow, M. *A Dictionary of the Targumim, the Talmud Babli and Yerushalmi, and the Midrashic Literature*. 1886–90. Reprint. New York: Jastrow, 1967.

Johnson, M. D. "Life of Adam and Eve." In *OTP* 2.249–95.

Kee, H. C. "Testaments of the Twelve Patriarchs." In *OTP* 1.775–828.

Klijn, A. F. J. "2 (Syriac Apocalypse of) Baruch." In *OTP* 1.615–52.

Knibb, M. *The Ethiopic Book of Enoch: A New Edition in the Light of the Aramaic Dead Sea Fragments*. 2 vols. Oxford: Clarendon Press, 1978.

Kugler, R. "The Levi–Priestly Tradition: From Malachi to *Testament of Levi.*" Ph.D. diss., University of Notre Dame, 1994.

Kümmel, W. G. *Introduction to the New Testament*. London: SCM, 1966 (translated from the 14th [1965] German ed.).

Kvanvig, H. S. *Roots of Apocalyptic: The Mesopotamian Background of the Enoch Figure and of the Son of Man*. WMANT 61. Neukirchen-Vluyn: Neukirchener Verlag, 1988.

Lambert, W. "Enmeduranki and Related Matters." *JCS* 21 (1967): 126–38.

McNamara, M. *Targum Neofiti 1: Genesis*. Aramaic Bible 1A. Collegeville, Minn.: Liturgical Press, 1992.

Maher, M. *Targum Pseudo-Jonathan: Genesis*. Aramaic Bible 1B. Collegeville, Minn.: Liturgical Press, 1992.

Marcus, R. *Josephus VI: Jewish Antiquities Books IX–XI.* LCL. 1937. Reprint. Cambridge: Harvard/London: Heinemann, 1966.

————. *Philo Supplement I: Questions and Answers on Genesis.* LCL. 1953. Reprint. Cambridge: Harvard/London: Heinemann, 1979.

Margulies, M. *Midrash Haggadol on the Pentateuch: Genesis.* Jerusalem: Mosad Harav Kook Publishing, 1967.

Milik, J. T. *The Books of Enoch: Aramaic Fragments of Qumrân Cave 4.* Oxford: Clarendon Press, 1976.

Neugebauer, O. See Black, M.

Neusner, J. *Genesis Rabbah: The Judaic Commentary to the Book of Genesis. A New American Translation.* 3 vols. BJS 104–6. Atlanta: Scholars Press, 1985.

Neyrey, J. *2 Peter, Jude.* Anchor Bible 37C. Garden City, N.Y.: Doubleday, 1993.

Nickelsburg, G. W. E. *Jewish Literature between the Bible and the Mishnah.* Philadelphia: Fortress, 1987.

————. "Son of Man." In *ABD* 6.137–50.

Reeves, J. *Jewish Lore in Manichaean Cosmogony: Studies in the* Book of Giants *Traditions.* Monographs of the Hebrew Union College 14. Cincinnati: HUC Press, 1992.

Sanders, E. P. "Testament of Abraham." In *OTP* 1.871–902.

Sasson, J. M. "Word-Play in Gen 6:8–9." *CBQ* 37 (1975): 165–66.

Schmitt, A. "Die Angaben über Henoch Gen 5, 21–24 in der LXX." In *Wort, Lied und Gottesspruch: Beiträge zur Septuaginta. Festschrift für Joseph Ziegler,* edited by J. Schreiner, 161–69. Forschung zur Bibel 1. Würzburg: Echter Verlag, 1972.

Skehan, P., and A. Di Lella. *The Wisdom of Ben Sira.* Anchor Bible 39. Garden City, N.Y.: Doubleday, 1987.

Stemberger, G. See Strack, H. L.

Strack, H. L., and G. Stemberger. *Introduction to the Talmud and Midrash.* Edinburgh: T. & T. Clark, 1991.

Thackeray, H. St. J. *Josephus IV: Jewish Antiquities Books I–IV.* LCL. 1930. Reprint. Cambridge: Harvard/London: Heinemann, 1967.

Tiller, P. *A Commentary on the Animal Apocalypse of* I Enoch. SBLEJL 4. Atlanta: Scholars Press, 1993.

Urbach, E. E. *The Sages: The World and Wisdom of the Rabbis of the Talmud.* Cambridge and London: Harvard University Press, 1987.

Vancil, J. W. "Sheep, Shepherd." In *ABD* 5.1187–90.

VanderKam, J. "Enoch Traditions in Jubilees and Other Second-Century Sources." SBLSP, edited by P. Achtemeier (1978): 1.229–51.

————. "Some Major Issues in the Contemporary Study of 1 Enoch: Reflections on J. T. Milik's *The Books of Enoch: Aramaic Fragments of Qumrân Cave 4.*" *Maarav* 3 (1982): 85–97.

————. *Enoch and the Growth of an Apocalyptic Tradition.* CBQMS 16. Washington, D.C.: Catholic Biblical Association of America, 1984.

————. "Studies in the Apocalypse of Weeks (*1 Enoch* 93:1–10; 91:11–17)." *CBQ* 46 (1984): 511–23.

———. *The Book of Jubilees.* 2 vols. CSCO 510–11. Scriptores Aethiopici 87–88. Leuven: Peeters, 1989.

———. "The Birth of Noah." In *Studies Offered to J. T. Milik to Celebrate Forty Years of His Scholarly Work on Texts from the Wilderness of Judaea,* vol. 1: *Intertestamental Essays in Honour of Józef Tadeusz Milik,* edited by Z. J. Kapera, 213–31. Krakow: Enigma Press, 1992.

———. "Righteous One, Messiah, Chosen One, and Son of Man in 1 Enoch 37–71." In *The Messiah: Developments in Earliest Judaism and Christianity,* edited by J. H. Charlesworth, 169–91. Minneapolis: Fortress Press, 1992.

———. "Biblical Interpretation in *1 Enoch* and *Jubilees.*" In *The Pseudepigrapha and Early Biblical Interpretation,* edited by J. H. Charlesworth and C. A. Evans, 96–125. JSP Supplement Series 14/ Studies in Scripture in Early Judaism and Christianity 2. Sheffield: Sheffield Academic Press, 1993.

———. "1 Enoch and Enoch in Early Christianity." In *The Jewish Apocalyptic Heritage in Early Christianity,* edited by J. C. VanderKam and W. Adler.—, consulting ed. *Qumran Cave 4, VIII: Parabiblical Texts, Part I.* DJD XIII. Oxford: Clarendon Press, 1994. CRINT 3.4. Assen/Maastricht: van Gorcum/ Minneapolis: Fortress Press, 1995.

Vermes, G. *The Dead Sea Scrolls in English,* 3d ed. Sheffield: JSOT Press, 1987.

Westermann, C. *Genesis 1–11: A Commentary.* Minneapolis: Augsburg, 1984.

Winston, D. *The Wisdom of Solomon.* Anchor Bible 43. Garden City, N.Y.: Doubleday, 1979.

INDEX OF REFERENCES TO ANCIENT TEXTS

Old Testament

INDEX OF MODERN AUTHORS

INDEX OF SUBJECTS